THE ILLUSTRATED GUIDE TO
HORSE TACK

Other books by Susan McBane published by David & Charles
Keeping a Horse Outdoors
Behaviour Problems in Horses
Effective Horse & Pony Management: a Failsafe System
Horse Care & Riding: A Thinking Approach

Other books by Susan McBane
Your First Horse: a guide to Buying and Owning
Keeping Horses: how to Save Time and Money
Ponywise
The Horse and the Bit (editor)
The Horse in Winter
A Natural Approach to Horse Management
The Competition Horse: its Breeding, Production and Management (co-author)
Horse Facts (co-author)
Know Your Pony
Understanding Your Horse
Pony Problems: how to cope
Grooming
The Outdoor Pony

Contributor to
The Octopus Complete Book of the Horse
The Pony Book
The New Book of the Horse

THE ILLUSTRATED GUIDE TO
HORSE TACK

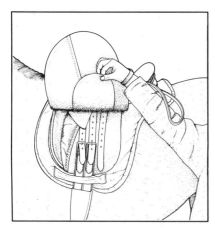

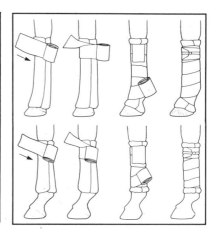

SUSAN McBANE

David & Charles

DEDICATED TO ALEX
The only man I send flowers to and the only uncle I have left!

Line illustrations by Sally Alexander

A DAVID & CHARLES BOOK

Copyright © Susan McBane 1992
First published 1992

A catalogue record for this book is available from the British Library.

ISBN 0 7153 99470

Typeset by ABM Typographics Limited, Hull
and printed in Italy by Milano Stampa SpA
for David & Charles
Brunel House Newton Abbot Devon

CONTENTS

INTRODUCTION

The subject of tack is one which can both fascinate experienced horse people and thoroughly confuse novices. The range of items is vast, and new ones are appearing all the time. However, up to twenty years ago the variety facing prospective purchasers was not too daunting; but developments in materials and designs in virtually every area of the horse clothing and tack industry since then have brought on to the market many new items and concepts which do, in fact, seem to have a real place and purpose in the horse world.

For example, we have many more types of specialist saddle now, and not simply show jumping, general purpose and dressage saddles plus old-type hunting and show saddles. The most recent innovations are probably in the field of endurance riding and in the development of adjustable saddles and flexible saddles which move with the horse.

The greatest improvement in clothing has been the development of permeable or 'breathable' fabrics. Although there is still no perfect fabric which will keep water out and allow sweat to evaporate, for example, up through a turnout rug when it is clogged with mud (interesting problem for the textile developers!), this is no more unthinkable now than synthetic fabric itself was for horse rugs a generation ago when it first appeared in the form of the Lavenham quilted nylon rug. This was originally denigrated by die-hards (as were rubber riding boots), yet it is now ubiquitous.

This book is certainly not intended to be a complete catalogue of what is currently available, but it does include a section giving illustrations and details of some of the more exciting products on the market. Basically, the book aims to guide readers through the subject, explaining the uses and aims of different items, how they should fit, be used and cared for, so that the reader may be in a much better position to decide what he or she needs, and what is appropriate for a particular horse.

It is still very much the case, particularly among young riders, that a piece of equipment will be bought for no better reason than that some prominent competitor is seen to be using it, so they think it must be good or even necessary. This is certainly not so. Every horse is different; the use of a particular noseband, say, on one horse may be not only unnecessary but also counter-productive, whereas the same noseband may suit another animal perfectly. Some of the more complicated schooling accessories and specialised aids in that field can be very dangerous if used inappropriately.

I do hope this book will help clarify the subject and enable readers to think clearly about the purposes and effects of any items they are thinking of putting on their horses. More to the point, I hope it will enable them to know, when faced with a specific problem or need, what equipment could help them overcome it (in conjuction, as always, with good riding and communication techniques). Understanding why a horse or pony has developed a particular fault is at the root of reducing or preventing it, but sometimes using a particular piece of equipment can help us get our message through to him about a better and more comfortable way of going.

The correct fit and use of equipment is detailed throughout the book: no matter how well designed and made an item may be, it can cause pain, discomfort and even accidents if it is not fitted and adjusted properly. We often see nosebands which are much too tight, saddles which cause pain because, although excellent in themselves, they simply do not fit the horse, and rugs which, although of good basic design, are the wrong size for a horse or have been put on incorrectly and are creating a danger and source of irritation.

Because most tack and clothing is expensive, it pays to look after it. From the safety point of view, too, equipment must be kept in good repair. Care and maintenance are therefore also covered.

Most horses, ponies and their owners do not need an extensive wardrobe of tack and clothing. Nevertheless, carefully chosen, good quality items suitable for both horse and rider are not only possessions to enjoy and take pride in, but they also have an important part to play in all spheres of equestrianism.

1
SADDLES AND ACCESSORIES

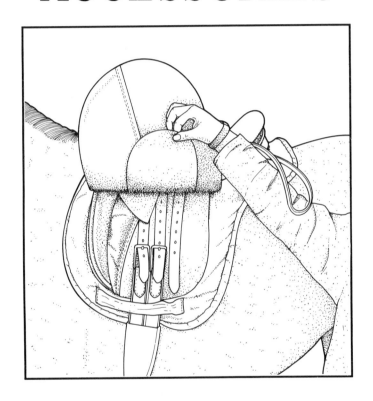

Domestication of the horse

It is thought that the horse was first really domesticated about 5,000 years ago in the Far East and/or Middle East. Archaeological excavations dated to that period and slightly later have produced padded animal-skin saddles and bridles, sometimes richly decorated. Not all civilisations developed at the same time and rate, and earlier European cave paintings show Przewalski-type horses or ponies wearing something similar to a headcollar, long before the period when horses are thought to have been actually domesticated.

The Scythians made the most impressive early saddles, consisting of two long cushions stuffed with animal hair, with either a leather piece joining them over the top, or with wooden arches at 'pommel' and 'cantle'. The principle of lack of spinal pressure was already understood at this early stage of development. Probably the most famous archaeological example of this type was found at the Frozen Tombs of Pazyryk and dated to roughly 500BC.

Saddles built on wooden frames came into being in the first century AD, and from this design developed the mediaeval saddle, on which in turn is based today's Western saddle and its relatives, the South American gaucho saddle and the Australian Stock Saddle. Modern military and endurance saddles are based on these, if not wholly intentionally.

The development of the saddle

The one invention which most assisted Man in his rise to power as an acquisitive empire-builder was the saddle, and its development from a mere animal skin to a craftsman-fashioned accoutrement which helped him sit, stay on and control his mode of transport in peace and war – the horse. Another significant addition was the stirrup to fit on that saddle, making for extra security, greater comfort and improved manoeuvrability, and which enabled the rider to stay on horseback longer without tiring unduly. Another clever idea was the girth, the like of which was not to be found on any basic animal skin and which proved much more effective at keeping the skin/saddle in place than the thongs, broad and narrow, around the breast and buttocks employed hitherto. The saddle and its accoutrements have certainly determined the course of history: those who had them were able to use their chariots or cavalry to much greater advantage, either to defend themselves or to conquer others who did not have them. There have always been, and probably always will be, those who have and those who have not in human society, and horses, saddles and other equestrian equipment have been crucial to the expansion and progress of human civilisation, and the sheer survival of Man himself until times still well within living memory. Not everyone is aware that horses served in the early years of World War II.

Nowadays, although there are still military complements of horses remaining in many countries, these are mainly for ceremonial and sporting purposes; however, our horses are thriving, though as a means to recreation, competitive or otherwise, in varied disciplines. Saddles have developed from a basic military pattern to suit those disciplines, and are designed in accordance with current thinking on the most appropriate position or seat of the rider: this varies from the true classical or the pseudo-classical seat used for competitive dressage, to the position adopted by flat-race jockeys where the actual seat rarely even touches the saddle.

The saddle, if of sound design and reputable manufacture, is certainly the most expensive item of equipment to be purchased – apart from the horse! Yet some of the expensive ones are not, in fact, that well designed, and it is still the case that many are thought up and made by people who do not ride and have never done so. However, consumer demand is becoming ever more discerning in part because of the increasing desire to succeed competitively, and also because such large amounts of money (not to mention kudos) are tied up, not only in racing but in all spheres of equestrian competition; thus we see saddles marketed in such a way as to be aimed at the more knowledgeable rider, and the product often endorsed by 'personalities' – usually successful competitors, sometimes trainers. Craftsmanship and skill in manufacture are no longer enough on their own: knowledgeable design techniques are also now essential.

Making a saddle

Animal skins in the form of tanned, curried, treated and dyed leather still comprise the most common material for saddle-making, although synthetic materials are now established and likely to increase. However, it has taken these a surprisingly long time to appear and gain a foothold in the admittedly highly conservative horse world.

The saddle tree

Saddles are made on a framework called a tree, and it is the shape of the tree which categorically determines the 'cut' of the saddle, which equestrian discipline and therefore riding position it will be suitable for, and how it fits the horse. Most trees are still very successfully made in separate parts from laminated beechwood, although other woods are now used as well; the parts are first heated and pressed into shape, then joined together and covered by muslin skrim fabric. Steel plates are added to strengthen the head (front arch or pommel) and gullet, also underneath the tree from the pommel to the rear arch (cantle). Saddles can come in for hard knocks should the horse fall, and are subject to continual lesser stress from the weight of the rider, so this strengthening is essential. The tree is coated with a glue-based waterproofing substance; and finally the all-important stirrup bars are rivetted to it.

Two views of the saddle tree. The shape of the tree determines the shape and use of the finished saddle. The side view of this tree (right) shows a fairly straight, upright pommel or head, indicating, with the fairly high cantle, its use for dressage or as one of the modern showing saddles

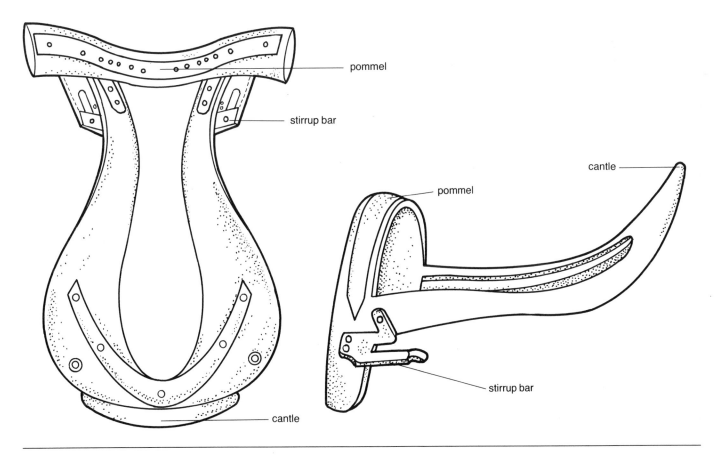

pommel

stirrup bar

pommel

cantle

stirrup bar

cantle

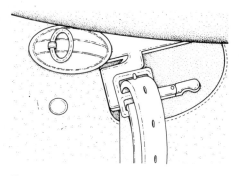

The **stirrup bar** underneath the saddle skirt (raised in this picture) showing the stirrup leather over the bar and the buckle in the correct position up as far as it will go. The safety catch is down to facilitate the leather sliding off the bar in an emergency.

The stirrup bars: The strongest, and therefore safest bars are of forged steel, and this should be stamped on each one. There will almost certainly be a little catch on the end of each, the so-called 'safety catch' which nowadays we are always told to leave down, horizontal with the bar. The purpose of the catch is to prevent the stirrup leather sliding off the bar whilst you are riding, so you don't suddenly find yourself with no stirrup. Older-style saddles had stirrup bars which protruded (uncomfortably) under the thigh and leathers did sometimes fall off if the catch was down or loose – and it wasn't always because the rider was incapable of keeping his leg in the correct position. Today's saddles have 'recessed' stirrup bars which avoid any tendency to such an unfortunate occurrence: the leathers are a tighter 'fit' over the bar and in normal riding will stay in place. The reason for having the catch permanently down is that should the rider get a foot through the stirrup in a fall, the stirrup leather will pull off the bar more easily and so the rider will not be dragged, quite possibly with fatal consequences. Whereas most 'old-timers' in the saddlery craft will express themselves in favour of keeping the catch well oiled and in the 'up' position, as it was intended to be, even with today's saddles, virtually any instructor will advise keeping it down. In fact some catches are badly fitting and will not come up completely even when oiled – and as the incidence of the leather coming off the bar would seem to be very unusual with a modern saddle, it probably *is* safest to leave the catch down.

The spring tree: Nowadays almost every saddle tree intended for an adult's saddle is a 'spring tree', where two light blades of metal are built in on each side of the seat from the pommel to the cantle. These give the tree greater resilience in use, and create greater comfort for the rider, and it seems that with a spring tree, the horse feels the seat aids more easily. An old objection to spring trees was that the constant, albeit slight, 'give' would cause the saddle to move unnecessarily on the horse's back and make the skin sore. I well remember when spring tree saddles first became widely available, but in practice I never experienced any such problem occurring, nor do I know anyone who did: like anything new, sceptics and diehards criticised it widely – but it is now used almost universally, and few of us can really recall the unrelenting ride of the rigid tree saddle; and those who can would never dream of going back to it!

The saddle seat

Once the initial formation of the tree is done, the seat can be set up, and this is a time-consuming and skilful process. Pre-strained canvas strips are tacked, under strips of leather, to the tree. The two webs to which the two rear girth straps are fastened are then fixed over the waist (the narrowest part of the tree around the centre), and the front girth strap stitched to a web which may be either wound round the two sides of the tree or fastened over it.

Girth straps: Most saddles have three girth straps (or tabs) and some people like to fasten the girth to the first and last tabs so as to spread the tension and stabilise the saddle on the horse's back. However, much depends on the

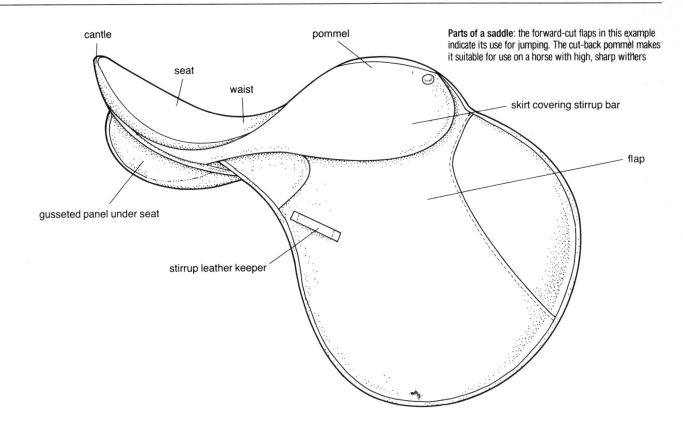

cantle

seat

waist

pommel

Parts of a saddle: the forward-cut flaps in this example indicate its use for jumping. The cut-back pommel makes it suitable for use on a horse with high, sharp withers

skirt covering stirrup bar

flap

gusseted panel under seat

stirrup leather keeper

Parts of a saddle, viewed from underneath

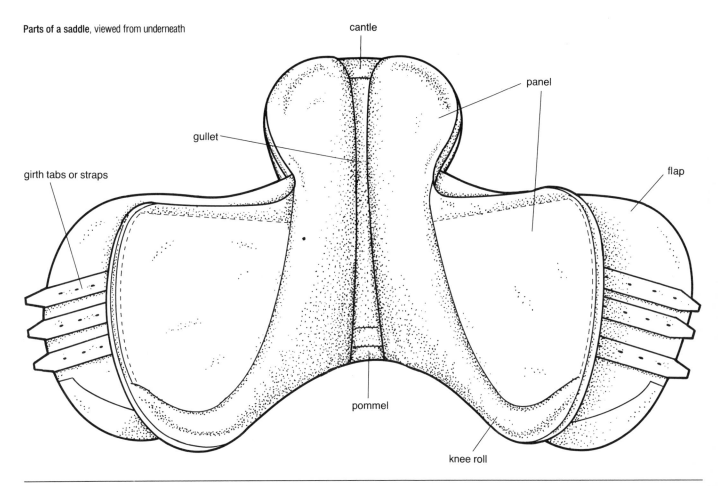

cantle

panel

gullet

girth tabs or straps

flap

pommel

knee roll

Buying tack

As in any field, there are good and bad saddles not only as regards design but also in the quality of materials and manufacture. If in doubt it is safest to purchase your saddle, whether secondhand or new, from a retailer who is a member of the British Equestrian Trade Association (in the UK – or the country's equivalent body elsewhere) and to be sure that any national standards marks are stamped on. National craft associations – in the UK this would be the Society of Master Saddlers – usually have their crest or badge displayed in their members' premises, and it will probably appear on stationery and catalogues. Signs like these should guarantee good quality goods, also that expert advice is available to guide your choice.

It is far better to buy a top-quality secondhand item (whether a saddle or anything else) than a new one of lesser quality. Most reputable saddlers will take tack in part exchange, and will repair and check all items before offering them for sale – and good tack can easily last several lifetimes if well cared for. It will probably go out of fashion before it wears out.

horse's condition and conformation: if he is tubby, fastening the girth to the first two straps will help keep it in position and prevent it being pushed forward by the horse's belly. Should the reverse be the case, if the horse is either very fit and fined down or in poor condition, the saddle may be inclined to slip backwards, in which case fastening the girth to the two rear straps will help keep it forwards. In croup-high horses, or those with poor shoulders, the saddle may slip forward; slab-sided ones may cause it to slip back.

Materials: The traditional way of building up the seat was with serge fabric stitched down to the canvas below, and stuffed with woollen stuffing through a small cut; however, very few saddlers now employ this method as modern economics have put its cost beyond the pocket of most customers. Various synthetic coverings and stuffings are now the norm and in some cases synthetic stuffing is fine, long-lasting and does not settle or go lumpy like its woollen counterpart, though the less satisfactory synthetic stuffings found in cheaper saddles can result in the saddle sinking alarmingly quickly, and the leather of the underseat panel (on the horse's back) going 'baggy' as a result.

The saddle seat can be made of various types of leather: suede is favoured by many as aiding rider security, but depending on use it can wear smooth in a matter of a very few years; the seat can also be made of non-suede pigskin; doeskin; or, like the rest of the saddle, some sort of cattle hide which is the hardest wearing. The leather is blocked and set (stretched) on to the tree and fixed securely in place; the skirts (covering the stirrup bars) are welted to the seat; the girth straps will have been firmly stitched to their webs before the flaps are fitted; and finally the panels will be fitted, and the sweat flaps, where used. Sweat flaps are properly intended to protect the more absorbent underside of the flap from sweat in a saddle where the panel only reaches part-way down it (called a half-panel). In fact, as nearly all full-size modern saddles have full panels, the sweat flap makes for unnecessary extra thickness under the rider's leg and would be as well abandoned.

The panels: To fit, little leather pockets are sewn on to the panel and the points of the tree fitted into these; the panel is then stapled or stitched in place. The panels must be very carefully and evenly stuffed whether the material used is traditional or synthetic as, lumpy uneven stuffing can throw the best designed tree out of balance and easily cause pressure points and a sore back. If the panel is over-stuffed the bearing surface – the part which touches the horse's back (or the numnah) – will curve too much and so reduce the actual area which contacts the horse's back; it may also be too hard, and if insufficiently resilient, may cause actual bruising. Too much stuffing in the front area can throw the saddle's centre of balance backwards, and vice versa.

Saddle designs for different disciplines

The ultimate design or shape of the saddle depends almost entirely on the tree and specifically on the angle of the pommel or head. Old-fashioned English hunting saddles, used for generations in the hunting field, had a vertical head and a flattish seat ('the plate') with a low cantle. The rider's position employed moderately long stirrups, and when this saddle was first produced and widely used, no one had heard of the 'forward seat' or the 'jumping position'. Riders were taught to lean forwards when taking off at a jump, but then to lean right backwards with the feet stuck forwards as the horse landed. Consequently there was no need for the now almost universal forward-cut flap to accommodate the shorter stirrup and, therefore, forward-protruding knee – and knee rolls had never been dreamed of. Nowadays, none but the most inveterate diehards would equally never dream of trying to cross a country in one of the unforgiving, grossly unhelpful and very uncomfortable old English hunting saddles, which positively encouraged the rider to lean backwards.

General purpose/event saddle

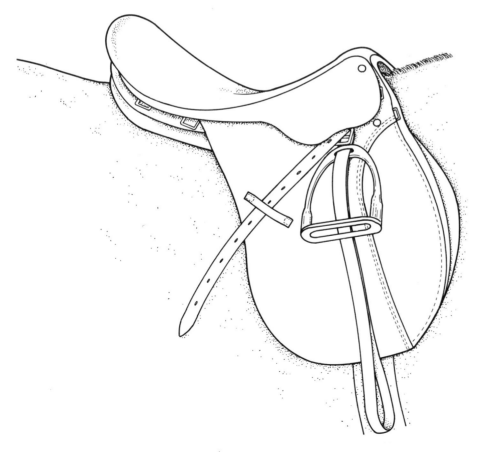

A general purpose saddle showing the stirrup irons run up their leathers, as they should be when the saddle is not in use. The moderate forward cut makes the saddle suitable for almost any purpose where an extreme seat position is not called for. Many general purpose saddles are used successfully for every discipline from dressage to show jumping

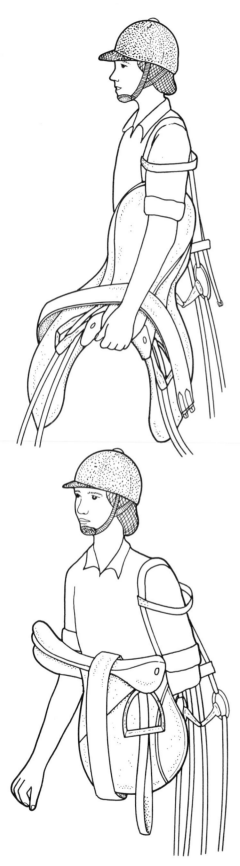

How to carry a saddle and bridle:
two different methods

The saddle which is most widely used for general riding is the general purpose saddle, now often called the event saddle. The head of the tree is sloped backwards at about 45° which enables a moderately forward-cut panel and flap to be fitted to the saddle. Knee rolls – a stuffed leather pad stitched to the front of each panel – certainly help rider security when landing over a jump or riding over tricky country (or on a 'stopper'), but forward-cut panels and flaps with their accompanying knee rolls make it even more important that a saddle fits the rider and not solely the horse. For example if you have short legs you may well find that on some saddles your knee does not make contact with the bulk of the roll at all when your stirrups are comfortably adjusted, so you derive no benefit from them. It is therefore equally important to try a saddle in the shop yourself, if at all possible, as well as on your horse (see p33, Fitting a Saddle).

Some saddles also boast thigh rolls, a vertical line of stuffed leather down the back edge of each panel under the flap. In most cases these are quite unhelpful, and certainly don't keep the thigh in any sort of position. More recently, angled rolls have been introduced (that is, angled ostensibly to support the underside of the thigh) but these are rather cumbersome if large enough to affect the position of the leg – and if they don't, they really serve no purpose at all.

A well balanced, modern, dipped tree will have the deepest part of its seat mid-way between pommel and cantle, the cantle will not be *too* high, and the rider will find that thigh rolls of any kind are largely superfluous, the fairly deep, central seat doing all that is necessary to keep him comfortably and without effort in the correct position. The deepest part of the tree should be over the horse's centre of balance, just behind the withers where the back is strongest and best able to bear the rider's weight with the least energy consumption. If the deepest part is too far back, the rider will find that his seat is also constantly slipping too far back, and he will need to keep making disturbing and annoying readjustments to his (or her) position. And if the deepest part of the seat is too far forward, the rider will slide towards the pommel which is obviously very uncomfortable.

The general purpose or event saddle is cut to accommodate a stirrup length which is short enough (depending on the rider's leg length) to allow for correct use of today's forward jumping or cross-country seat, where the knee should be firmly *on* the flap and not in front of it as often happened when, in days gone by (though not *that* long ago!) riders tried to use the 'new' jumping position on old-fashioned hunting saddles. There will still be 'enough leg below the knee' (as an instructor once put it to me) to give some security in the event of problems, but the rider can adjust his balance to stay more forward with the horse at faster paces, or in the more general upright position for slower paces.

As their name implies, these saddles are very good for general, all-purpose riding: jumping, schooling on the flat, hacking out and so on; and offering, as they do, a versatile seat, they are deservedly popular.

The showjumping saddle

The saddle devised purely for show jumping (arena or stadium jumping) has a more sloped-back head to allow for a more forward-cut panel and flap, so accomodating the more forward knee resulting from the use of shorter stirrups as used by some riders (although not many nowadays use the rather exaggeratedly short stirrup seen in earlier days, even for show jumping). These saddles are very specialised and are based on an initial design by Italian Major Piero Santini, a pupil of the 'inventor' of the forward seat and the 'natural' riding system in its entirety, Federico Caprilli. They are uncomfortable for general riding and hacking as the leg is not correctly positioned on the flap when the stirrups are lengthened, which for greater comfort and practicality they would be for such purposes; and as many have very narrow waists or twists (the narrowest part of the saddle and the area on which the rider's weight may be mostly borne) they tend to dig in where it hurts! They are superb for periods of short duration such as when schooling or competing over fences when the seat may not, in any case, be much in contact with the saddle; but they are neither suitable nor intended for sitting and riding in for longer periods.

Saddles of any type with excessively narrow waists also cause the problem of concentrating the rider's weight onto a smaller bearing surface of the saddle, which means that the weight is being borne by a smaller area of the horse's back. If you press a sharp needle into your hand it will hurt, but if you press a blunt pencil into your hand with the same pressure it does not hurt at all. This is because with the needle, the weight is concentrated into a much smaller area (the needle point), whilst with a blunt pencil lead it is more spread out and is therefore easier to bear. The same principle applies to the horse's back: the wider the waist and the greater the bearing surface, the more easily the horse can bear your weight. An excessively wide waist, however, forces the thighs apart and the rider up in the saddle and this can be equally uncomfortable;

The Caprilli system

The Caprilli system of riding was excellent for its original purpose of training troops to ride across a country. It was certainly revolutionary, and was the breakthrough from the old, backward 'hunting seat' used not only in England but also in most other Western European countries. It relied on the rider being in the forward 'jumping' position most of the time and appearing immobile as the horse galloped and jumped.

This may still be fine for moderately high fences – say up to about 3ft 6in – but most trainers and instructors today teach more participation on the part of the rider, particularly when higher fences are to be jumped. The forward jumping seat may only be adopted when the rider is actually approaching the fence. A more upward seat and, today, with longer stirrups throughout, is used between fences to give the rider more contact with and control of the horse.

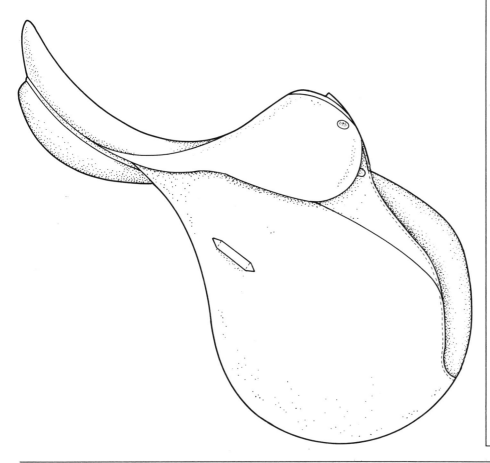

A show jumping saddle with forward-cut flap and knee rolls, in this case on the outside of the flap.

unless, as sometimes happens, the saddle is carefully made to permit closer contact with the horse's back by skilful panel design and stuffing. Most modern saddles, whether general purpose or jumping, do in fact have rather narrow waists, particularly the latter design as we have seen, and this is a point to be watched for in saddle fitting. Fortunately, there now seem to be enough designs on the market to enable purchasers to avoid over-narrow waists.

The dressage saddle

Dressage saddles have probably been victim to more misunderstood theories than any others. Like the old English hunting saddles, they have a vertical or just slightly sloping head to permit the straighter panel and flap used to accommodate the longer stirrup length typical of the dressage seat – but there the similarity ends. A dressage saddle is intended to place the rider in a more upright position with the weight on the seatbones, which should settle in the deepest part of the saddle without conscious effort on the part of the rider. To this end, some of them have ridiculously high cantles which in fact push the rider forward too far, onto the pommel. Others have off-centre seats (usually too far forward) and some are specifically stuffed, it seems, to tilt the saddle backwards on the horse's back to compensate for a dip which is too far forward. In a correctly designed and comfortable dressage saddle the cantle should be very little higher than the pommel, and with a dip which can be seen to be central when viewed from the side.

A dressage saddle. Note the upright pommel and straight-cut panel and flap. The saddle has knee rolls for comfort and some security, and these may also influence the leg position, helping the rider keep the knee back. The flap has been lifted in the drawing on the left to reveal the panel and knee rolls. The saddle has long girth tabs or straps, in this case both on one piece of leather although they are often separate. There are also so-called thigh rolls running down the back edge of the panel – a common feature which, however, does nothing to influence the position or stability of the thigh!

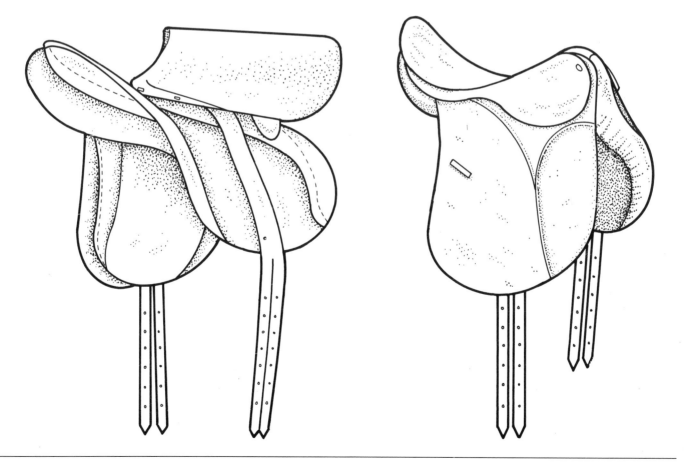

The seat of a dressage saddle is usually gusseted to allow for a flatter bearing surface and greater stability on the horse's back (it also helps spread the pressure), and particular effort is made to keep stuffing to a practical minimum to allow for close-contact riding. Recessed stirrup bars – fixed to the underside of the tree rather than the top – are virtually universal in all saddles now, and are employed on dressage saddles to avoid the sometimes actually painful bulk of stirrup leather and buckle being right under the thigh. Some saddles may have thigh rolls on top of the flap itself, and there are knee rolls on the panel positioned to accommodate the longer stirrup length used for dressage and to help the rider maintain his position and stability in the saddle. The whole design is intended to keep the rider in the correct basic position without him consciously having to think about it, thus leaving him (or her) free to concentrate his/her energy on going with the horse and giving the appropriate aids.

It has been usual for dressage saddles to have long girth straps – in which case only two will be present – to permit the use of a short belly girth; the girth buckles will then be down below the panel (depending on the precise length of the girth) and so out of the way of the rider's leg, removing another undesirable bulky obstruction between rider and horse. However, some dressage saddles now have conventional short girth straps, since not everyone feels that belly girths and their buckling arrangements are necessary, and then three will be present, allowing for finer positioning on the horse's back as described earlier. It is all a matter of personal preference.

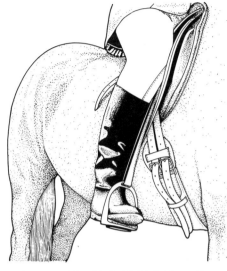

A dressage saddle with short belly girth in use. The idea is to remove the bulk of the buckles from under the rider's leg, but with carefully designed trees and positioned stirrup bars and girth tabs that problem is less common on modern dressage saddles, and many now have normal, short girth tabs

The fitting of the **short belly girth** on a dressage saddle

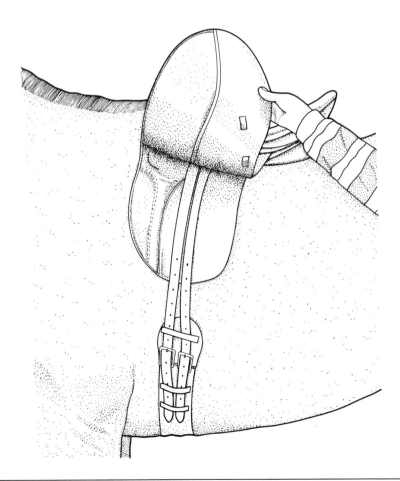

Endurance riding

Depending on the rules of the ride entered, it can benefit both horse and rider if the latter can dismount and lead the horse some way. This takes the strain off the horse's back muscles and allows them to rest, gives the horse psychological relief and relieves the rider's leg and back muscles.

Sustained pressure on the back can create 'deadened' skin and flesh as the blood circulation is interfered with. Although this should not happen with a well designed, properly fitted and padded saddle, it is certainly not unknown, even with today's higher standards of management, in endurance riding.

Dismounting and loosening the girth or girths a couple of holes (so that they do not feel tighter without the rider's weight on the saddle) gives the blood a chance to flow gradually back into the capillaries and 'refresh' the back by providing oxygen and nutrients and removing waste products.

Another refreshing practice is to change the numnah at each stop.

Saddles for endurance riding

Endurance riding is now firmly established as a specific competitive discipline requiring its own specialised tack. Horses are often under saddle for many hours in endurance riding and an exact, *comfortable* fit is essential. In their early stages of development most endurance saddles were based on the old military saddle similar in concept to the Western saddle, which in turn stemmed from the high-front-and-back medieval saddle. The military saddle has well padded bars (rather than a conventionally shaped tree) joined by front and rear arches, and these extend further back on the horse, spreading the weight and allowing for small pack attachments and other accoutrements. The seat is, to put it very simply, rather like a leather hammock slung between the arches, and is supremely comfortable for the rider whilst allowing free air circulation down the horse's back. Some endurance saddles are made on this principle, but others are now being designed and produced on more conventional trees; they have special 'therapeutic' qualities and specialised synthetic materials and stuffings aimed at increasing resilience and spreading weight as the horse moves to create a constantly even pressure. Small 'massage balls' are built in to some saddles, on the same principle as the car seat covers designed to massage the thighs, seats and backs of, initially, long-distance and taxi drivers; in fact these are now used regularly by many people who spend any length of time in their cars. Of unlikely benefit in theory to the uninitiated, in practice they work beautifully, and saddles made on this principle are currently finding favour with horses and riders alike.

The head of an endurance saddle made on a conventional-type tree is vertical or, in a few designs, very slightly sloping, depending on preference and the country of origin. Many endurance riders outside America like Western or Australian stock saddles which are similar in concept and, of course, specifically designed for working riders who would spend most of their daylight hours in the saddle.

Many endurance riders like to adopt a semi-forward position and keep their seat off their horse's back in trot and canter; also, to relieve their own muscles and to change the 'feel' they give to their horse, they like to be able to alter their stirrup leathers up or down a hole or two and ride at different lengths. Modern endurance saddles make this a comfortable possibility by not favouring an extreme long-in-the-leg seat as does a Western saddle – though if the rider wants to ride this way he can. Of course, his weight is still transmitted to the horse's back via the stirrup bars and is no less, even with an off-the-back position; but its distribution is changed, particularly if the stirrup bars are placed correspondingly a little further forward, being more closely concentrated around the strongest part of the back and over the centre of balance instead of perhaps a little behind it. Moreover when the rider's seat is fully in the saddle the horse feels every slight shift and bump, in a way that he does not when the seat is held just above it; and whilst this position does need an obviously fit rider to maintain it for significant distances, it does seem to be preferred by many horses who, in fact, learn to recognise it as a signal that the miles are there to be eaten up!

Side saddles

About thirty years ago, along with many other 'out-moded' aspects of the horse world, side-saddle riding as a technique and an art form was destined to disappear. Despite its elegance and precise sartorial etiquette, and its role as an attraction at major shows, and the fact that many intrepid ladies for generations had hunted fearlessly side saddle, it could not compete as a technique in the evolving fields of horse trials (eventing), show jumping and (a moot point this) dressage.

Now, however, it has its own organising body, The Sidesaddle Association, and has made a significant comeback not only as a showing class but as a technique in its own right. It is particularly suitable for those (gentlemen and ladies) who have had to give up riding because of arthritic hips, many of whom find they can ride quite comfortably and effectively side saddle. The numbers of teachers of the art are increasing, and show classes are now quite well established.

Many who would like to practise riding side saddle experience problems in finding suitable saddles, however. Despite the fact that new side saddles are now being made, most in current use are pre-World War II. They can be expensive, and are difficult to obtain as they do not come on to the market very often. In addition, side saddles were always made to measure for a particular animal and rider. Years of neglect, coupled with the fact that the old wooden trees are very fragile compared with the modern laminated wood ones, have resulted in many good old saddles being irretrievably damaged. However, the increasing interest in side-saddle riding is encouraging production of new side saddles, so enthusiasts can still pursue the sport today.

Nearly all side saddles are nearside ones, that is, the lady sits with her legs on the near side of the horse. Offside saddles are seen, but are very rare.

The tree is made of wood, reinforced with metal, usually cast iron. The newer laminated wood trees are lighter than the older ones, and stronger. The head is cut back, and the top pommel, or fixed head, over which the rider's right leg is placed, is fixed on the left. The lower pommel or leaping (jumping) head is screwed into the tree (rather than being part of it like the fixed head), and can be adjusted to suit the width of the rider's thigh, or to accommodate either flatwork or jumping. Sometimes a saddle will have two screw-in sockets for the leaping head so that adjustments can be made easily. The thread on leaping-head sockets should always be a lefthand one, as this is stronger.

The seat of a side saddle should be quite flat, and covered with doeskin or some sort of suede leather for security and to help stop the rider sliding down to the left. Some experts say that the offside of the seat should be built up slightly to prevent the rider's seat sliding over, but the opposite problem is the more common and most saddles will be, or need to be, built up on the near-side to prevent this. Imbalance in the rider is a very bad fault which can easily give the horse a sore back and stiff muscles as he tries to counteract his lopsided rider.

As with any other saddle, the gullet must leave a clear channel of air down the horse's back as spine pressure is so damaging. The tree points must not interfere with shoulder movement nor must there be any pressure on the loins

Development of the side saddle

Historian, horseman and author Anthony Dent has suggested that the original side-saddle riders were the women of early civilised, nomadic tribes, particularly the pregnant ones, and also probably the young children, who were perched sideways on pack animals as the tribes followed their herds to new grazing grounds.

When women did ride properly in the early times they rode astride, and also played polo, one of the very earliest equestrian sports. There were, though, examples of women riding side saddle, and in Britain the practice was widely adopted after the example of Queen Anne in the fourteenth century.

However, the saddle was nothing like the side saddle of today. The rider sat truly sideways, with her feet resting on a little plank or *planchette* on either the near or off sides of the horse. For hunting, hacking out and long journeys, however, astride riding was used.

It is said to be Catherine de Medici who introduced the now familiar pommels to the side saddle in about 1500, and they underwent various changes of design and position until the modern system evolved.

In the early part of this century the side saddle was developed further to make it easier for the rider to adopt a more forward seat out hunting, and during the current revival lighter, stronger and less bulky saddles are being produced.

The Side-Saddle Association

Learning to ride side saddle was not easy until the present revival of interest in the discipline came about, as few people could teach the art. Now there are more trained instructors but they are not exactly widespread. The Side-Saddle Association at Highbury House, 19 High Street, Welford, Northampton, NN6 7HT is a very useful organisation for anyone interested in side-saddle riding, and can give help in finding instruction.

Although Ladies Hack and Hunter classes were always open to side-saddle riders, there are now special side-saddle horse and pony classes at shows large and small up and down the country, plus regional and national championships. The Association can also help you get your own and your horse's turnout exactly right – the sartorial aspects are crucial in this discipline.

at the back. If the shoulders are interfered with this can cause the saddle to move, and possibly slip back on to the loins.

The best saddles are lined with linen, but serge can also be used. These are not so easy to clean as, of course, they cannot be removed easily, but they should be given a good brushing with a stiff brush when dry. They can be cleaned to some extent by damp sponging and brushing, but actually to wet them can be bad for the stuffing and they will then take a long time to dry. Newer saddles have a leather lining, but this material can cause a sore back due to the increased pressure from a side saddle and the fact that it is less absorbent than fabric.

The nearside saddle flap must be large enough to keep the rider's right leg off the horse's shoulder, so is cut well forward and sometimes has padding underneath the front part. There is usually a flap or belly strap stitched to the bottom edge of the nearside flap which fastens with a hook and eye to the smaller offside saddle flap, the object being to keep the flaps down and secure.

Normally a Fitzwilliam, or an Atherstone type or a three-fold baghide girth is used and, unlike astride saddles, the girth is fastened first to the nearside girth tabs or straps. There are two main girth straps plus a very important third one – the point strap – which is angled backwards at 15° from the vertical. This is attached at the top to the point of the tree and a strap called the balance strap is buckled to it. The balance strap is stitched to the rear part of the saddle on the offside and passed obliquely below the horse's belly before being buckled to the nearside point strap. Another arrangement, though not considered safe for strenuous work but which is neater for showing, is to have the balance strap stitched to the girth (rather than the saddle) on the offside. This obviously does not keep the saddle so steady as the former arrangement. The balance strap has a buckle and keeper at each end, one end buckling to the nearside point strap, as described, and the other to the short length stitched to the offside rear of the saddle, or to the girth if this method is preferred. Sometimes the balance strap will be stitched directly to the girth on the offside. When girthing up on the offside, the front girth buckle is fastened to the offside point strap to help keep the saddle in place.

There are several variants in side saddles according to who made/makes them, and the stirrup leather attachments are perhaps more diverse than any other aspect. Basically, whatever patented pattern appears on the saddle, it must have a quick-release mechanism which is kept well oiled, and the user must practise using it, as they all differ. Side-saddle stirrup irons must have larger eyes than other stirrups to accommodate the adjustment hook which is an integral part of these stirrups and leathers. According to make, there will be a fitting at the top end of the leather to take its 'mate' on the saddle, with a metal hook at the other end which threads through the eye and back on itself, being adjusted according to the required length by means of holes in the leather near the stirrup itself. A little leather cover or sleeve protects the saddle flap and the rider's boot.

The saddle flaps usually cover the girth tabs, but there are now saddles on which the offside girth attachments are visible on the outside of the flap. These are used mainly for showing and the girths used with such saddles have high-quality buckles and keepers for elegance with, very often, the balance strap stitched to the girth.

Most horses take well to being ridden side saddle with its lack of an offside leg aid (the whip is used for guidance) and different weight distribution. It should always be remembered, though, that the horse can easily develop a sore back in the early days of adjusting to side-saddle equitation. His stints under saddle should be short at first to help his skin and muscles get used to it.

The rider has a leg-up and it is recommended nowadays that she (or he) sits astride in the normal way at first, absolutely straight in the saddle, and then brings the right leg over the fixed head. From behind, the rider must appear to sit as straight as on an astride saddle, but with the offside leg missing. In this position he or she will be balanced securely, and the weight distributed as comfortably as possible for the horse. The tendency to raise the left heel and grip with the left leg must be avoided (except possibly when jumping, or for momentary security in an emergency) as this encourages the rider to sit to the left which is bad for the horse's back.

Saddling up

The saddle should be carried with the right hand holding the fixed head, and the lining down the hip and thigh, the seat under the right arm. The girth and balance strap can be attached on the nearside and held, with the flap strap if there is one, in the left hand. The saddle is placed carefully on the horse's back a little too far forward and slid back, as with an ordinary saddle. The balance strap is buckled to the point strap, and the girth to the first two girth straps.

Next fasten the girth on the offside, from which all adjustments are made. The balance strap lies on top of the girth and must not be tighter than the girth. The flap strap should, likewise, be fastened no tighter than the girth and balance strap. If the horse wears a martingale, the girth, balance and flap straps all pass through its girth loop.

Ideally two people should saddle up the horse: one to hold the saddle in place, and the other to move around the horse carrying out the various steps involved in fitting the saddle. The girth and balance strap are finally adjusted on the offside once the rider is mounted. It is important not to have the balance strap too far back or too tight, as some horses will buck against it.

General care of the saddle

The leather part of the saddle is cleaned in the usual way, and the doeskin or suede seat brushed. Care must be taken not to drop or misuse the saddle because of the comparatively fragile nature of most side-saddle trees. If it has to be put on the ground (it will not balance conveniently over a stable door like an astride saddle) put it down pommel first, resting on the girth. Do not leave it on the horse's back if the girths are undone. Take care not to bang the pommels against door jambs and so on, and if you are transporting the saddle in a vehicle with the horse, keep it well stacked away from the animal, and protected by other equipment so it cannot fall about. Do not place the girths over its seat, as with other saddles, as this can leave a mark. It is well worthwhile seeking out a saddler experienced with side saddles for a yearly check, and The Society of Master Saddlers or The Sidesaddle Association should be able to help here.

Riding side-saddle

Your first impression on being 'put up' (given a leg up) on to a side saddle is how far up off the horse's back you are. The seats of these saddles are much more thickly padded than astride or cross saddles. The seat of a side-saddled must be flat, not dipped in any way, or you will find staying put and in balance much more difficult.

As mentioned elsewhere, the most common way to be put up these days is to have a normal leg up and sit astride the side saddle. Centre and balance yourself properly, then bring your right leg over to the left over the pommel so that, from the back, you seem to be riding astride but minus your right leg. Your instructor will check the correct adjustment of the pommels and your stirrup length.

Some riders take to the side saddle immediately, whilst others feel unsafe due to having no right leg available. The unusual balance sensations this produces can be a little disconcerting, but with good instruction and a reliable horse this can soon be overcome.

On the safety question there are pros and cons: a side-saddle rider will stay put during many forward pecks on the part of the horse, as the right thigh across the front of the body anchors the rider in place. On the other hand, should the horse actually fall a side-saddle rider is less likely to be thrown clear. Correct instruction on emergency action, and stress on properly fitted and adjusted tack, as with astride riding, makes the likelihood of serious accidents much less.

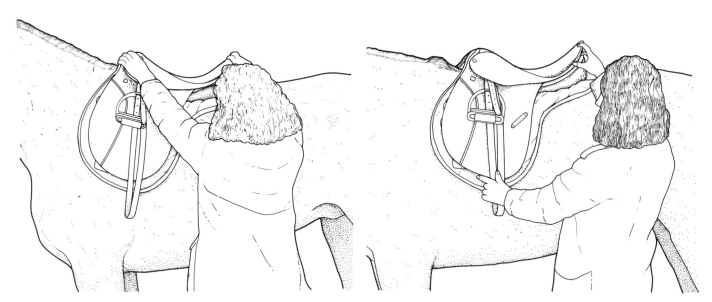

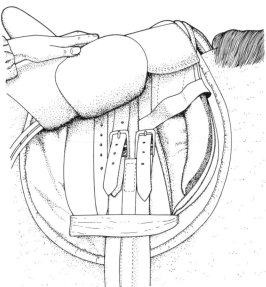

Top left: Hold the saddle (with the numnah, if used) and place it on the withers, too far forward. Slide it back with the direction of the hair to its correct position so that the pommel is above the back part of the withers. Usually, the saddle finds its own 'natural' spot on the back

Top right: It's easy to push the saddle too far back, like this. If this happens do not push it forward again as this will ruffle the hair underneath and cause discomfort. Lift the saddle up and start again

Right: It is normal to leave the off (right)-side girth buckles done up, passing the girth under the girth groove and fastening it on the near (left)-side. This view of the saddle from the off-side shows the flap and the buckle guard (in this case attached to the saddle) lifted up to show that the girth has been fastened to the first two tabs (the most usual way), with the first tab having been passed through the loop on the numnah to help keep the latter in place. The girth itself has been passed down through the bottom loop on the numnah for the same purpose

Bottom left: It is correct to rest the flap on your head whilst buckling up the girth. The girth has been passed up through the loop on the bottom of the numnah, again to keep the latter in place. Above the flap and under the skirt, the stirrup leather can be seen over the stirrup bar

Bottom right: When fastening the girth on a saddle with three girth tabs (which is common) it is important to ensure that you use the same two tabs on each side of the saddle. This is the near-side of the saddle shown in the third illustration, and the girth is fastened on the first two tabs on each side so that the saddle will sit straight (unless the horse has an unevenly developed back) and pressures will be as even as possible

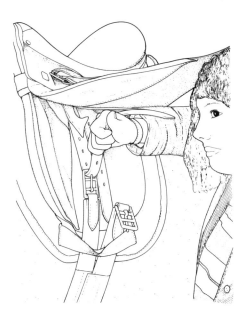

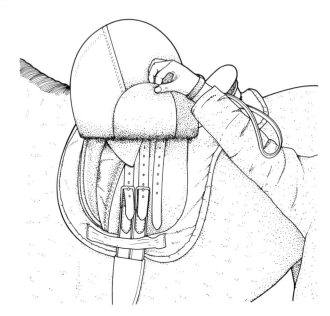

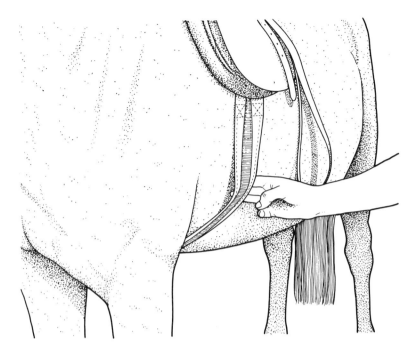

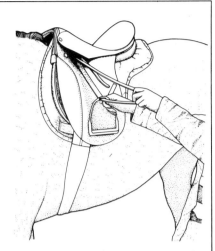

Tighten the girth one hole at a time to accustom the horse to the feel before mounting. Check that before trying to mount you can just slide the flat of your fingers between the girth and the horse. This girth is too loose and would slide down the horse's side when the rider attempted to mount

Before mounting, slide your stirrups down the leathers, and before or after dismounting slide them up again right to the stirrup bar. Note that on this saddle the numnah has correctly been pulled well up into the front arch or pommel to remove pressure on the withers

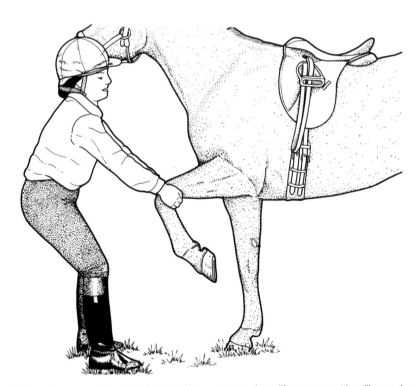

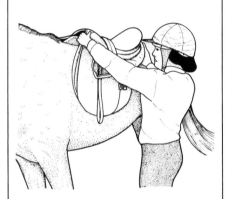

When removing the saddle *lift* it up off the horse's back as this is more comfortable for him than sliding it round. . .

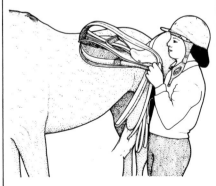

After girthing up to mount, stroke your horse's shoulder and leg down to the knee and pull his foreleg out from the knee so that his elbow moves forward as far as it will go. This will smooth out the skin under the girth to prevent wrinkles and discourage galling, and also to increase the horse's comfort and action in front. Here the elbow has not moved forward as the horse is resisting, possibly being unused to this exercise. With calming words and encouraging pulling on your part he will soon relax and allow his elbow and shoulder to be pulled forward. Do this on both sides, of course. It is often done from the fetlock with a straight foreleg: this, however, is difficult for a horse as he cannot lift his foreleg straight but has to bend it at the knee to lift it, then straighten it out. Pulling the leg out from the knee, as shown, is more comfortable for him and more effective

. . . and as the girth comes over the back pick it up and put it, sweaty side down, on the saddle seat. If you put it muddy side down you could scratch the seat leather

The effects of the stirrup bars

The effect the stirrup bars have on the rider's seat can be crucial, particularly in dressage saddles and those intended for non-jumping riding. Old-fashioned showing saddles were designed to show off and exaggerate the horse's front, and would specifically position their riders towards the cantle; as the stirrup bars were never, proportionately, set as far back as the deepest part of the seat, the rider had little choice but to ride with the feet well forward from the under-hip position commensurate with a balanced classical-type seat. There are still riders who use this old-fashioned position even today, and this includes the American saddle seat.

The true classical seat requires that the rider's body is in balanced harmony with the horse's centre of gravity: it should be possible to drop an imaginary vertical line from the rider's shoulder, through his hip and the horse's centre of balance and down through the rider's heel. Even with a fairly straight-legged seat and long stirrup the knee will protrude forward a little, but the stirrup bar should be positioned so that when the leather hangs vertically downwards the stirrup allows the rider to place his or her foot in it on the ball of the foot with the heel directly under the hip. Another rule of thumb with a central seat to the saddle (as opposed to a set-back one) is that the leather should hang vertically down the middle of the flap.

If the stirrup bars are set too far forward – and this happens even in some quite expensive and supposedly 'top-hole' dressage saddles – the rider will have to make a conscious effort to keep the heels back under the hip, rather than the feet

The effects of weight and its distribution

Obviously horses are much better able to move without the weight of a rider on their backs; moreover, Nature designed the horse's spine to have dependent structures such as the abdomen and contents slung *from underneath it* and the tops of the ribs – it was never intended to bear weight placed on it from above. However, although when we look at a fully fleshed horse from the side the back appears to curve downwards in a slight arc from withers to croup, in fact it does the reverse: the chain of vertebrae forming the backbone actually curves very slightly upwards, something which can be seen clearly in the skeleton. Physically this is a very strong structural design, and one used by engineers in the construction of, for example, suspension bridges. In the horse there are bony 'fingers' called 'processes' which protrude from the top of each of the vertebra: these are of differing lengths, shortest in the dorsal and lumbar (back and loin) regions, and highest at the withers, and in the living horse the slight downward curve we see is formed by the tops of these processes, not the vertebrae themselves. In a horse with good to reasonable conformation this is a very convenient shape for us because the saddle will sit easily in the best place, with the pommel just above and behind the highest point of the withers; and if it is well balanced with a centrally dipped seat, the rider will, as already mentioned, be carried directly over the strongest point of the back, a position which requires the least effort from the horse.

There are two difficult points of conformation to cope with: firstly, if the horse has exceptionally high and sharp withers; and secondly, if he is croup-high, where his croup (the highest point of his hindquarters) is higher than his withers.

To cope with the first point, a saddle can have what is termed a 'cut-back' head, where the front is 'scooped out' to accommodate the withers without injuring them or setting the saddle too far back on the horse. Cut-back heads were once common in the old traditional Lane Fox showing saddles, and undoubtedly some are still used; they could be used on any horse, and reduced the effect true of some saddles of obstructing the judge's view of the withers under the pommel. They were more 'discreet' and, along with the very straight-cut flap, flat seat and rearward positioning of the rider, would show off the horse's front to best advantage. Nowadays however, most people feel they are unreasonably uncomfortable, and they are certainly not conducive to a modern/classical balanced seat. Also, some showing professionals feel that if the judge is uncomfortable when riding their horse in the ring, he (or she) – being human – is bound not to give it as many points as if he had experienced a comfortable ride. For these reasons the highly specialised showing saddle with cut-back head is going out of favour in many show-rings and being replaced by a close-contact dressage, or some other comfortable but fairly straight-cut saddle, often with a plain normal girth as opposed to the short belly girth which does look a little untidy for the show-ring. In such cases, obviously, a saddle with three short, rather than two long girth straps is used.

The second conformational fault of being croup-high is much more difficult to deal with, and mature horses like this should not be selected if they are required to carry a saddle for long periods: despite the best efforts of rider and saddler, the saddle will constantly slide forwards and dig the horse behind the shoulders, sometimes – and particularly, it seems, with Western-type saddles – to the extent of causing callousing. Certainly bruising can occur, and in any case, a horse of this conformation gives the rider a most uncomfortable feeling of tipping downhill all the time; combined with a poor, short front it makes for a most unpleasant ride. The saddle can, of course, be stuffed to lift it at the front, but its general downward urge will not be affected and there is always a chance of bruising to the area behind the shoulders.

An important point to appreciate is that croup-high conformation is quite normal in youngsters; many do not 'come up' in front until they are about four years old, and their fronts do not develop fully until after their quarters. When young horses are first backed and saddled, particular care should therefore be taken over the saddle used. This factor can also make rug-fitting difficult. However, as youngsters should not be worked for anything like long enough to cause a problem, perhaps this is not a serious consideration; although I feel it should be borne in mind nevertheless.

Horses with withers which are poorly defined, or low and wide, and animals of a generally rounded shape (whether because of conformation or an over-fat condition) will have trouble keeping the saddle in place. A well-defined girth groove on the breastbone is a definite help in 'wedging' the girth, and so the saddle, in place, and is a good point to be looked for in a horse. On the other hand, a slab-sided animal may well have a good girth groove but be so narrow that however carefully the saddle is fitted, it is never particularly stable on its back. Horses with sway (dipped) and roach (arched) backs cause problems of their own, and extremes of these conformation faults are very difficult to deal with; they will need the help and advice of a very competent, experienced saddler. Generally, the time-honoured advice holds good: avoid buying horses with serious conformation faults.

How much the saddle moves around on the horse's back is exacerbated by the rider's weight and movement. We want the horse to move freely, but a good rider will move in the saddle as little as possible and will do his or her utmost to sit in balance over the centre of gravity. Even this simple-sounding feat is not easy but it is a fact that, in the words of Geoffrey Hattan FBHS: 'a rider should not be permitted to do anything until he is capable of doing nothing'. In other words, until he can stay in complete harmony and balance with the horse, and not disturb its movement in the slightest, he should not be giving aids or attempting to influence it. Wouldn't it be wonderful if this actually happened with every rider?! In practice, to reach this stage involves careful instruction on the lunge, and the majority of riders will not have the patience to wait that long before 'attempting to influence the horse'. In the highest echelons of every single equestrian discipline we will see riders who throw themselves around to a quite unreasonable degree, partly in their attempts to influence the horse, but also in their efforts to keep their own balance on his back, be this unintentional or even subconscious.

Every tiny movement is felt by the horse, and sensitive animals will not

positioning themselves naturally, encouraged by the correct drop of the leather. In forward-seat saddles such as event/general purpose/cross-country and jumping saddles this is less important, of course.

Adjustable stirrup bars are a more recent development, where the leather can be moved forward or back as required. These are made by at least one firm at present, and may well become more common as inventions continue apace in the field of tack. Most saddlers prefer their old familiar designs, however, so this positioning of the stirrup bar is a point to be watched when buying and trying a saddle.

Saddles and Accessories

① Brown's Performance Saddles of Nevada, USA have made their saddles available in the UK through top endurance rider Yvonne Tyson (address, p195). Ortho-Flex saddles allow the rider to custom fit each horse easily by balancing the saddle and letting flexible panels do the rest. The panels are bolted on to the tree and extend fore and aft of the tree, giving a greater weight-bearing surface and allowing fewer pounds per square inch of pressure on the back, so making the task of carrying a rider much easier for the horse.

When the rider is in position, the panels flex to the horse, enabling him to move more freely yet with contact at all times over the whole back area. This flexibility allows the horse to move more naturally and with greater comfort and ease. Each panel has a cover which, on the bottom surface, is made from medical fleece which does not absorb moisture and needs little cleaning but can be washed by machine with no adverse effects. The Ortho-Flex saddles have proved popular in endurance riding in the UK and the USA for several years.

stand for such treatment; neither will some highly trained ones, although 'schoolmaster' horses will tolerate it as part of the job and others of a more placid temperament will not react so strongly – but feel it they do. Every movement also affects the way the saddle feels on the horse's back, so any small unsuitability will be magnified, maybe to the extent that actual problems are caused. It is a known fact that poor riders cause sore backs in the form of rubbed skin and bruised muscles.

For the horse, every movement of the rider is felt as weight redistribution in the saddle and on his back, and necessitates a counteracting movement if he is to keep himself not only in balance but physically in a position to carry out whatever movements the rider is asking for. This means he is often using muscles and energy unnecessarily. Sometimes if a movement is needed quickly to counterbalance a sudden lurch by the rider, muscle damage can occur as the muscle contracts in an unco-ordinated way as an emergency measure. This sort of thing also happens if a horse slips on mud or slippery roads under saddle; strong, quick muscle action is needed for him to keep his feet, and muscles and other soft tissues can be wrenched, putting him out of action for some time or causing a sore back which, sadly, may not be recognised either by the rider or by the manager of the horse. It is obvious, therefore, that no matter how expensive, luxurious, well designed and meticulously made is the saddle, a poor rider can still damage his horse through incorrect and inappropriate weight distribution. In a saddle which is not correctly designed these faults will be made even worse.

When a horse has been under saddle for some time, say two hours or more, we are now advised not to remove the saddle as soon as the rider dismounts, but to leave it on for a while so the blood vessels in the back, which have been compressed under weight, can return to their former shape and 'tone' gradually. It is said that if the saddle is removed immediately blood will rush back into the tiny capillaries too quickly and rupture them, causing tissue injury, congestion and a sore back.

It is certainly true that compression of the skin under weight can deprive it of blood to the extent that areas subjected to unreasonable pressure can die off (a condition sometimes known by horsemen as 'sitfast'); occasionally this necessitates surgical removal of the dead tissue, or the back may be scarred, with white areas where the hair follicles have been damaged and subsequently a bare or perhaps hard, calloused area. However, if the saddle distributes weight and pressure evenly and is adequately padded either through its own panels or, if a Western-type saddle, a decent blanket or pad, this sort of thing is far less likely to happen. Nevertheless, I still feel it is a good idea to dismount and walk the still-saddled horse for the last half-mile or so home (or round the showground, or wherever you are, for a good ten minutes) with a slightly loosened girth (and with the stirrups run up their leathers for safety, of course!) to ease pressure and to try and counteract the occurrence of any 'blood rush' (for want of a better expression!). This has other benefits, too, such as helping the horse wind down and cool off – provided the rider can control him from the ground! I must admit that in practice my horses have never experienced a sore back from having the saddle removed immediately; but then, it is no extra trouble to walk the horse home, and will ease a rider's possibly stiff leg muscles too, after a long ride. Horses seem to like it, and to

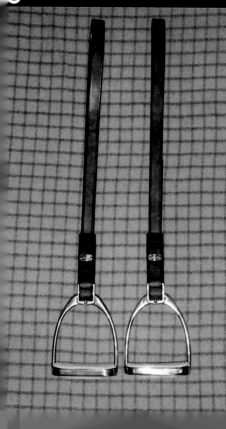

② With the increasing interest in Britain in true classical equitation, A. J. Foster Saddlemakers (address, p195) have made available the Lauriche Dressage saddle, which has, in fact, been available in the USA and on the continent of Europe for many years. The seat is broad with a low pommel and cantle (unlike conventional competitive dressage saddles) so is supporting and very comfortable, but not restrictive.

The saddle panels have a wide bearing surface, fitting the horse's back well from front to rear and from side to side which gives stability with dispersed weight-bearing. There is also a wide gullet to leave the horse's spine totally free of contact. To add to the stability, balance and even pressure, the saddle has girth tabs attached to the front of the trees (at the point) and also from the swell of the tree at the back, an arrangement which takes a standard dressage girth with no problem.

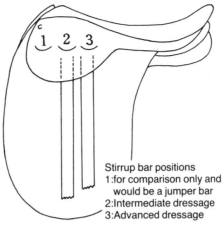

Stirrup bar positions
1:for comparison only and would be a jumper bar
2:Intermediate dressage
3:Advanced dressage

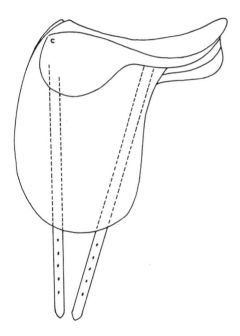

The Lauriche dressage saddle is available in two models, the Intermediate and the Advanced, the difference being in the seat bone to stirrup bar relationship. The Advanced saddle is intended for the advanced classical rider or the novice who aspires to that position, and the Intermediate has its stirrup bar a little further foward in what Fosters describe as the 'standard dressage position'. The stirrup bar on the Advanced saddle is set a little further back to enable the rider to sit in the advanced seat and leg position unhindered by the stirrup's pulling the leg forward, as can happen on some dressage saddles. The Advanced saddle also allows for the fact that the rider's own seat shape changes from one position to the other, claim Fosters.

Two quotes from authorities may be of interest. Sylvia Loch, author, teacher and lecturer on classical equitation, says of the Lauriche Dressage Saddle: 'I have been riding in a Foster's Lauriche Saddle for some time now and I am able to enjoy the depth and comfort of seat hitherto undreamed of in a conventional dressage saddle. This is the seat of maximum adhesion and broad-based support, which the great European Masters always referred to as the Classical Seat. My horses like it, too, and I am delighted now to be able to recommend the Lauriche range of dressage saddles to all my pupils and readers of my books.'

Physiotherapist Mary Bromiley says: 'More riders are now realising that the many training problems they are experiencing are due to unhappy horses. Foster's Lauriche Saddle is such that with its unique panels it allows the horse to round up its back and lower its head with complete comfort, leaving it free to work. Reverse this and make him uncomfortable and he will hollow his back and raise his head which, of course, will restrict him greatly.'

③ Fosters also supply the Lauriche Stirrup Leather. It is described as being designed for style and comfort with no buckle beneath the skirt of the saddle, so preventing bruising and inner-thigh soreness. There is no loose tongue and, therefore, one less thickness of leather under the rider's thigh. This contributes to a much closer 'feel' with the horse. Although intended for an elegant appearance in the dressage arena or show ring, the leathers are claimed to be robust and practical for eventing or showjumping and, with a full 12-hole adjustment, come in sizes from children's to gents.

④ The Ajustree Saddle, from G. Fieldhouse Saddlery (address, p195), has a traditional laminated beechwood tree with an adjustment mechanism consisting of two hinges on either side of the pommel which can be moved to alter the width of the tree to fit the horse's back but producing no change in the wither region. The adjustment mechanism corresponds with the horse's back below and behind the withers which is where the horse gains or loses weight and muscular development during the year,

according to his feeding and work programme.

Once the tree has been adjusted to fit the horse, the hinges are secured in place with a pair of bolts which are part of a fitting kit held at retailers selling the Ajustree saddles. There are two basic saddle widths, narrow to medium and medium to wide, and the fitting kit permits the saddle to offer ten adjustments to each saddle width which in practice means they can be made to fit virtually any size and shape of horse or pony.

This allows purchasers much more leeway when buying a saddle and the saddler will be able to quickly and easily alter your saddle when necessary.

G. Fieldhouse Saddlery also produce a 'Supersoft' elasticated leather girth which has a spongy foam inside a chrome-tanned soft leather hide for hard wear but greater comfort for the horse, particularly as it is in the shape of a traditional Atherstone girth. They have produced a saddle for ridden Arabs which gives a deep, supportive seat but with a low cantle to ensure that the saddle keeps a low profile on the horse so as not to detract from the horse's conformation. The front arch has a keyhole shape deep cut back and a low pommel for rider comfort. The points of the tree are angled to allow the panels and flaps of the saddle to fit behind the horse's shoulders, allowing him to move freely and show himself off. As Arabs are often broad-backed the saddle is slightly wider than normal which gives a larger weight-bearing surface along with comfort. There is a small knee roll.

The company's Endurance Saddle, too, has a supportive seat, recessed stirrup bars which cannot be felt under the thigh and provides comfortable leg contact for riders wishing to go for long periods 'out of the saddle'. It has a foam seat moulded for comfort, but is not over-padded. As the panels have a large bearing surface, no tree fans are needed at the rear of the saddle. The flaps are straight cut so that there is no interference with the horse's shoulders and there are large knee rolls to provide support for downhill going. The stirrup leathers can be worn under the flaps for extra rider comfort and there are large dees on the front and rear of the saddle to attach various items of equipment.

Another interesting item produced by this company is the Hartley show saddle in two versions, one for show hunters with a detachable knee roll and one for show hacks which is slightly straighter cut. The saddles provide close contact with a wide weight-distributing panel. They have a 2½in cut back head to accommodate a wide variety of horses and the tree has been specifically designed with a flat seat which allows the horse to be shown properly but will accommodate and suit a judge in comfort.

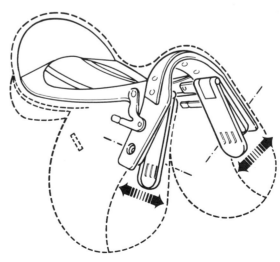

Back injuries

Recognising back injuries is a very important part of horse management. It may be true that the nearer the ground you get the more likely are you to find the source of any lameness, and back problems may not be as common as some think (particularly in cases of obscure or hard-to-diagnose lameness) but it is important to be able to recognise the symptoms of back injuries in general so that further injury, and mental problems, can be avoided by not continuing to work the horse.

The signs of back injuries of any kind, and however caused, can be very varied. The horse or pony may not be actually lame in the accepted sense of obviously saving one leg and favouring another. He may go short, with stiff paces, pottery gaits and general bodily stiffness. He may look anxious, hold his head higher and more stiffly, refuse to accept the bit or the rider's aids or at least do so unwillingly, be unwilling to work, may start refusing fences, running out, rushing fences, kicking and bucking on landing (often a source of much amusement to show-jumping audiences) or rushing off on landing. Depending on the actual injury, going up or downhill can also create problems for the horse.

He may be unusually stiff and unwilling on corners, bends and circles, or start having difficulty in performing some movement he usually does easily and well. His temperament might change and he could become irritable or defensive. He may well cringe downwards when attempts are made to put on the saddle, or sidle away from it. He might start attacking (even if mildly), anyone trying to tack him up or groom his back. Reining back may become particularly difficult and painful for him, with or without a rider. Lunge work often

like having company at their heads. One horse I used to ride would chunter to me all the time I walked at his head; though perhaps he was just relieved to get me off his back!

Although this practice is fairly widely known, and teaching organisations quite commonly advise leaving the saddle on for a while, you will see riders doing quite the opposite at formal competitions; for example in horse trials, as soon as a horse completes the speed and endurance phase, the rider removes the saddle and saddle-cloth to go and weigh in. Similarly, after the steeplechase and roads-and-tracks phases, most are quick to whip off the saddle and sponge the horse down before the cross-country. Endurance competitors vary in what they do, some leaving the saddle on and others taking it off. And whether your ride has been short or long, once your saddle does come off it's a good practice to rub over the horse's saddle patch gently, in the same way as you might rub yourself after removing clothing after hot exercise or long wear. Horses appreciate it – though not the hearty hand-slapping which used to be taught by the 'Old School' and which surely can't do those fragile, compressed little capillaries any good!

'Cold back' syndrome

When a horse hollows his back to avoid the saddle, the usual reason given by many in the horse world is that he has a 'cold back'. Of course the horse does not have a cold back in the literal sense and the expression is meant to indicate that he objects to the cold feel of the saddle leather when it is put on his back. Even when a numnah or saddle cloth is used and the horse still flinches away from it, the owner/rider will continue to maintain that the horse is anticipating the cold feel of the saddle and that this is why he tries to avoid it. Like so many old excuses and theories in the horse world, this one must surely be doubted by anyone with an eggcupful of intelligence. In the first place, the horse's back is covered with hair which in winter, when the saddle is most likely to feel cold, is often quite thick unless the horse has been clipped right out; even then most people must surely suspect that the real reason the horse resents having the saddle put on, and may also resent being mounted, is that his back hurts.

Back problems have been under investigation by the veterinary profession for many years now, and can still be difficult to diagnose. They may involve injury to the bony vertebrae themselves, to the soft tissues such as the tendons and ligaments, or to the muscles and the skin. Such injuries can be caused by a variety of mishaps: the horse may have wrenched himself during work or play, he may have slipped up or fallen or have over-jumped; he may have been made to carry too heavy a rider (a horse should be able to carry a third or slightly more of his own weight without trouble), or been worked too strenuously for his stage of fitness (which includes being worked too young) or for too long, causing excess fatigue and loss of strength and energy in the muscles.

However, there is undoubtedly one major cause of back injury which I'm sure often goes undetected, either because people don't think about it sufficiently or because they find it inconvenient to admit to it, and that is an ill-fitting saddle. Badly fitting saddles can cause deep-seated bruising of the back muscles, badly bruised and even damaged spinal processes – and not only on the withers (such damage is known as fistulous withers) but down the backbone – and rubbed or even raw skin due to friction and pressure. Horses with white marks on their backs or even bare patches have evidently suffered quite severe saddle injuries in the past, and have ended up with no hair on that spot or previously coloured hair growing white – a sure indication of previous bad management.

If ever a horse you are tacking up tries to swing away from the saddle, or tries to flatten or arch his back downwards away from it, or even tries to lie down, put the saddle away and arrange for a vet to examine his back thoroughly, and carefully examine the saddle, either yourself, or ask an expert to do so. Certainly do not give the horse ridden work, or any other work if the vet advises against it, until the back has recovered. You will not necessarily be able actually to see the injury; deep-seated bruising, for example, may show no obvious outward sign of damage, nor may spinal injuries. With bruised or even fractured vertebral processes, however, there is usually heat and swelling (although these can be caused by trauma other than the saddle).

A horse with slight but chronic (ie long-lasting) back injuries may not actually cringe away from his saddle, but these can cause all sorts of problems: he may go short, be unwilling to work and particularly to get his hind legs under him or to jump, or he may dislike being groomed and become bad-tempered when you try to do so. He may start to run out at fences, to refuse, or to buck and kick on landing (looks funny, but it isn't if your back is killing you), and he may appear intermittently lame. The trouble is not bound to be related to the saddle, of course, but this is certainly one area you should investigate.

Fitting a saddle to horse and rider

The saddle should provide the rider with a secure, comfortable place to sit, while at the same time causing the horse not one iota of discomfort. Horses' and ponies' backs come in all shapes and sizes, and the back of any one animal will vary considerably throughout the year according to its condition and workload. It may be fat and blubbery when it is out of work; hard, fined-down and muscular during work; or if it has been underfed or ill, thin and bony.

Many people buy one saddle for their horse and may overlook the fact that as his condition changes it no longer fits quite as well. It is possible to compensate for very minor deficiencies by using thick or thin numnahs; this doesn't alter the fact that the saddle doesn't actually fit, but then to have a different saddle for each season of the year or to suit our horse's changing condition is hopelessly impractical for most of us, even if we have different saddles for different pursuits (though see p38 for modern developments which overcome these difficulties). Probably the best solution for the one-saddle owner is to fit it when the horse is in normal, moderate working condition, so that variations either way won't be disastrous. As many 'ordinary' horses work most of the year they will be in similar condition most of the time, and there will probably not be too great a problem.

shows up back problems in the form of unwillingness or lameness or stiffness, and trying to turn the horse sharply in hand often produces a horse who seems frozen to the spot, unable to move.

Watch for his behaviour in the stable or field. Reluctance to lie down or roll, or difficulty in doing so, are signs of possible back injury, as is difficulty in rising again. If his bedding has obviously not been lain on and he has no stable stains on his coat or clothing, he has not slept or rested flat and the reason could be a back injury.

The cause of an injury could be the saddle itself; carelessness when tacking up (such as leaving the panel folded up under the girth which can cause a sore); or the horse may have rolled on a stone or grooming kit left in the bedding. His work can obviously cause back injuries as can a simple slip-up on mud or an icy or slippery surface. Cornering too sharply or quickly can also do it and falls and stumbles most certainly can.

Although the symptoms mentioned can all be due to other causes, they are recognised signs of back problems and should alert any owner or groom to the need for further expert investigation.

Professional tack fitting

Professional help in fitting tack to horses, ponies and riders can go a long way towards acquiring a satisfactory item which will give many years of excellent service if well cared for.

Shopping at a retail outlet which is a member of the British Equestrian Trade Association will enable customers to obtain qualified help in tack fitting. The BETA runs courses and awards qualifications, in module form, in various aspects of the equestrian retail trade, including the fitting and safety of tack, so it is a good plan to ask about this qualification and staff holding it on the premises.

A qualified instructor, with either or both British Horse Society and/or Association of British Riding Schools qualifications, will also be able to offer sound advice.

Premises displaying a trade badge or crest (such as, in the UK, the Society of Master Saddlers) will have staff qualified in the making of tack whose knowledge and experience will be able to guide customers towards the right choice.

If you are in any doubt about your own ability to fit tack, take a suitably experienced or qualified friend or professional adviser with you if the retail outlet you are using cannot offer qualified or experienced assistance.

Saddles come in wide-, medium- and narrow-tree widths, and this variety will usually provide something to accommodate most animals fairly well. Either a normal or a cut-back head is available, and the length of the saddle also varies: it is usually measured in inch increments (although many are now sold in metric sizes), up to 18in or even 19in for large occupants, though most adults are probably suited by a 16in or 17in saddle.

Fitting the rider

It is usually easier to fit the rider than to fit the horse where saddles are concerned. You can try a prospective saddle in the shop, or carefully on a saddle-horse at home, or on the horse itself. Basically you should sit on it and snuggle down with relaxed seat and legs (none of this 'toes-up' business which automatically stiffens you up!) then take up the stirrups at your normal length. Provided you feel comfortable (and the new saddle may feel a little strange at first), you can then check the following points: you should be able to fit the width of your hand between the front of your body and the front arch of the saddle, as also between the back of your body and the rear arch. Your knees should not protrude off the front of the flap when your stirrups are adjusted to the shortest position in which you are going to use them, nor should they be too much (eg several inches) behind the knee rolls (if present – and they usually are these days) when your stirrups are at their longest length. Do the stirrup leather test mentioned earlier and make sure that, in a normal position, your leathers are vertical when your heels are in line with your hips. If normally you don't ride like this, then have a few lessons and try it (I am not being facetious) and see how much easier riding becomes, and how much more willingly your horse goes. And if your saddle militates against this, don't buy it. Don't buy it, either, if it seems to force your thighs too far apart and prevent a deep seat.

All riders have faults, even the best, and one of the worst when it comes to causing back problems in the horse, apart from constantly banging up and down, is to ride with your body twisted or lopsided. So sit straight when you are trying your saddle, and persuade a friend to study you critically from behind and in front and give you an honest opinion! Further, before you even sit in it, check that the lowest point of the seat is midway between pommel and cantle so you know you are at least starting off with a central seat.

If the saddle passes all these tests and you feel comfortable, you can try it on the horse.

Fitting the horse

It is much more difficult to fit a saddle to the horse, if only because he cannot tell you, in the same way as a child, what it feels like: if it is alright, if it pinches, digs in, or presses on anything. It is entirely our responsibility to spot problems, and this may well be quite difficult. If you have any doubt at all about your own ability to do this, it is best to ask an expert friend, colleague or instructor to help you, as this really is a critical subject. The saddle must:
(a) be the correct width for the back;

(b) leave a clear channel of daylight down the spine from withers to loins (spinal contact must at all costs be avoided in saddle fitting);

(c) not interfere in any way with the horse's movement;

(d) be the correct length for the back so that it does not press on the loin (kidney) area; and

(e) have resilient stuffing of the correct amount so that there is neither too little which would result in insufficient cushioning effect, nor too much, so that it is rounded downwards – not only is this uncomfortably hard to the horse's back, but it actually reduces the bearing surface of the panel, thus intensifying pressure on those areas of the back which the panel touches most.

Most saddlers will want you to try a saddle over a piece of cloth, a saddle-cloth or a thin numnah to avoid marking the underside with sweat or grease, and this is a reasonable enough request. And if you get a saddle on approval through a mail-order firm it would be advisable to do this, because if you return it stained you may have to buy it. Some firms have on-site fitting facilities with expert advice on hand from a saddler or other expert to help you, although it is unfortunate that some of the newer 'tack supermarkets' seem to be staffed by salespeople who know little about the stock and even less about horses and are simply there to sell the goods. If this is the only type of salesperson available, shop elsewhere, unless you are confident of your own ability to check the fit of the saddle.

Fitting Procedure: Place the saddle in the usual way – forward of the withers, sliding it back into place – and consider first how it sits on the back. If it comes impossibly high above the withers and seems perched on the back (even allowing for newness) with little room around the withers, the tree is probably too narrow. If it sits very low and there is a lot of room round the withers but

Badly fitting saddles

Although some people try to lessen the effects of a badly fitting saddle by placing various pads under the parts which do not fit (to either lessen pressure or friction, or take up space where the saddle is too big) this can only be a very temporary measure.

Wither pads under the pommel do take some of the pressure off a very sensitive and thin-skinned area of the spine, one which is very susceptible to injury from badly-fitting saddles, but they merely *lessen* pressure on an area which should have none at all.

Thick numnahs of various materials can disguise lumpy, uneven or inadequate stuffing in the saddle but not even it out altogether.

The only remedy for a badly fitting saddle is to change it completely or to have it adjusted by a competent saddler if the faults are minor.

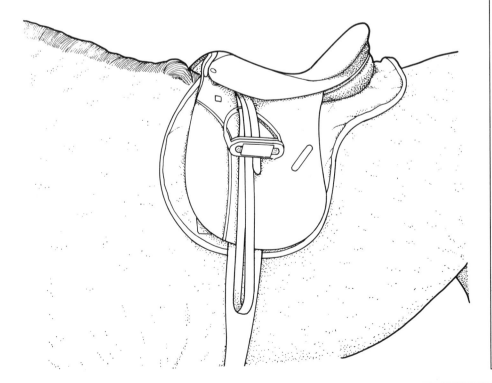

A well-fitting saddle which sits centrally on the horse's back and is of a good design for general riding. The numnah has been pulled well up into the gullet all the way along to remove pressure on the spine, and the stirrups are run up their leathers because the horse is not mounted

Buying used tack

Purchasing used tack can save a considerable sum of money but can be quite risky.

Buying from sales is probably the most risky procedure of all. If you do not know the field well enough you should take someone with you who knows sale procedure and who can check the tack, as a good deal of faulty tack passes through sales and is offered 'as seen' with no guarantee of quality. The better auctions give some form of guarantee. In any case, you will not be able to try the tack on your horse before purchase.

Buying from private sellers may not be as 'safe' as it at first seems. They are not governed by the same consumer laws as commercial retail outlets; you have to check items offered very carefully indeed and there will, of course, be no guarantee.

The safest way to buy secondhand equipment is from a reputable saddler. Many have good stocks, can give advice on fit and suitability and offer some sort of guarantee.

not much clearance above them, it is probably too wide. When girthed up the saddle should appear neither to pinch (when it is too narrow) nor to rock from side to side (too wide).

The best way to start is to put up the horse's heaviest rider and ride around in the saddle for a good half-hour, if you possibly can, to let it settle on the back. Initially, check the following points with the rider up:

1 When the rider leans forward and back, there should remain that tunnel of daylight all the way down the spine. Furthermore when the rider leans forward you should be able to fit the width of three fingers (four if your hands are slim) between the withers and the front arch.
2 You should just be able to slide the flat of your fingers around the sides of the withers.
3 Ask someone to hold the horse's foreleg up and out in front of him, making sure he is extending his shoulder: you should be able to fit the width of your hand between the top of his shoulder blade and the front of the saddle to be sure that the latter will not hamper his movement. Do this both sides.
4 The saddle should sit on the back only, and not extend backwards to the loin area which is not strong enough to bear weight.
5 Bearing in mind that the horse's flesh and skin are vulnerable, it should not be possible to rock the saddle from side to side on the horse's back to any great degree: if you can, it is too wide, or is stuffed incorrectly.
6 Without a rider, you should check that the saddle sits straight on the horse's back, a point best checked from behind and slightly above the horse. This vantage point is also the best from which to study the muscle development and condition of his back. Most horses – except very well schooled and conditioned ones – are at least slightly better muscled up on one side than on the other, and this can affect saddle-fitting and make the saddle appear lopsided or twisted. Schooling is the way to improve muscle development and therefore saddle levelness, though in a particularly bad case the saddle stuffing can be adjusted to take account of the unevenness until things improve.

Check that the saddle itself is not twisted: view the saddle from the rear, adjusting the level of your eye-view so as to check that the centre of the pommel is in the dead centre of the cantle when you are looking straight down the horse's spine. A twisted tree can occur if a rider always grasps the cantle when mounting instead of the pommel or waist; it can also be a fault of manufacture. Mounting from a block or with a leg-up obviates this, and is a mark of consideration for both horse and saddle – *not* an indication that the rider is incompetent or 'past it'!
7 Check that the stuffing of the saddle permits as wide a bearing area on the back as is reasonably possible and that it is level, as much as it can be allowing for the natural shape of the horse's back – no horse, except a few show Arabs, having a back entirely like a table-top. If the stuffing causes the panel to curve away from the back where it ought to be touching, it will decrease the bearing surface and concentrate the rider's weight over a smaller area, intensifying its undesirable effects. As much of the back area as is reasonably possible should be used for bearing weight so as to spread the pressure.
8 When the saddle is off the horse, be sure you can fit the width of a lady's fist into the gullet all the way down. Some gullets on poorly designed saddles

almost meet in the middle, making the clear tunnel of daylight down the spine impossible to achieve.

After a saddle has been in use for a few weeks or months, it will have settled into the shape of the horse's back and may well appear to have sunk down. This is normal, particularly with wool-stuffed saddles but also with some synthetics. Take the saddle to a good saddler and get more stuffing put in. Ideally, the rule should be: one horse, one saddle – in other words, the saddle should not be used on any other horse so the stuffing can conform to one horse only. The new stuffing must be carefully put in to maintain the central balance of the seat and the 'sit' of the saddle both laterally and longitudinally.

Another point to remember is that when the rider posts or rises in trot his weight is taken alternately by the saddle seat and the stirrup bars. As the bars are positioned a little further forward than the deepest part of the seat, this means that the horse will feel the weight in two close but distinctly different parts of his back with each 'forward – down' sequence performed by the rider. If the saddle stuffing is not even and level, this will cause the saddle to rock forward and back slightly all the time, and this in turn will cause concentration of pressure and also a certain amount of friction, both of which can cause soreness.

Check also that the tree of any saddle you are considering buying has not been broken, either; this is possibly more likely with a secondhand one but not impossible in a new one if it has been dropped or otherwise misused. Hold the pommel firmly in one hand and the cantle in the other, then twist the saddle firmly to and fro to see if there is any movement or if you can actually hear a creaking, scraping noise. Rest the cantle on your thigh and, grasping the pommel firmly with both hands, pull the pommel back towards you, watching and listening for movement or noise. The tree should stay firm and silent!

The stuffing, whilst effectively protecting the back, should still allow you to sit as closely to your horse as is reasonably possible. With a newly stuffed saddle you may, for a while, feel as though you are sitting on a platform, but it will soon settle.

Felt pad saddles

Although not at all common these days, old-fashioned children's felt pad saddles are still used occasionally for young children.

They are made of thick (about 1in) felt (usually green or brown) and have a leather or leather-covered metal hand loop or arch at the front for the child to hold on to. There are stirrups and leathers and, of course, a girth, and sometimes a crupper. There is no tree, and they are really one step up from blanket riding.

Many children who learn on a pad saddle and are used to the very close contact they give find it quite difficult to adapt to a saddle with a normal tree. With good instruction which stresses the value of learning to feel the pony's actions through the pad, children to develop quite deep, sensitive and natural seats, and it seems a shame that pad saddles are not used more often these days.

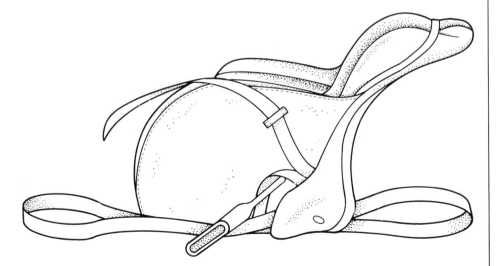

When removing the saddle it's best to put it over the stable door or on a fence. If you have to put it on the ground, place it pommel down, like this, and ideally fold the girth under the pommel to avoid scratching and damaging the leather

New developments

Probably the two most significant developments in the field of saddlery in recent years are these: the fairly widespread introduction of saddles made from synthetic materials; and saddles with adjustable trees which take account not only of the varying shape of different horses' backs, but also the change in shape of an individual horse's back at different stages in its condition and fitness.

Synthetic saddles

At the present moment, synthetics are made on nylon trees, though other materials will probably be used in future. They can be made with wool or synthetic stuffings (at present mainly wool is used) and the covering is a special nylon fabric which is non-slip and so helps the rider stay put. To clean they can be hosed or sponged down, they are very comfortable, mostly very well designed, and are lightweight and inexpensive compared with well designed and nicely made leather saddles. In the early stages there were complaints which surfaced after a year or two's wear concerning the trees which in some cases spread, but this problem now seems to have been overcome and these saddles are certainly developing and improving all the time. Dressage, general purpose and jumping models are available from different manufacturers, and other designs will doubtless soon be widely available.

New parts can be obtained for synthetic saddles with little trouble so their maintenance is not a problem, and although no one claims that they will last as long as a good leather saddle, their price makes this less crucial. With synthetics being widely available, inexpensive, and improving all the time, poor quality leather saddles will soon have no market slot, since their only advantage has always been cheapness. On the other hand, leather always looks good, though it may transpire that riders will decide to keep leather for 'best' and to use synthetics for everyday riding, the latter having all the advantages given, and in particular of being quick and easy to clean – this scores hands down with working owners who are saved the undeniably time-consuming chore of washing, soaping, and maybe dressing a leather saddle. When synthetics get wet there is no extended drying-out period, and no leather to dress to prevent hardening; and if you live and ride near the sea as I do, there is no fear that you are spoiling a leather saddle with salt water.

Adjustable-tree saddles

These are currently all-leather models with a mechanism in the front arch which, by the insertion of a little key, will cause the tree to narrow or widen so as to fit virtually any horse or accommodate the changing condition of any one horse. Obviously the advantages of this are tremendous. Furthermore it is claimed that this enables less stuffing to be required in the panel, and so the rider can obtain a closer contact with the horse; though you should always keep an eye on this point, and maintain the saddle stuffing in reasonable order and amount by regular (yearly?) attention.

Other advances in saddle design include an improved dressage saddle which permits a wider bearing surface on the back without either forcing the thighs too far apart, or pushing the rider up out of the seat, or forcing him or her to ride on the fork instead of the seatbones; also a saddle specially designed for women, which takes into account the anatomical differences in the female pelvis and hip joint.

A: Shows the narrow male pubic arch, the wide female arch and how the standard pommel arch comes into contact with each
B: Each pelvis seen from below is superimposed over a standard saddle seat, demonstrating how the wider female pelvis causes the seam line to lie against the inner thigh, causing great discomfort (see Female Riders, opposite)

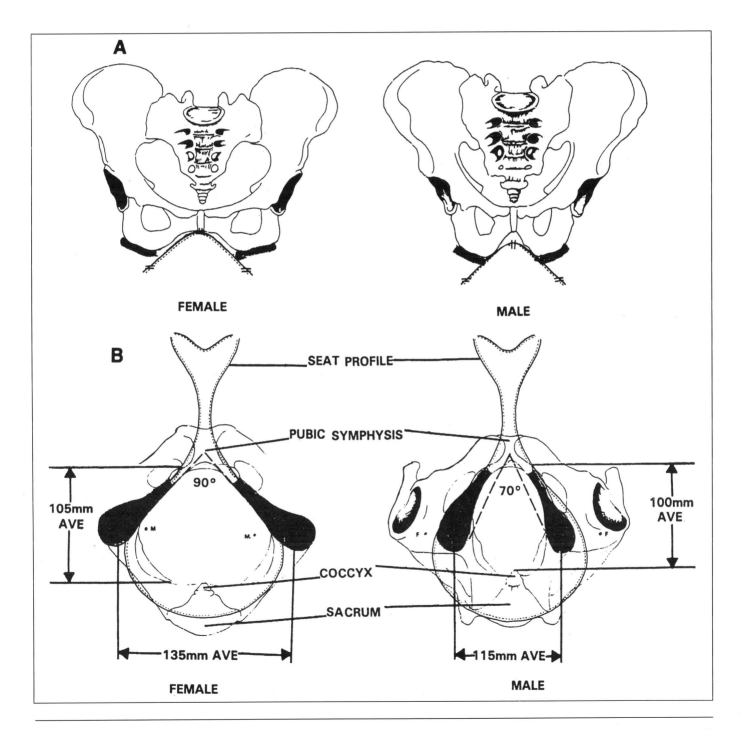

Riding without stirrups

When riding without stirrups, simply cross the left stirrup over the horse's withers to his right or off side, and vice versa.

It is much more comfortable for the rider if the buckle is first pulled downwards a few inches so that it and the doubled-over stirrup leather do not create an uncomfortable bump under the front of the thigh. This is due, particularly in the case of the less experienced rider, to the weight being less in control without the support of the stirrups.

When the stirrups are taken back again the buckle must be pulled back up to the stirrup bar, or it will cause the same discomfort and could bruise the thigh.

Dressage stirrup leathers (detailed later in this book) have the adjustment down near the stirrup itself rather than up by the rider's thigh to remove any bulk, and this obviates this problem.

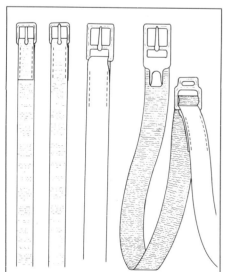

Narrow **childrens' stirrup** leathers on the left. On the right is an **extending stirrup leather** (normally fitted on to the nearside) which unhooks during mounting to make life easier for rider and horse, and hooks up agin once the latter is mounted. A plain leather is fitted to the offside.

Saddle accessories

Stirrup leathers

Some people make the mistake of buying a really good quality saddle, whether new or used, and think they are economising by then buying less-than-top-quality stirrup leathers, irons and girth. This is not just false economy, it is undoubtedly a potentially dangerous practice because your life could well depend on the reliability and strength of these accessories: all of them play a major part in keeping you and your horse together.

Certainly, it is possible to ride without irons or girth at all – I have seen more than one impressive display of High School riding where the saddles had neither, and did not budge an inch because of the riders' exemplary seats and techniques; but most of us feel happier with them!

Stirrup leathers come in various types of leather and synthetic materials, and in different lengths and widths, for small children starting at about ⅝in, up to 1¼in for large gentlemen (note that in all areas of saddlery metric measurements are also now used). The leather may be buffalo-hide, rawhide or oak-bark-tanned ox-hide; and synthetics come in plastics, nylon web and occasionally other materials, too.

Red buffalo-hide leathers are so strong that they are often sold as unbreakable and it is, indeed, hard to imagine a normal riding circumstance when they would break. All leathers have a smooth (grain) side and a rougher (flesh) side, although in top-quality leathers the flesh side should not really be noticeably rough. Leathers made of ox-hide and rawhide are made with the flesh side outwards so that the considerable wear they receive from the eye of the stirrup is borne on the tougher, grain side; but with buffalo-hide leathers the reverse is the case because they are so strong that this point is insignificant. New buffalo-hide leathers do, however, stretch more than others. *Ox-hide leathers* stretch least; *rawhide leathers* (less easy to find) come somewhere between the two.

Buckles: The buckles on leathers and girths should be of strong stainless steel, with a firmly located tongue and a little groove on the top bar of the buckle for the tongue to lodge in. Nickel buckles should be illegal in my view as they wear, crack and break alarmingly easily, as do nickel bits and stirrups; in fact nickel items should only be used by those who like living dangerously! The term 'solid nickel' (as opposed to, presumably, 'nickel-plated' – like cheap cutlery) gives the impression that they are strong and reliable, though nothing could be further from the truth. If the all-important consumer market refused to accept nickel it would soon go out of common usage, and the sooner the better; surprisingly, some otherwise good quality items have nickel buckles. Maybe *you* could make the point, by refusing to buy unless the shop supplies 'the real McCoy' – stainless steel ones. So, look for a good item and insist on stainless steel buckles. As with so much else when riding, your life *is* at stake here.

Good quality leathers will have evenly-punched holes in them (and if they are *not* even, you will always be riding lopsided, of course!) and these will be numbered; so if your leathers are on the same number you are more likely to be riding 'even', even though you may not feel like it! (If they continue to feel unlevel, either the saddle is unevenly stuffed or is twisted, or your horse is very unequally muscled-up, or your riding is at fault.) Some people have one leg significantly shorter than the other, a surprisingly common feature, and they will adjust their leathers accordingly; also, jockeys usually adjust the stirrup on the inside of the course they are riding to a hole or so shorter – this makes riding the turns at speed with short stirrups easier: for a left-handed course the left leather will be shorter, and vice versa.

As all new hide leathers stretch initially, they should really be changed round every time the saddle is cleaned or every time you ride (which, following the counsel of perfection, should be one and the same thing, really). Moreover, if you habitually mount from the ground, the leather on the near-side is constantly being subjected to considerably more weight and stress than the off-side leather and will stretch accordingly if they are not changed round regularly. Of course, you could follow the excellent advice of mounting alternately on the near- and off-sides.

Once the leathers have stretched to their full extent, you may use one hole more than the others for much of your riding, and a crease will probably develop where the leather passes through the eye of the stirrup; should this start to show significant signs of wear, it is a good idea to get ox-hide and rawhide leathers shortened from the buckle. With buffalo-hide leathers this is much less important.

Extending stirrup leathers (see illustration) are available for those who have to mount from the ground – for example, arthritis sufferers, or for those who, quite simply, are not as agile as they once were. These are a boon for such riders if they have to dismount (or are dismounted by their horse!) when out, and have no access to any sort of mounting block or bank.

Getting a leather through the stirrup the right way up can sometimes perplex the inexperienced, so here are step-by-step instructions: take your leather with the buckle towards you and the pointed end away with the smooth side upwards (if of ox-hide or rawhide, the reverse for buffalo hide), with the tongue of the buckle downwards, and thread the pointed end away from you through the eye on top of the stirrup. Bring it up and back towards you and through the top bar of the buckle, putting the tongue through one of the holes.

Now, attaching a leather to the saddle: push or slide it over the bar (really hard, if necessary; some bars are most unco-operative unless their ends are slightly angled outwards, and this is a rare feature) and, by pulling down firmly on the piece of leather lying next to the saddle flap, pull the buckle right up to the stirrup bar where it is less likely to dig into your thigh, particularly if the saddle is not too well designed. Also available are leathers which fasten in various ways down by the stirrup (a military idea), thus avoiding altogether any possible discomfort; this feature is popular with dressage riders.

The spare end of leather should be passed back on top of the two looped pieces to lie behind your leg, preferably in the little leather 'safe' set diagonally for this purpose on the back edge of the flap of any good saddle. Don't double it under the rest of the leathers first, as this will create an uncomfortable lump under your thigh. Some horses get really irritated by a loose end which is in the safe but is long enough to flap about or touch their side, so in such cases don't use the safe – the leather is less annoying if it hangs down straight.

Left or right?

It is traditional to mount, lead and handle horses and ponies mainly from the left or near side. However, horses should be handled from both sides to prevent difficulties.

There seems to be a rather inefficient exchange of information between the right and left sides of the horse's brain across the linking cord of tissue – the *corpus callosum*. For this reason we have to teach horses everything twice, from both sides. This is one reason why a horse may, for example, shy at an object when passing it on the left rein but not when passing it on the right rein.

The practice of mounting a horse on the near side seems to have evolved from the time when swords were worn. They were carried on the left, and so mounting on that side prevented the sword getting caught up or flying about.

Horses who dislike being mounted usually give no resistance when tackled from the off side as they seem to associate the problems with the near side. If the general problems (such as rough handling, painful mounting and so on) are not removed, the difficulties may well recur on the off side.

Accustoming a horse to being mounted from both sides is good for both rider and horse, and develops agility in the former and adaptability in the latter.

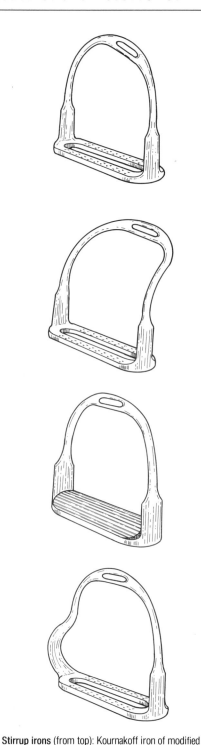

Stirrup irons (from top): Kournakoff iron of modified form, with the eye set off-centre to the inside (this being a near-side iron) so that the sole of the foot slopes towards the horse. In true Kournakoff irons the stirrup tread is also sloped upwards so that the foot has to be held with the toe up and heel down.
Bent top iron, which also has the effect of positioning the foot with the toe up and the heel down.
English Hunting Iron, the most common stirrup seen and satisfactory for most purposes, although normally regarded as too heavy for racing.
Australian Simplex Safety Iron with forward bulge, making it difficult for a foot to become caught in the stirrup

Stirrup irons

These are no longer made of iron, of course, but should be of high quality stainless steel; and *never* nickel, for the reasons already given. It is easier to find a good, heavy iron with your toe should you 'lose' one when riding, especially if you have 'trained' your leathers to hang at the correct angle, something which can be done quite simply: leave the irons down when the saddle is put away, twist the left leather twice round to the left and the right one twice round to the right, and tie them in that position under the saddle with a piece of string. Gradually, you'll find that when you are mounted but with your feet out of the stirrups, the latter are hanging at right angles to your horse's sides, with the leathers turning naturally flat against your shins; like this you can very easily find a stirrup and slip the toe in without having to fumble inwards with the foot.

Various irons are shown and explained in the captions to the accompanying drawings. There are all sorts of irons aimed at helping you keep your foot in the 'right' position, and they will have various effects depending on your individual physical qualities: they can be a real advantage, can stiffen you up, cause pins and needles, make your feet and ankles numb, or even, as in my case, cause almost excruciating pain in the ankles because they force your feet into what is, for you, an unnatural position. I walk very slightly splay-footed, and any stirrup iron designed to make me keep my toes to the front and the outside of my sole slightly lower than the inside (both of which old-fashioned instructors still exhort their pupils to do) is absolute torture and, of course, totally mitigates against relaxed, harmonious riding.

The various safety irons on the market are an excellent idea, and are all designed to help you free your foot should it become jammed in the iron in a fall. In fact if you make sure the treads (bottoms) of your stirrups are just one inch wider than the widest part of the sole of your riding boots or shoes (measured from the *inside* of the stirrup branches), your foot will be unable to slip through and will be most unlikely to get stuck. And even though modern riding trainers are now available, it is still advisable to use stout footwear with a proper heel which will help prevent the foot slipping through. Rubber stirrup treads which slot into the base of the stirrups are almost universal these days and certainly help you keep your stirrups – as well as being marginally warmer in winter.

Probably the most common safety iron is the Peacock Safety Iron; this has a thick rubber band instead of an outer branch, hooked to the top of the stirrup near the eye, the idea being that when pressure is put on the band it will become unhooked and will free the foot. Although the idea is basically sound, the stirrup seems to 'miss' the strength of its metal outer branch and in time does bend slightly, even if stainless steel, causing the tread to slope a little downwards and inevitably affecting the foot position.

The Australian Simplex stirrup is designed with an outward and forward loop on the outer branch and so does not have this failing – the extra room the loop provides on the branch prevents the foot becoming stuck. However, it would seem to be rather more likely that the foot might go right through the iron.

Probably the most suitable iron is still the English Hunting Iron, as also the heavy dressage iron which originates in Germany. If the irons are the right size, and the rider's boots or shoes also, they are probably as safe and suitable as anything else available. When buying irons make sure that the eye on the top will allow your chosen width of leather to run easily through it, without causing either annoyance to you or wear to the edges of the leather.

Breastplates

A breastplate or breastgirth is sometimes needed when a horse has a particularly well developed shoulder or a good front but little behind the saddle – perhaps due to natural leanness, lack of condition, or peak fitness – to keep the saddle from slipping back. There are 'collar' type breastplates called 'hunting pattern' breastplates, and the sort which fit round the chest as a horizontal strap attached to the girth on each side, and supported by a thinner strap which passes over the withers. The collar type have a strap passing round the base of the neck like the neckline of a rug, with two short straps attached at the top, one each side of the withers, which go back to fasten to the metal dees or loops on the front arch of the saddle (to stop everything sliding up the horse's neck), as well as a strap attached at the bottom which passes down between the forelegs and loops round the girth, this strap being adjustable. It is possible for this type of breastplate to have a running or a standing martingale attachment (see Chapter 3).

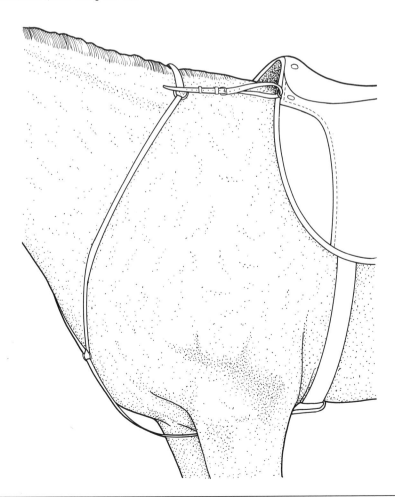

Feet first on safety

There have been instances reported occasionally in the press and among the author's contacts of some of the newer styles of riding and mucking-out boots and shoes sticking in stirrups with rubber treads.

Some of the shoes have rubber soles themselves, usually ridged or patterned, and some have low heels. Apparently the patterns are causing sticking, and the absence of a heel allows some shoes which seem to be of the right size in accordance with the stirrup base to slide through the stirrup nevertheless.

Shoes and boots intended for stable work rather than riding should not be used for the latter particularly if they have rubber soles and/or low heels.

Normal stable 'wellies' are often used for riding but the heavily ridged pattern of the sole is not, in the author's opinion, really safe because of the possibility of sticking.

Ordinary rubber riding boots have a virtually smooth sole in comparison and if of the correct size should cause no problem.

A **breastplate** correctly fitted, fastened to the saddle dees and the girth and adjusted just tightly enough to keep the saddle in the correct place. It is obviously useless if too loose

A sheepskin-padded breast girth of the type which fits over the withers and fastens round the girth tabs or straps at the sides. It should be adjusted so that it lies above the points of the shoulders but does not press on the horse's windpipe

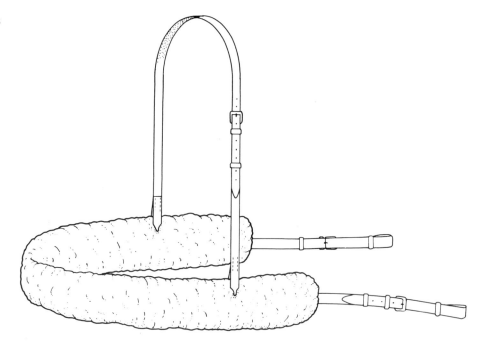

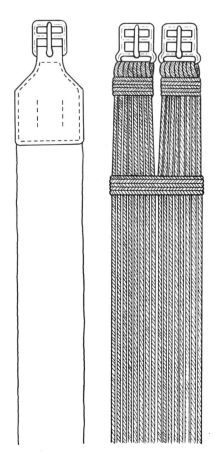

Left: **Elastic girth** which requires a strong enclosing leather fastening at each end and usually only one buckle at each end. Take care when putting these on, that pressure is even. Two are often used together
Right: **Cotton string girth**, easy to care for and as cool as anything else in summer

The other type of breastplate is sometimes padded with sheepskin or synthetic fleece to lessen friction. It is important with this type that it is fitted high enough so as not to interfere with the movement of the shoulder, but low enough to avoid pressure on the windpipe which could interfere with the horse's breathing. On each side a short strap continues from the end of the chest strap, and fastens round one of the girth straps.

Neckstraps for novice riders (children or adults) are an item of equipment not used as much as they very well could be. They follow the collar-type breastplate design with usually only the two short straps fastening to the front dees, but both purposes would be served with the girth strap attached too. A neckstrap is a real boon to a novice, not to mention the horses and ponies whose riders might otherwise try to keep their balance by hanging on to the reins and jabbing the mouth – most painfully for the animal.

Girths and surcingles

The girth could well receive more attention than it does as far as type, length and width is concerned, not to mention the stuff of which it is made. Leather girths are traditional and still in use, although the three-fold baghide girth seems to be hard to obtain, probably because it is now very expensive. If you have a good saddler, he may make one up for you. It is fitted with the closed edge behind the elbow and the open side of the girth towards the rear. Inside a piece of oiled fabric is placed between the layers, which effectively keeps the leather supple. Leather is used for almost any pattern of girth, but it has very little 'give' in it and is hardly absorbent at all. However, although leather girths may compromise a horse's comfort, particularly when he is breathing hard, it has to be said that a clean, soft leather girth will not normally cause galling unless there is stitching lying next to the horse which is coarse or coming undone.

I feel a girth should be either absorbent or permeable (of one of the 'breatheable' textiles) so that sweat – which softens and therefore weakens the skin – is soaked up as much as possible or is transmitted away from the skin. Weak skin is obviously more prone to galling, and the practice of hardening up the skin by the application of surgical spirit to the saddle and girth areas seems to have been abandoned in most yards these days. Salt water can be used instead, to good effect.

The old-fashioned type of nylon girth was completely non-absorbent from a practical point of view, and had the propensity to be very rough on the skin, but it seems to be out of fashion now, thank goodness. Nylon string girths positively caused soreness and galling, and despite the intermittent cross-bands built in to keep the strings in place, they often narrowed in use and so offered a similarly narrow area of pressure concentrated round the girth area. A girth should be comfortably broad enough to spread pressure without being over-restrictive.

If a horse has a somewhat upright shoulder and perhaps an insignificant girth groove, not to mention a large belly or croup-high conformation, there is every likelihood that the girth will dig in behind the elbows and cause galling. For such horses in particular the Balding and Atherstone pattern girths are to be recommended. These are narrower in shape behind the elbows so as to present less material (whatever it is) to this constantly moving and thin-skinned area.

Textiles for girths, apart from the leather and permeable ones of various types already mentioned, also include soft fabrics such as lampwick and mohair; wool, serge and cotton webbing, though this can be rather harsh and weak; and fabric string girths of various sorts. The obvious advantages of

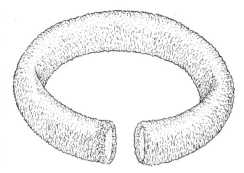

A fleecy girth sleeve to help prevent galling and to absorb sweat: these can be made of real sheepskin or synthetic fleece

Selection of girths (left to right)
Wide webbing girth needing two buckles
Narrower webbing girth with one buckle; two girths must be used together
An elastic insert. To even up pressure it is best to have inserts at both ends of the girth
Lampwick girth, absorbent, soft and easy to care for
Atherstone girth shaped behind the elbow to help prevent galling
Balding girth with crossing leather pieces, again to help prevent galling behind the elbow

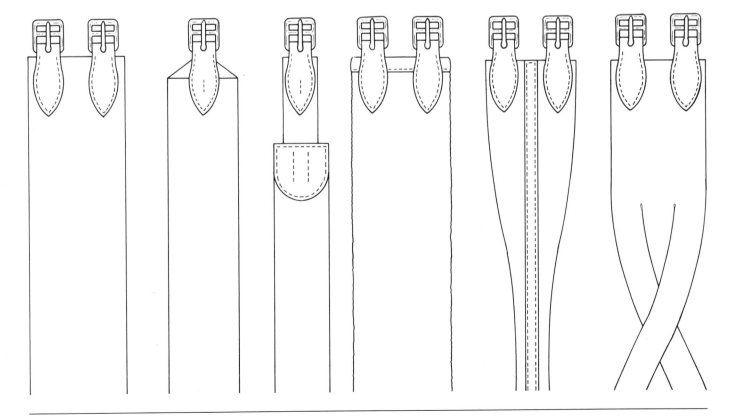

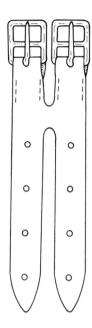

A **girth extender** which buckles on to the girth tabs, useful if you have a fat horse or a too-short girth, but only as a temporary measure

lampwick and mohair girths are their softness and absorbency, but they are also strong. The idea behind string or stranded girths is that they permit air to circulate between the strands and so keep the horse a little dryer in this area, as well as supposedly providing extra grip; whereas the permeable fabrics – now also used for rugs and numnahs – actually claim to take the moisture away from the skin and help it evaporate to the outside, and they do work extremely well in practice.

The design of a girth is equally important. As previously mentioned, the Balding and Atherstone patterns are good, and come in various materials; and the material of which any girth is made should be comfortable to the horse – some of the early brushed-nylon types are actually abrasive as well as being non-absorbent. Also, the buckles of a girth and the way they fasten should receive more consideration; the so-called 'humane' girth for example, with V-shaped straps on to which the buckles are stitched, would do well to find a wider market: this type of fastening allows the strap to move a little in accordance with the horse's movements by sliding on its ring, and by accommodating itself a little thus, it also makes the saddle more secure – you can therefore girth up a little less tightly with it, to the increased comfort of the horse.

Elastic inserts (at both ends to balance up the girth) are a good idea too, and fully elasticated web girths are also available; these are used mainly in racing

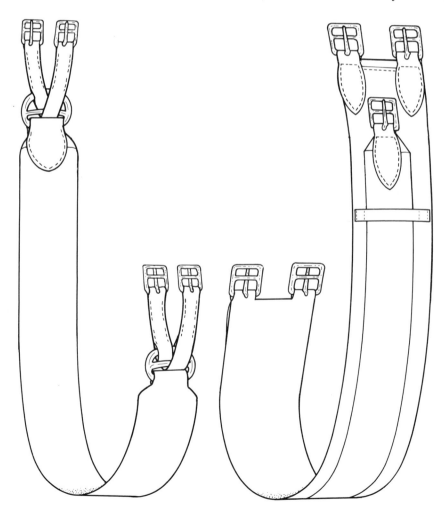

Left: **Humane girth** which, because of the sliding buckle straps, provides a more comfortable, 'giving' feel to the horse and enables the girth to be fastened less tightly than normal as it feels more secure

Right: **Fitzwilliam girth**, normally used on side saddles but sometimes used where extra security is felt necessary as all three girth tabs can be used with it if the girth is long enough. Not a common girth today

where their added grip and give are appreciated by horses at peak effort. However, the rubber content of these girths perishes fairly quickly, so keep an eye on their condition.

Web girths are sold in pairs to provide extra security in the (highly likely) event of one of them breaking, but are not as popular as they used to be. They can come in cotton (very weak) or wool and wool/cotton mixtures, but can harden badly if not kept really clean. However, web is used for the longer surcingles which completely encircle the saddle and girth area of eventers as an extra safety precaution. Web is also used in a narrow, tubular form, often white, which crosses over under the breastbone where there is a pimple-rubber section aimed at giving extra grip. These are used on show ponies, and the intention (as with most show tack) is to cover up as little of the animal as possible. Some fine-skinned ponies, however, do react to the pimple-rubber section which can cause soreness.

The short belly girths used on some dressage and showing saddles do remove the buckles effectively from under the rider's leg, but they can look a little clumsy, and create an ungiving lump which in some horses, is rather near the elbow for comfort. In fact it is quite easy to work out just how long a girth you need, which will avoid lumpy fastenings under your leg yet be hidden by the saddle flap and will not interfere with your horse's action by getting in the way behind his elbow: simply ask a friend to measure carefully from just behind the angle of your knee, under your horse's belly and up to just behind the angle of your other knee. Most saddles will have girth straps long enough to permit this, but if not, they can easily be replaced by a good saddler.

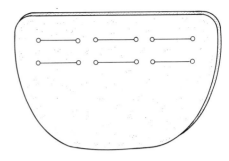

Girth safe, also sometimes called a buckle protector. It actually protects the saddle flap from damage by the girth buckles. It is threaded on to the girth tabs and pulled down the tabs over the buckles when the girth is fastened. Obviously, you need one on each side of the saddle

Numnahs

At one time it was considered very *infra dig* to use a numnah, despite the fact that both numnahs and saddle cloths have been used for generations by the

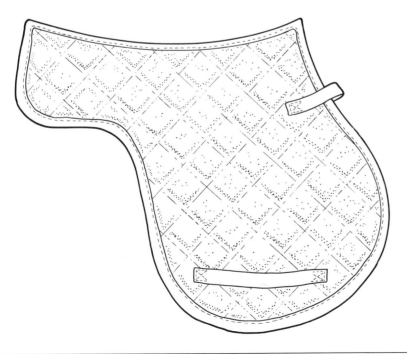

A useful type of numnah for everyday riding, made of quilted cotton and shaped to comply with the horse's spine. It is absorbent, light, unobtrusive and easy to launder

Colour co-ordination

The colour of the saddle girth can certainly make a surprising difference to the horse or pony's appearance. If unsure what colour to choose in a fabric girth, pick the one nearest to your animal's coat colour. Very narrow, whitened showing girths are used on show ponies, but for everyday use white is hopelessly impractical unless you are prepared for it to look murky. Grey horses, however, suit white.

Show horses look better in brown, or sometimes beige girths rather than white, the object being to make the girth as unobtrusive as possible.

Bandages still look best, I feel, in conservative colours such as navy, dark green or dark grey depending on the horse's colour. White look lovely in dry weather when they have more chance of staying clean.

Numnahs too should be unobtrusive and so in conservative colours – perhaps navy or black for grey horses, brown for most others. Although brightly coloured numnahs, bandages and synthetic boots are commonly seen on children's ponies and teenagers' mounts, garish colours never seem to look good on horses or ponies, particularly when under saddle.

military and others in 'high places'. Nowadays, however, numnahs are regarded as a positive advantage provided they are of good style, fit and fabric; and they do protect against sweat, which doesn't do the leather lining of a saddle any good (hence the recommendation to clean any tack after every use).

The old-fashioned, thick, stiff felt ones are appalling. They remove virtually all 'feel' between you and your horse, and positively encourage the saddle to slip out of place. Real, unsheared sheepskin ones are now washable and easier to care for, but they undoubtedly heat up the back a great deal and make it unacceptably hot and wet; and sheared sheepskin only a little less so. Thick, synthetic fleece (usually acrylic) numnahs may be a little better, and those of cotton fleece and filling are probably the best as they are absorbent, soft (if kept clean) and do not hold the heat.

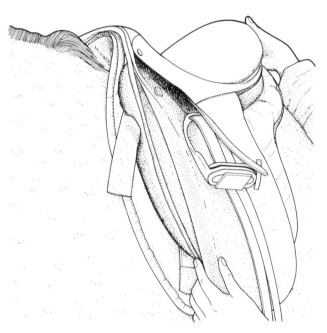

This picture shows the numnah pulled well up into the saddle gullet to avoid spinal pressure, the stirrups raised up their leathers correctly to secure them (as they should always be when the horse is not mounted) and the loop on the numnah waiting to be threaded on to the girth tabs when the girth is fastened, to secure the numnah

In a saddle with a leather lining (panel) – as most are these days, except the synthetics – a thin cotton, quilted numnah does absorb sweat and is probably more comfortable for the horse as it is a little softer; and being thin it is also very discreet if the shape is chosen to go with that of the saddle. Even winners at big shows use them!

Probably the most significant and helpful advances are the 'therapeutic' numnahs with special fillings and of specialised materials which are designed to spread pressure, alleviate friction and carry away sweat. They were largely developed in answer to the needs of endurance riders.

2
BRIDLES AND BITS

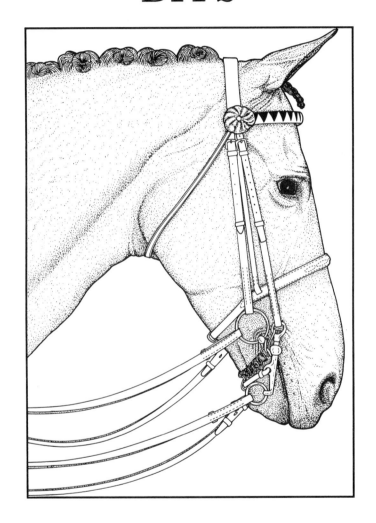

Bitting materials

Some of the newer types of metals just coming on to the market in the manufacture of bits and stirrups are stainless steel alloys, some with a yellowish tinge, which are claimed to be extremely strong. Other alloy products (metal mixtures) are also being developed and should be fairly widely available before too long.

Probably the most interesting developments, however, are the newer plastic and nylon materials which far supersede the older types of nylon bits which wore rough and were easily damaged.

As further steps are taken to bring other synthetic materials into the field of tack and harness manufacture, the over-riding considerations must be strength, suitability for the job and, where bits are concerned, palatability to the horse.

Horses accept all sorts of unpleasant things into their mouths. Rawhide and leather both taste revolting yet leather-covered bits are still used and rawhide thongs were always used by earlier peoples on their animals.

Copper, as mentioned in this book, also tastes revolting, yet is readily incorporated into the mouthpieces of certain bits today, maybe in the form of inserts, ports or rollers.

This may not be a popular suggestion, but perhaps it would be a good idea if, before putting any material into our horses' mouths, we put it in our own first for a useful length of time to check how it *really* tastes!

Materials

The first method of control used on the horse by early civilised man was simply a rope or thong round the top of its neck; however, although this may have been adequate for slow-moving pack animals (many of which are used, even today, with nothing on their heads or necks at all), once man had begun driving horses in harness it must have quite soon become obvious that this did not offer anything like enough control over an animal which was perhaps not 100 per cent co-operative, nor fully trained. Versions of halters and headcollars are depicted in early carvings and illustrations; and the horse's bit must also have evolved from a simple rope or thong which passed through its mouth or looped round the lower jaw – it was obviously known to the civilisations flourishing when the horse was first domesticated about 5,000 years ago.

Early developments from the simple thong included braided leather, wood, bone and horn, all of which were used before metal came into use. Iron was obviously the first metal to be employed; then bronze, and brass and copper too were tried, though the last two were nothing like strong enough for any such job where both strength and durability are required. Copper is today used in some bits for covering part of the mouthpiece, because it is said to be 'soft' and to have 'good mouthing qualities' (where horses are seen to salivate and play with the bit). Soft it certainly is, for a metal, but I feel the so-called good mouthing qualities may well come, in this case, from the fact that copper tastes absolutely revolting (try it yourself), and moreover induces a feeling of nausea if kept in the mouth for even a few minutes; this is not something I should want to inflict on my horse.

The invention of *steel* produced a revolution, not least in the craft of lorinery (the manufacture of spurs, stirrups and bits), and steel is still used by the military in many countries of the world. However, perhaps current cutbacks in manpower will finally see the Services universally adopt *stainless* steel, which requires hardly any labour to keep it clean and shining: unlike its ordinary steel counterpart which has to be burnished and polished daily to keep it from rusting and maintain it in decent enough condition to be put into a horse's mouth (or to be seen as stirrups and harness accoutrements on a smart animal).

Stainless steel is very strong; it is also rust-free, and although a dull film may develop over stirrups and bit-rings (though not the bit mouthpiece which the horse himself keeps 'clean' every time it is used), this is soon removed with hot soapy water or a specialist stainless steel cleaner such as is used for stainless steel saucepans.

The shortcomings of 'solid' *nickel* have been mentioned in the previous chapter, although sadly there are many bits still available made from this wolf in sheep's clothing. The correct term for it is 'nickel silver', and you do not have to be Yuri Geller to be able to bend a spoon made from it very easily! In my view it is simply not strong enough to be used for the manufacture of bits and stirrups: it breaks without warning, and bends easily; also joints (such as in jointed snaffles) wear very easily, as do bit-rings, so that the corners of the lips between the ring and the mouthpiece are much more likely to be pinched with – obviously – the most excruciating pain to the horse.

Aluminium is often used in the flat-racing world, a practice fraught with considerable risks because aluminium is a weak metal, its only advantage being is lightness (considered crucial in racing).

Non-metal materials most commonly employed are rubber, vulcanite, nylon and plastic. *Rubber* is obviously a comfortable, mild and soft material, but older bits (and more modern ones, of poorer quality) have a metal chain running through their centre which can break without warning, leaving you without a bit at all! So if you want a rubber bit, make sure it bears a guarantee ticket that it contains a strong reinforcing thread of strong *nylon* – not of metal – running through it as the best do.

Rubber is good for covering mouthpieces: it is possible to buy a rubber-covered mullen or half-moon-shaped mouthpiece and also a jointed one covered with rubber. These give a soft, non-threatening feel to a horse, and many go well in such bits.

Vulcanite is a type of hardened rubber which is nonetheless softer than metal and is therefore gentler and more forgiving when used as a bit. However, both vulcanite and rubber bits do wear more quickly than metal, and a sharp eye must be kept on their condition. Vulcanite is most usually seen in mullen-mouthed snaffles and pelhams.

The early, cheap nylon bits were not a success as they tended to wear rough and could seriously cut an animal's mouth. These days, however, the type of nylon used is extremely strong but at the same time very light, smooth and with no unpleasant taste; it has about the same 'hardness' as vulcanite, and the bits made from it are justifiably popular with horses and riders alike. Along with the new plastics, these bits also have a degree of flexibility which is more comfortable.

Inside the horse's mouth

Whatever people may say, it is no easy matter for the inexperienced to examine the inside of a horse's mouth, and then to understand fully what they are looking at, and how it will affect their choice of bit. Most horses will resist to some extent when you open their mouth – they will wriggle the tongue around, move their head away and so on, and so it is always best to get expert help. Call your veterinary surgeon, and also maybe an experienced, knowledgeable instructor or trainer; the vet certainly will have an instrument called a 'gag' – nothing to do with a gag snaffle, but to keep the horse's front teeth apart and therefore his mouth safely open for examination or treatment. This might be rasping the back teeth, the need for which should be checked once or even twice a year and carried out, when required, by the vet. Certainly a new horse or a youngster should have his teeth checked and attended to before you even try to put a bit in his mouth.

The vet will be able to tell you many things, particularly if he or she is also a rider: whether or not your horse has a proportionately large or small mouth for

Bitting problems

A fairly freak situation turned out to be the cause of major bitting problems in a young horse bought by an acquaintance of the author.

The normal arrangement of teeth in the horse's mouth, as described here, leaves a toothless space, the bars of the mouth, where the bit can rest conveniently.

If the bit is fitted as normally recommended, it is practically impossible for the horse to 'get the bit between his teeth' as the saying goes, thereby negating virtually all the rider's control. The bit can be marked or even damaged, depending on the material from which it is made, if pulled up against the back teeth, and in an extreme case the horse might just manage to grasp it between his back teeth, but this is really not common.

The young horse mentioned earlier had given regular mouthing and bitting problems ever since my acquance had tried to back and ride him as a three-year-old. As the horse grew stronger he regularly took off with his rider, who seemed to have no control at all, and gave virtually no response to the bit.

It was not until expert help was called in in desperation that it was discovered, through a very cursory examination of the horse's mouth, that he had teeth growing almost all the way down the bars to the tushes which were just erupting.

The bit, therefore, had been resting on teeth instead of the bars all the time, and the horse's owner had never even thought to look inside his mouth for the cause of the problems!

Titbits

Most people like to give their horses and ponies titbits for doing well or as a sign of affection, but what they often get – sugary treats such as mints or sugar lumps – are as bad for their tooth enamel as for our own.

Chocolate has problems where competition horses are concerned as it contains caffeine which is a prohibited substance under competition rules – and, of course, also contains sugar.

It is worth looking out for the special non-sugary looking out for the special non-sugary horse treats on the market in various flavours such as clove and cinnamon, and finding out which ones your horse likes.

It is also worth noting that horses who are mainly grass-kept do appreciate grains such as oats or barley, or a little flaked maize, as titbits, rather than nuts or cubes which contain a lot of grass meal. Stabled horses, conversely, usually fed that type of concentrate, appreciate grass, herbs and other plants such as dandelions as a titbit.

his size; whether the branches between his lower jaws are unusually narrow, with little room for the tongue (necessitating a bit allowing for the tongue), also whether the tongue itself is unusually big and fleshy. He or she will tell you if the upper and lower jaws are sufficiently wide apart (particularly in youngsters) to allow for a thick mouthpiece; or whether for example a youngster is suffering from *lampas*, a condition in which the roof of the mouth may swell, often during teething, thus making it an altogether uncomfortable process for the horse to take a bit at all.

If you know what you are doing it is quite possible to open a horse's mouth and keep it open without a gag: you simply stand on one side of the horse's head (say his right) with your back to his tail and pass your nearest (left) hand under his jaw. By inserting your fingertips into the corner of his mouth on the left side, you can open his mouth and gently but determinedly grasp his tongue, bringing it out of the left side of his mouth though without actually pulling it hard and causing discomfort. As a horse will wriggle his tongue considerably, you do have to keep a firm hold without annoying him too much. Your right hand is then free to move the lips and have a good look at the conformation of the mouth.

Some people are experienced and brave enough to put their hands right back in the horse's mouth and feel the edges of his back molars, using only this method and not a gag. However, as it is certainly not impossible for the horse to wangle his tongue out of your hand and close his mouth on your fingers without warning, I feel this practice is rather risky! A horse, and even a tiny pony, is quite strong enough to crush your fingers to irreversible pulp without even knowing about it!

Position of the bit: the bit lies in the convenient space between the incisors and molars (in a mare) or tushes and molars (in a male horse), but the size of the tongue is often overlooked when fitting the bit. It may take up much of the space available and will not be comfortable with, for example, a straight-bar bit

Whichever method you choose, examination of the mouth to determine its condition and conformation really is a must, and you should be able to perform the 'tongue-grasp' method so that you can examine regularly the front half of the mouth, the bars and tongue and maybe the insides of the cheeks without putting yourself in danger.

Mouthing problems can often be solved in this way: by examining the mouth with and without the bit, you may be able to see more or less just what effect the bit is having, and why the animal is having trouble accepting it or is unwilling to react in the way you would wish. Problems such as napping, rearing, generally bad or unwilling behaviour, head-shaking, and getting above or behind the bit are all forms of resistance, but should certainly not be punished until an exhaustive examination of the whole horse, not least his mouth, has been carried out. Remember that when we ask the horse to do or to wear something, he can only say 'Yes' or 'No' by either accepting or rejecting it: he cannot give an inbetween answer to the effect that he would say 'Yes' if only we could just change something slightly; nor can he categorically say 'No' if he finds something really unbearable. It is up to us to find out why he is saying 'No' – and with an open mind, too, not a biased attitude of 'making him have it in the long run'.

Problems which precipitate a 'No' or a 'Help!' from the horse can have many different causes: maybe the bit is unsuitable or the wrong size or fitted wrongly, or roughly or inappropriately used; it may be rough, broken or cracked, or worn; and if the problem is not the bit itself, it may be because the horse is teething and has sore gums, or has sharp teeth or wolf teeth or has injuries to the mouth however caused; there are also various nerve diseases which can cause trouble; also problems in other areas such as back injuries, lameness, unsuitable shoeing or trimming – in fact any other physical discomfort however caused may be a contributory factor: so you have quite a list already to help you solve any problems. Most horses are essentially willing to please, so it is as well not automatically to blame the horse and his attitude of mind without first going into every other cause thoroughly.

Headshy horses

Headshy horses are often difficult to examine and their resistances can prevent novice owners from even trying to look inside their mouths.

Putting a twitch on a horse can certainly help if properly done (see *Behaviour Problems in Horses* by Susan McBane, David & Charles) and a neck twitch, where you pinch up a fold of skin on the side of the neck, twist it firmly and move it (twitch it) about a little, can have the same effect of quietening down a horse in a very few minutes.

Simply passing the headcollar rope over the withers and bringing it up the neck to the poll can also give you initial control of the head.

The snaffle bit should normally fit up into the corners of the mouth, making contact with the skin but causing only one wrinkle

In that position the bit rests conveniently on the toothless part of the horse's jawbones (called the bars). If correctly used the bit is unlikely to come into contact with the front or back teeth, with the possible exception of wolf teeth in certain individuals

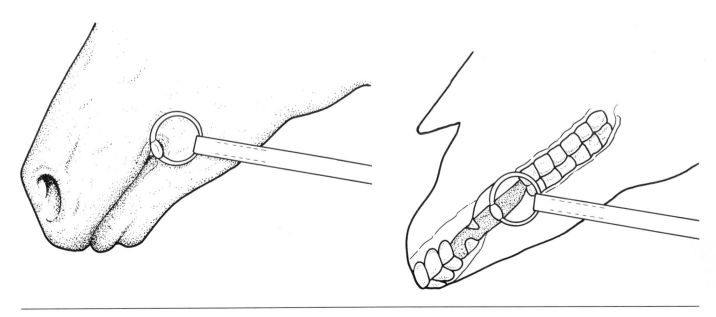

Types of bit

There are three main bit 'families' and two subsidiary groups.
The three main families are: snaffles; curb bits and double bridles; and pelhams.
The minor groups comprise gag snaffles; and bitless or nose bridles.

Snaffles

The snaffle normally has one mouthpiece, although the Y-mouth or W-mouth has two thin mouthpieces attached to the same bit ring on each side, with one joint on each mouthpiece, one each side. A snaffle is very direct in its action because the rings to which the mouthpiece is attached are directly on the ends of the mouthpiece and the reins, in turn, fastened to the rings. There is no leverage action with a snaffle, although the effect a snaffle has on the mouth varies according to the design of the mouthpiece, and also whether or not the bit has rings or cheeks on each end of the mouthpiece. The mouthpiece itself may have one joint in the middle, or two, joined by a flat central link or spatula; it may have no joints at all and be a simple straight-bar, or it may be curved – the half-moon or mullen mouthpiece. As a child I remember riding a pony which used to go in a snaffle bit with a port, a little 'hump' in the centre of the mouthpiece to accommodate the tongue; until a few years ago I had never again seen such a bit, the nearest to it being the Kimblewick (see Pelhams p70) with its D-shaped ring and ported mouthpiece, although it also has a curb chain, unlike the old ported snaffle. Until the late fifties and early sixties it was possible to have bits specially made to your own design, and the one I remembered had probably been made to order – a system which the economic climate now precludes. However, the style has reappeared and the German KK range, illustrated here, includes ported snaffles.

The rings may be joined to the mouthpiece by simply passing through a hole at each end, or by means of what is called an 'eggbutt' joint, where the ends of the mouthpiece itself are fashioned to form a T-shape thus becoming a part of the ring and so preventing any possibility of the corners of the lips being pinched. Eggbutt snaffles have a fairly steady feel in the horse's mouth, and he is not able to move them about and play with them as much as a mouthpiece where the rings pass through the holes.

The latter type of fastening has two sorts of ring: a flattish ring, when the bit is called a 'loose-ring' bit; and a larger, thinner, rounded ring called a 'wire-ring'. Both types are more moveable in the mouth, and many horses like being able to play with their mouthpiece and move it about. Quite a few horses learn the habit of leaning on an eggbutt, and for these a more freely moveable ring may encourage a wetter, more sensitive mouth because they will mouth it more readily, and this encourages the production of saliva. The larger ring of a wire-ring bit means it will pull through the mouth less readily, and is suitable if you have a rough-handed rider or a horse with different ideas from his rider about which way he wants to go!

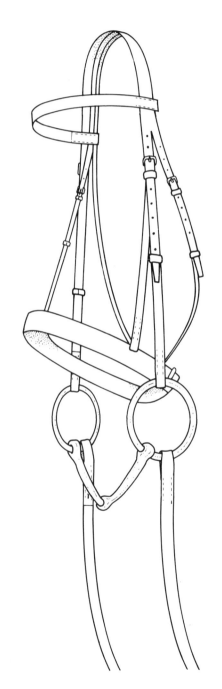

Snaffle bridle with loose-ring snaffle bit fitted

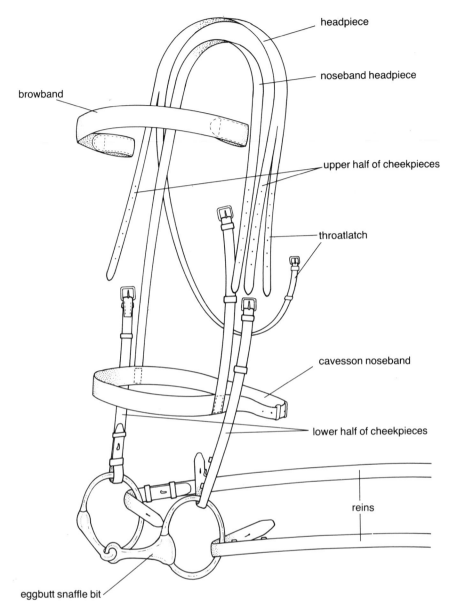

browband

headpiece

noseband headpiece

upper half of cheekpieces

throatlatch

cavesson noseband

lower half of cheekpieces

reins

eggbutt snaffle bit

Parts of a snaffle bridle, showing an eggbutt snaffle

Tack tangles!

If you find taking a bridle to pieces a daunting task because you aren't sure you'll be able to put it back together again, simply write on the underside of each piece what it is and which is left and right. Then use this drawing to help you reassemble everything.

It does not take long to learn what each piece looks like on its own and to put it back together. It is easiest to start by putting the noseband headstall through the browband loops, then the bridle headpiece with the upper halves of the cheekpieces and the throatlatch. Do up the noseband, then attach the lower halves of the cheekpieces to their upper havles, attach the bit and finally the reins.

You can do this on a proper bridle rack, bridle hook or a table, whichever you find easiest.

Cheeks on the end of the mouthpiece – so that the bit looks rather like a capital letter H – are also designed for this purpose as they are impossible to pull through the mouth. The most usual sort is a full cheek, employing the full left and right arms of the H, but there are also half cheeks, comprising either the upper half or the lower half, which serve a similar purpose. Full cheeks should be secured, usually by little loops or keepers which are stitched to the cheekpiece of the bridle and slot over the top branch of the cheek; this keeps them in position and steadier in the mouth, but it does then give the more fixed effect of an eggbutt snaffle. If the keepers are left off, the bit 'mouths' more like a loose- or wire-ring snaffle, which some horses prefer.

Although cheek snaffles – and particularly those with full cheeks – are most effective when extra turning control of strong, unco-operative or green horses is required, many people do not recommend their use during jumping because should the horse fall, there is a chance that the upper branch could actually pierce the horse's cheek.

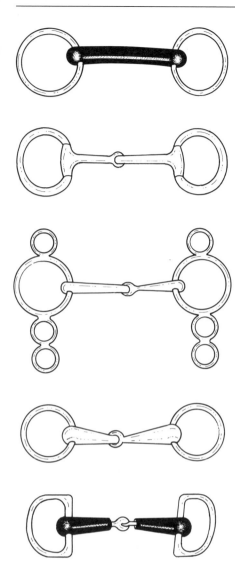

From top: **Loose-ring rubber snaffle**; an **eggbutt jointed snaffle**; a **3-ring snaffle** which creates poll pressure when the reins are changed to the lower rings; a **thick-mounted, jointed, loose-ring German snaffle** and a **rubber-covered, D-ring, jointed snaffle**

The snaffle mouthpieces in most common use are the single-jointed, the mullen-mouth and (though less so) the double-joint and sometimes the straight-bar. There are very many different mouthpieces and designs for snaffles, and whole books have been written about bits alone. Many are very obscure, perhaps no longer even made, and anyway unnecessary in their action. A few are exceptionally strong (some would say cruel)– but it also has to be said that even a smooth, mullen-mouthed bit can cause great pain if roughly used. In bitting, almost everything depends on how sensitive the rider's hands are on the other end of the reins, and also on his standard of equestrian education and his attitude of mind. All sorts of complicated theories exist about bitting, but as one experienced loriner said, nine out of ten bits are probably for men's heads and only one for the horse's. It is certainly true that no matter how much you learn about theory, until you put a bit into a horse's mouth and ride or drive him in it, you cannot tell whether or not he will like it, respect it, feel comfortable in it or go well in it – given good hands on your part, of course.

In former days, great pride was taken in having 'hands like silk' and in schooling a horse to go in the classical way – from the hindquarters, in self-carriage, and manoevrable on the weight of the reins alone. Today (although the fashion does seem to be turning yet again) there is great emphasis on maintaining a heavier bit contact, and having the horse 'on the bit': this gives a mental impression to many riders that the horse has actually to seek pressure on the bit, almost lean on it a little – or a lot, as far as some horses and riders are concerned. This trend seems to have developed since World War II, along with generally lower standards in riding combined with an increasing use of the snaffle, the latter probably compensating for the fact that most 'ordinary' riders today cannot handle a double bridle with the skill of their counterparts of a few generations ago.

In very general terms, it may be said that a poor rider can do less damage and cause less pain with a snaffle than with a bridle comprising any kind of curb action. Unfortunately the 'new' emphasis on contact, contact, contact and leg, leg, leg to go with it, conspires against the very lightness we are all supposed to be striving to attain, according to the written rules of modern dressage. The practical application of dressage riding as seen in many lessons and also in the public spotlight of the competitive dressage arena, is often quite different from the theoretical concept; and in my view it is particularly horrifying to see that today's emphasis on contact is extended to horses wearing double bridles, which are then obliged to perform against several pounds or kilos of bit pressure – the complete antithesis of going on the weight of the rein alone, the ultimate criterion of former generations and the way that a horse properly educated to wear a double bridle *should* go. Indeed if your horse *did* go on the weight of the rein in a dressage competition, albeit from the back end and in self-carriage, you may well be marked down for not having your horse 'properly on the bit'!

The snaffle is always used in racing, although horses raced in double bridles in bygone centuries, and in point-to-point races earlier this century. However, its proper use should be considered as for starting young horses, those learning about bits, balance and humans, and developing their musculature so that ultimately they can go in self-carriage under the weight of a rider. The idea should be that as their education continues, they learn to wear a double bridle with the extra finesse this offers the rider. However, nowadays many horses will never see a double bridle in all their lives; nor will many riders ever get the chance to use one, for the snaffle will always be a safer bit for both the novice and the less educated and sensitive rider to use. Excellent results can, of course, be obtained with snaffles; but riders should always be aware that even a snaffle is not, in itself, 'mild' and rough hands can still very easily seriously bruise a horse's mouth or even draw blood.

The feel a particular snaffle will give a horse depends on the design of the mouthpiece and the make and shape of his mouth, and these, combined with the horse's attitude of mind and standard of schooling, will dictate how he responds to aids given via the bit.

The simplest action is that of a **straight-bar snaffle** which acts almost entirely on the tongue and lips. The horse can also use his tongue to push the bit up and prevent its pressing on the bars of his mouth, the toothless area between the front (incisor) teeth and the back (molar) teeth on each side. The bars correspond with the corners of the horse's lips where the bit will lie. Just behind the incisors, male horses will have tushes (canine) teeth: these are of no use in the modern horse, being a vestige of an early ancestral feature. It is very rare, but not unknown, for mares to have tushes. Both sexes, however, can develop wolf teeth, small, rudimentary molars in the upper jaw (and very occasionally in the lower) just in front of the true molars. Wolf teeth can cause problems with the bit and are best removed by a vet.

The straight-bar snaffle is not always a particularly comfortable bit for many horses, however, as the tongue can be squashed and even pinched between the bit and the bars if it is so large that it overlaps the bars. Generally, a **mullen** or **half-moon mouthpiece** will be more acceptable to most horses. Again, the horse can jiggle it about with his tongue if he wishes, but not as much as he can with a straight-bar; being curved, the mouthpiece has some pressure on the bars whilst leaving more room for the tongue to rest in comfort between the lower jaws. Both mouthpieces also act on the corners of the lips.

A single-jointed mouthpiece bears more on the bars and on the lips, but less on the tongue because of the room left by the 'broken' shape of the mouthpiece; its action is therefore said to be 'stronger', as the bars are more sensitive than the tongue. A single-jointed mouthpiece that is too large will also press upwards when pressure is put on the reins to any extent, into the roof of the mouth, and can certainly then cause pain. The action of a single-jointed mouthpiece is often described as a 'nutcracker' action: this is not quite accurate but is near enough to make the point, that the more the reins are pulled (what an awful expression!) the more the joint is closed, so the mouthpiece presses on and squeezes the bars between its two 'arms'. Moreover if excessive pressure is used with this bit, the horse's cheeks can be trapped between his back teeth and the rings or even the mouthpiece of the bit; this is obviously extremely painful, and can cut and seriously bruise the cheeks, especially if the teeth have been neglected and allowed to become sharp. And if a single-jointed mouthpiece is too wide for the mouth, it can hang down and bang on the front teeth; this will also happen if it is fitted too low in the mouth.

A double-jointed mouthpiece acts on the bars and the lips; because of its less extreme shape it has no so-called nutcracker action, but it leaves less room for the tongue and, depending on the shape and angle or 'set' of the

Teething troubles

When youngsters are teething their mouths are often very sore and it may be felt that work involving the wearing of a bit should be stopped.

It will be found, however, that although a rest will do a young horse no harm at all, it is possible to work him effectively in a bitless bridle or simply give him lunge or long-reining work from a well-fitting lungeing cavesson.

As mental education is just as important as getting him to learn commands and aids physically, it can be very useful to take him for a walk in hand, perhaps in the company of an older, steady horse who will set a good example.

He can be walked around the yard and paddock premises, particularly to spots where there may be something unusual going on such as haymaking, machinery being repaired, buildings being maintained etc to accustom him to all sorts of sights and sounds.

Watching other horses being schooled, particularly those he knows, is certainly known to make the youngster's education easier as messages seem to 'sink in' when watching other horses working.

For these 'walkies' the youngster can wear a well-fitting lungeing cavesson, as described, with a long leadrope clipped to the front ring. If you are expecting problems, use two ropes and handlers and do take that experienced schoolmaster horse along as well.

The development of bits

Although no one can be exactly sure when and how bits came into being, the process has been thought out and detailed by equestrian and historical experts and seems logical enough.

Initially, horses were probably controlled by a simple rope around the top of the neck, a method still used today by some peoples and tribes. It will have been noted that the nearer to the head the rope was the more control was possible.

It was only a small step from this to putting a rope round the horse's face and jaw, linking it together and also passing it up over the poll, making a rudimentary halter.

Perhaps a little more thought was involved in the next stage – passing the rope or thong through the mouth. This may have been done in an upward direction at first, with the rope passing through the mouth and back up the sides of the head. Then further consideration will have produced a loop round the lower jaw. American Indians often rode horses with this jaw-loop arrangement and a single rope or thong passing back to the hand but adapted to 'rigid' bits when they got their hands on escaped horses of the Spanish Conquistadores.

Earlier civilisations must have realized that leather, rawhide, plaited hair and fabric ropes did not last long when wet from a horse's saliva, and various materials such as wood, horn and bone were tried and employed extensively before metals were used.

connecting link or spatula, can press on it to a greater or lesser degree. The 'official' view of double-jointed mouthpieces seems to be that they are milder (because less extreme) than single-jointed ones; but I know many very experienced horsepeople inside and outside the Establishment system who maintain that they are more severe, and some horses simply refuse to go in them. The severity in fact depends on the angle of the spatula or middle link: in a Dr Bristol snaffle it is angled so as to press down into the tongue when pressure is put on the bit, and is therefore more severe; in a French snaffle mouthpiece it lies flat across the tongue and is therefore milder and should cause no trouble. Only study of the individual bit, preferably in your horse's mouth, can solve this.

Fitting and comfort

The mouthpiece of the bit should protrude just a quarter of an inch each side of the horse's mouth. If it is too wide it will slide about and bruise the mouth, and will also change the action due to the altered position in the mouth. If too narrow, it will pinch the lips and cheeks and may press them against the teeth (as already mentioned).

How high the snaffle should be in the mouth is still a point of disagreement among experts. It is felt by some that the bit should just touch the corners of the lips without actually wrinkling them; others feel that it should just wrinkle them – and yet others like to see a 'good wrinkle'! Again, much depends on the horse and how he goes, and how his rider rides him. For example if the bit is fitted fairly low and the rider tends to take a firm contact, the cheekpieces of the bridle will loop outwards – this is not important in itself, although it is unsightly. On the other hand, if you and your horse agree on a light contact, this will not happen. Some horses do not like the constant pressure on the corners of the mouth caused by having them wrinkled (as opposed to simply 'touching'); others do not mind. And if the bit is too low, it will encourage some horses to put their tongues over it, when they will become almost impossible to control.

The thickness of the mouthpiece should also be considered. When considering standardised bits of inferior quality available today, virtually all mouthpieces will be seen to be more or less round (in the past you could get flat and oval ones, too); naturally this means that only a small part of the mouthpiece will actually touch the bars of the mouth (like drawing a tangent off the edge of a circle). If the horse has flattish bars, as many pony, cob and more coarsely bred horse types may have, there will be more bit contact than in finely bred animals which may have rounded or even quite sharp bars, more thinly covered in flesh than those of their more plebeian cousins. For these better bred horses, the actual area touched by the rounded mouthpiece will be quite small.

According to the principle of spreading the weight to reduce the pressure (as discussed in Chapter 1), it is obvious that the thinner the mouthpiece and the sharper the bars, the greater will be the pressure brought to bear on one particular small spot. A thicker mouthpiece and/or flatter, fleshier bars will mean less pressure, even though the tension on the rein which creates that pressure may be the same.

With better quality bits, the arms of the mouthpiece are more oval in shape and this obviously provides an increased bearing surface on the bars of the mouth and a slightly milder effect. The fashion for using very thick mouthpieces seems to be over, many people having realised that this is not the only criterion for bit comfort. Horses with small mouths often find a thick mouthpiece too much of a mouthful; also, a very thick mouthpiece can be uncomfortably heavy unless – as is often the case – it is hollow to relieve this problem.

Except for some driving bits, most mouthpieces these days are quite smooth – and in your daily inspections pay attention that the ones you use have not become roughened in any way. Bits can still be found, though, with a smoothly ridged or 'rough' side, and a smooth side, for example the Army Universal Pelham. Normally these are curbs; as far as snaffles go, probably the worst roughened mouthpiece was the **twisted snaffle**, which often had genuinely sharp ridges.

Snaffle mouthpieces which are square (the edges vary in degree of sharpness) and those with rollers (oval or rounded balls, usually of metal) obviously have a more concentrated effect on the mouth, providing an erratic or greatly reduced bearing surface. The **cherry roller snaffle** and the **Magenis** are two examples, the cherry roller with the rollers fitted round the narrow foundation which serves for the mouthpiece, the Magenis with them inside a squared-off mouthpiece with no sides. The cherry roller snaffle (particularly in the form of a gag snaffle) is used on hard-pulling horses, and many riders maintain that it is not so much the more severe effect of the bit which brings results, but the fact that because the rollers are moveable the horse feels he cannot trust the bit sufficiently to lean on it and so does not take such a hold.

Curb bits and double bridles

The snaffle has, as we have seen, a fairly direct, simple, straightforward effect and is used mainly to indicate to the horse that we wish to turn or stop, although other nuances are possible depending on the skill of the rider. When it comes to nuances, however, the curb bit is infinitely superior: it is much more sophisticated and requires a truly balanced, independent seat so that the rider is not in any way using the hands to stay 'with' the horse, a high standard of equestrian education and a truly sympathetic attitude of mind towards the horse; it also requires a clear understanding of how the curb bit works and how it affects the horse – what it does to his mouth when in active use or simply in passive wear.

Design of the curb bit

In shape the curb bit is similar to the cheeked snaffle and looks like the capital

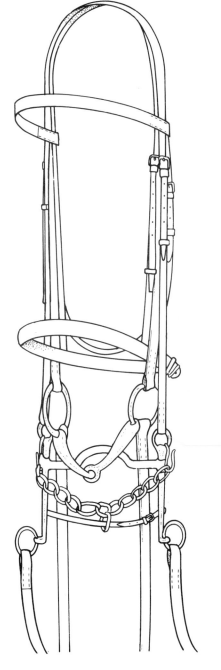

Double bridle, curb chain and lip-strap fitted

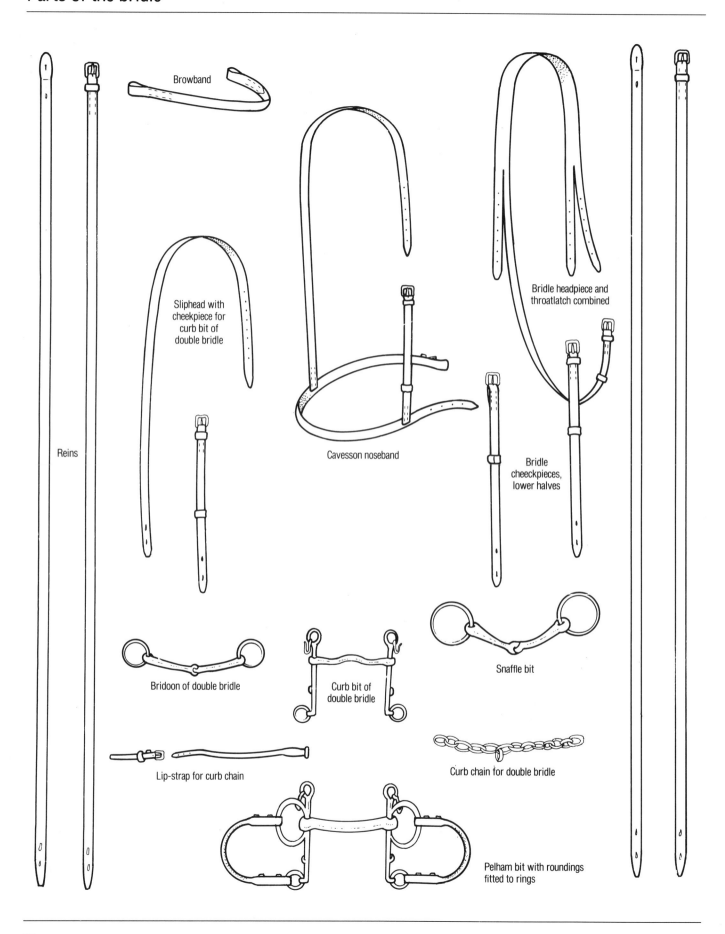

Browband

Reins

Sliphead with
cheekpiece for
curb bit of
double bridle

Cavesson noseband

Bridle headpiece and
throatlatch combined

Bridle
cheeckpieces,
lower halves

Bridoon of double bridle

Curb bit of
double bridle

Snaffle bit

Lip-strap for curb chain

Curb chain for double bridle

Pelham bit with roundings
fitted to rings

letter H, although the centre bar is higher up the two vertical arms. It has rings on the top of the arms (or 'bit-cheeks', as they are called) to take the bridle cheekpieces which support it; rings on the bottom to take the curb reins (usually narrower than the reins used for a snaffle or the snaffle rein of a double bridle where two bits are used, the curb and a thin snaffle known as the 'bridoon'); and small rings on the cheeks below the mouthpiece to which the lip-strap fastens (see p59). Hanging from the top rings are two hooks to take the curb chain.

The mouthpiece of the curb used today in English-style riding (as opposed to western, including South American, riding) is normally quite smooth with a moderately low port to allow room for the tongue. By lessening tongue pressure, this sort of mouthpiece puts more pressure on the bars of the mouth. The port must not be so high that it presses forwards and upwards into the roof of the mouth, although sadly some of this sort are still used today. In past centuries, horrendously high and even sharpened ports were the norm, together with sharp ridges and even spikes on both port and mouthpiece, in the barbaric and totally erroneous belief that the more severe the bit the more likely was the horse to behave! Normally, of course, the opposite is the case, although it is certainly possible to dominate most horses with a combination of severe ('sharp') bits, restricting nosebands, tight martingales and various other mis-used 'gadgets'. However, this can in no way be termed 'horsemanship' – although in my experience it is seen all too frequently in the training of children's show jumpers and in the polo world; and in polo this is the case during actual play, when there are very few rules as to what tack a pony may or may not wear.

Mullen-mouthed curbs are also available; like the snaffle, these place more pressure on the tongue, with only some on the bars. Horses find them easier to manipulate and often go kindly in them as a result, although horses with large tongues or who dislike tongue pressure will probably prefer a ported mouthpiece.

How the curb works

The curb bit works by means of the leverage principle: pressure put on the curb rein does not produce the same amount of pressure in the mouth as does the snaffle, but a much-multiplied one. It is not even like adding two and two and getting four, because in fact you get something like eight or ten: this is why working a horse with an extremely light contact on the curb rein, the proverbial weight-of-the-rein contact, does *not* mean that you have *no* contact since the weight of the rein itself is multiplied in the horse's mouth to create the pressure. In Western riding, silver decorative weights are sometimes added to the reins; or sometimes part of the rein (usually near the bit) is made of chain, which increases its weight and therefore the pressure felt in the mouth. When riding, it is usual and correct to ride with a slacker curb rein than bridoon rein, first because there is no need for such pressure and also because the resulting pressure in the mouth would be too great if the curb contact were the same.

When pressure or contact is applied to the curb rein, attached to the bottom ring of the cheek, the cheek is pulled backwards and the top branch moves forwards, creating a pull on the cheekpiece attached to it (on both sides if both

Riding on the curb rein

Riding horses mainly on the curb rein, or entirely so, is a skill little taught today. Apart from Western schools of riding where a curb bit of some sort with a single rein is the norm, we normally see curb bits used in double bridles and pelham bits which also provide a curb action.

This form of riding, on the curb only, is not cruel as often thought by novices and the uninitiated. It takes a truly independent, balanced seat and independent, sensitive and sympathetic hands to do it successfully. You also need supple wrists and, as riding on the curb is often done with one hand only, you need to be adept at handling each rein independently in that one hand.

We sometimes see top show hacks at national-level shows being ridden this way by professional showmen, the reins in the left hand and the right hand resting lightly on the right thigh. Usually, though, the curbs in question are part of a double bridle but the principle is the same.

If you watch any military parade or display you will often see one or more officers' chargers ridden mainly on the curb. In these cases, although horses are no longer used in battle, the rider has to handle a sword often, depending on the occasion, and it is essential that the horse be light in hand and the rider able to handle him with finesse and control.

As a much lighter contact is used with a curb bit, the method is often found suitable for horses with very sensitive mouths who go happily forward ridden on the curb but may rear or give other problems if ridden mainly on the bridoon, or in a snaffle.

Bridles and Bits

A **showing double bridle** with velvet-covered, patterned browband and matching rosettes at the end, a raised stitched cavesson nose band, a loose-ring bridoon and a sliding-cheeked curb bit. The author would like the throatlatch a little looser and the nose band lower, away from the horse's facial bones

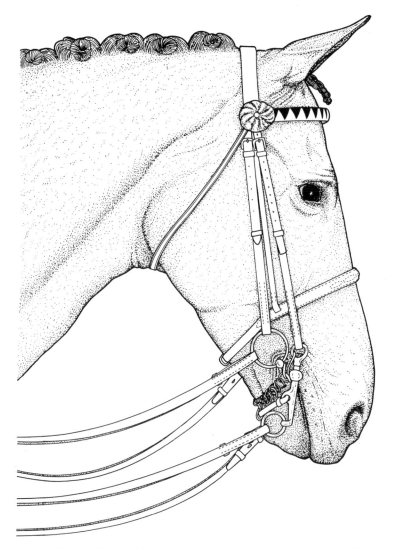

⑤ A Paragon long-distance saddle which shows a generous bearing surface on the horse's back, extra dees fitted to the back of the saddle to take small items of equipment, a padded seat for additional rider comfort, a slightly cut back pommel, a stirrup leather extension hooked up into place and ordinary English hunting stirrup irons. The knee rolls and padding over them will give extra comfort and security when travelling over varied and maybe rough, hilly terrain.

⑥ Despite taking care to buy strong, heavy stirrups of the correct width for the boot (an inch wider than the widest part of the sole of the boot), many people justifiably like to have an additional safety factor in their stirrups and the new Step Out stirrup from Safehorse (UK) Ltd (address, p195) provides an ingenious answer to getting a foot caught in a stirrup during a fall.

The stirrup has a hinged mechanism which opens up the side of the stirrup to release the foot in a fall but which keeps the stirrup tightly closed at other times. The stirrup is fitted with a replaceable dove-tailed non-slip tread. Made of specially hardened stainless steel, the stirrups look like any ordinary stirrup in use and, because of their strength, there is no problem with the base of the stirrup gradually being strained downwards towards, for example, an outer elastic branch or in a nickel stirrup.

reins are used) and, inevitably, downward pressure on the poll. But the most crucial point is the fact that the lower jaw is held between the mouthpiece and the curb chain fastened to the hooks. The mouthpiece should be slightly lower in the mouth than the bridoon, but not so low that the horse can get his tongue betweeen the bits which would result in considerably reduced control and possible injury to the tongue; the ideal place is said to be exactly above the curb or chin groove in which the chain lies. This all-round pressure on the tongue and lower jaw is the signal to the trained horse to relax his lower jaw and flex at the poll. It is quite possible to get a well-schooled horse to do this with just a snaffle, but the idea of the double bridle, using two bits, is that the bridoon (snaffle) can be used to regulate the pace and give instructions as to direction, while simultaneously asking for flexion and lightness with the curb. This all makes for extra finesse, for great lightness when the bridle is used properly, and for improved collection and movements from the horse.

This is necessarily over-simplified: various other factors also come into play, such as the use of the rider's back, seat and legs, and whip and spurs if used, the direction of the rein aids, and the voice when schooling (and surreptitiously and very quietly in the competitive arena, in some cases!). When the horse goes with the front of his face approaching the vertical, about 5° in front of it,

5

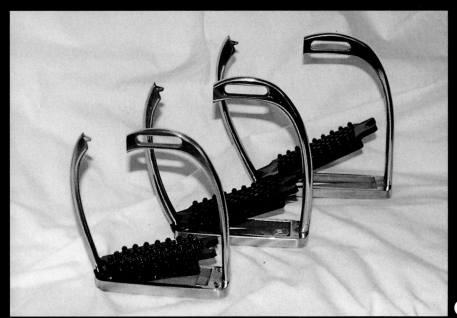

6

7 A side saddle with the balance strap sewn to the girth and the offside flap missing to show the girth buckles.

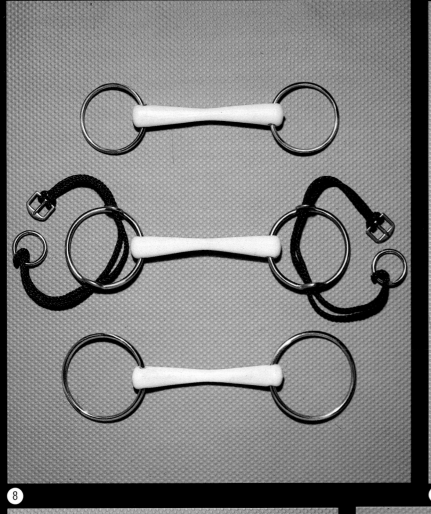

8

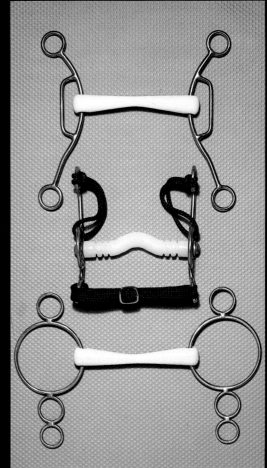

9

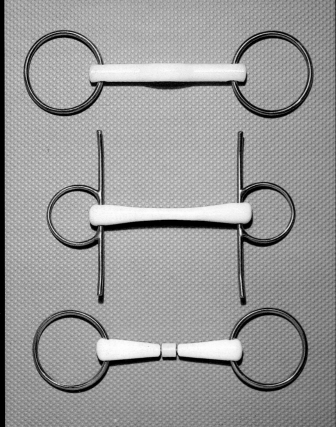

10

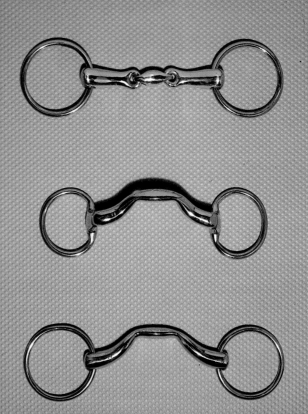

11

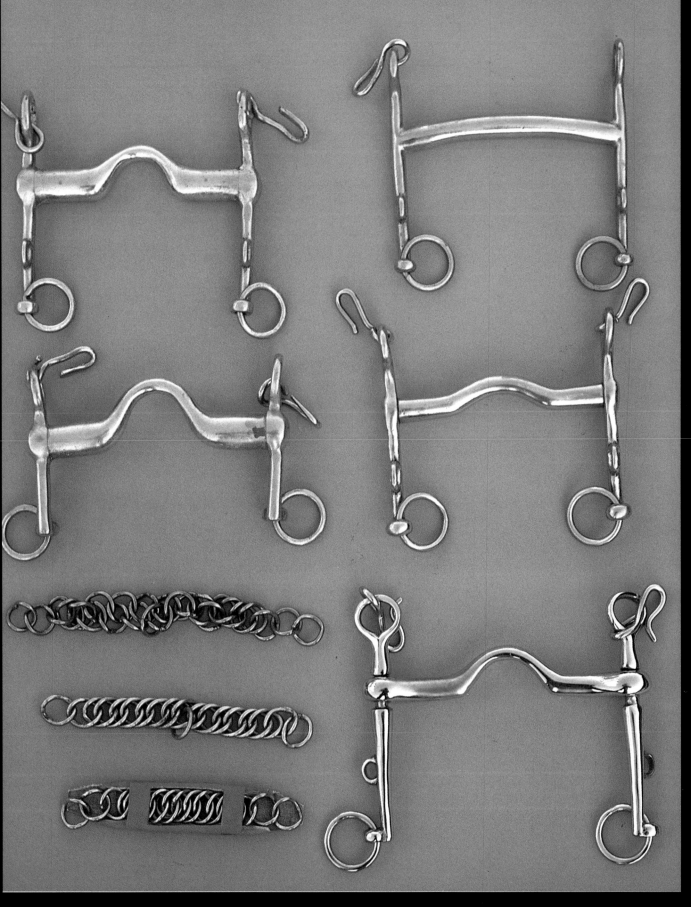

the bars of the mouth are in the best position to take the contact of the bit/s. If the horse goes with his head nearer the horizontal – called 'poking his nose' – the bit/s will ride up the bars and act mainly on the corners of the lips; they will not have their maximum effect, or allow much lightness.

Fitting the curb bit and chain

The proportions of the curb bit, and the tightness or looseness of the curb chain, are also important factors. The longer the lower cheeks of the curb the more exaggerated will be the pressure felt in the horse's mouth, and the longer the upper part of the cheek the more poll pressure there will be. In 'olden days', cheeks of potentially jaw-breaking length were used. As a guide, the following are considered good proportions: the lower branch of the bit cheek about 3in long and the upper part no more than 1½in long; if the upper part comprises one third of the total length of the cheek (or less) and the lower (obviously) two-thirds, this is about right.

The width of the mouthpiece – like the snaffle – should be such that the bit protrudes just ¼in each side of the mouth. All mouthpieces, for any bit, are measured across the width from the inside of the cheeks or rings. To avoid expensive mistakes when buying bits, or being refused an exchange by a saddler on the grounds of spreading disease, you can measure your horse's mouth either with a piece of string, or – though this is more objectionable to the horse – a tape measure or rigid joiner's measure; then buy a bit just ½in wider. With curb bits, it is better to buy a good quality bit which has the upper parts of the cheeks angled slightly outwards to avoid rubbing the cheeks.

To attach the curb chain, first make sure that the hooks are hanging down straight. Then take the curb chain and straighten it out so that the links are smooth and the little fly-link meant for the lip-strap is at the bottom. With your right thumb pointing upwards, take the chain in your right hand and slip it over the offside hook so that when it is positioned horizontally (as it will be when on both hooks) the upper part of the right-hand end link is on the inside of the hook; the chain will then ultimately lie flat. Then, standing on the horse's near side, twist the chain clockwise till all the links are flat (this is unnecessary if you straightened it out in the first place) and the fly-link is hanging at the bottom.

Next, thumb still upwards, slot the left end link onto the nearside hook, again so it lies with its highest side upwards on the inside of the hook. If the chain is too loose, you will need to hook on a link further down the chain – you will discover how tight it needs to be by trial and error. The main point is that *this* link is put on the hook with your thumb pointing *downwards*, so that you put the link on with an anti-clockwise motion. In this way you will avoid twisting the chain, and the links will lie flat and smooth even though there are two of them on the hook. The lip-strap buckles to the little ring or metal loop on the offside branch of the bit, passes through the fly-link and buckles to its other half (another separate strap) which you will have fastened to the left branch.

The actual length of the curb chain is critical to the functioning of the bit and its effect on the horse. The tighter it is the sooner and the more unmistakably the pressure is felt; the more severe the pressure capable of being inflicted; and also the less the rider needs to use the rein. But there are obviously limits,

PAGE 65:
Hydrophane Laboratories Limited (address, p195) introduced into the UK, the German synthetic Nathe bits and stainless steel K.K. bits which are now firm favourites with many serious amateur and professional riders. The synthetic Nathe bits (illustrations 8–10) have very light, comfortable mouthpieces with a soft feel, encouraging horses from young to old to accept the bit with confidence, yet the bits are very strong and do not distort in use.

⑧ Top: Large loose-ring standard snaffle. Middle: Gag bit. Bottom: Small loose-ring snaffle bit.

⑨ Top: American gag. Middle: Pelham. Bottom: Three ring bit.
The gag has the same direction as a conventional gag, the two pairs of reins being attached to the bars at the ends of the mouthpiece and to the lower rings on the ends of the cheeks, the upper rings being used to attach the bit to the bridle cheekpieces. The three ring bit attaches to the cheekpieces by the top rings and differing amounts of poll pressure, or none at all, can be applied according to whichever ring the reins are fitted to.

⑩ Top: Jumping bit, loose-ring. Middle: Full-cheek snaffle. Bottom: Jointed loose-ring snaffle. The tapered mouthpieces give a comfortable amount of room for the tongue without the necessity for a port or the type of joint which can cause damage to the roof of the mouth in certain cases, or create the so-called 'nutcracker' action when squeezing, and possibly bruising, the bars of the mouth.

⑪ The K.K. stainless steel bits were designed in collaboration with riders and veterinary surgeons to shift the pressure away from the lips and corners of the mouth more to the centre, making a milder bit in which horses appear to go happily and willingly.
Top: Training bit with thick mouthpiece, loose-ring and double joint. Middle: Eggbutt schooling bit. Bottom: Loose-ring correction bit.

PAGE 66:
⑫ Left, from top: Thick-mouthed, fixed-cheeked, ported curb with, below it, a similar shorter-cheeked, higher-ported curb. The different types of curb chain are shown at the bottom, the last one having a rubber cover.
Right, from top: Fixed-sided, mullen-mouthed curb; fixed-sided, ported curb and sliding cheeked, ported curb.

Adapting to the curb rein

When teaching a horse to go solely or mainly on the curb it is important to make sure that the bit rests comfortably in his mouth in the right position. Some horses will prefer a ported curb mouthpiece, and others a mullen mouth; few will like a straight-bar mouthpiece.

It is also essential that the mouthpiece be exactly the correct width for the horse's mouth. If it is too narrow its action will be inhibited and it may pinch, and if too wide the action of the curb chain will be affected as it will be held away from the sides of the jaw and act only on the jawbones.

If the rider has any inclination at all to pull on the reins, riding on the curb is out. The pain caused would be unbearable and the horse, if he had no problems already, would soon develop them.

Schooling the horse to neck-rein is also part of riding on the curb and information on this can be obtained from any good book on polo or Western riding.

It is also a good idea to make sure the horse is absolutely obedient to the command 'whoa' to obviate any instinct or tendency on the part of the rider to feel the need to pull on the reins.

Once these matters have been absorbed by the trainer/rider the use of the snaffle or bridoon of the double bridle can be gradually lessened and the curb rein can take over. If using a Scawbrig bitless bridle or a true Western bosal (hackamore), both of which are detailed in this book, the curb can be used immediately.

Self-carriage (or, at least, self-balance) are most important in a horse to be ridden on the curb and there should be no rush to dispense with the bitless bridle, if used. If using a double bridle, the bridoon can be gradually dispensed with.

and the general teaching is that the chain should be adjusted so that it and the bit mouthpiece combine in their effect when the cheek of the bit forms a 45° angle with the line of lips. In other words, the curb and chain do not act until this angle is reached.

It is also worth remembering that the very presence of a well designed and fitted curb bit in the horse's mouth, together with a carefully fitted chain, acts as a gentle reminder to the horse of what is required of him, whether the rider uses them or not. If the horse understands, through careful preliminary schooling, what the action of this combination requires him to do, the reins can be taken up so that they are only acting on the bit through their weight alone – in theory the horse will go with a more flexed poll and relaxed jaw than he would were they absent, without any effort or action from the rider. The weight of the rein alone, when multiplied by the gentle leverage action which will inevitably occur due to the horse's movements and the simple fact that the rider is holding the reins, will give a slight effect on the bit; so when the rider actually uses the rein, the slightest touch is sufficient because of the multiplied pressure. Whether or not the horse responds to that pressure is down to his schooling, his physical condition and his attitude of mind. Be aware, too, that the degree of pressure normally given on a snaffle bit these days will cause the horse considerable pain if exerted on a curb rein.

There is a good case for fitting the curb chain tighter than the 45° recommended and allowing for an angle of only about 25°, but only when it is used by skilled riders on well-schooled horses. This degree of tightness permits even less use of the rein, and extra lightness and finesse when it *is* used. It may also keep the bit steadier in the mouth, and prevent the chain moving too much and possibly irritating the horse when not actually in use. Thus the 45° angle may be considered suitable for horses and riders well versed and competent in the use of the snaffle and starting to learn about double bridles, with the lesser angle gradually brought in as the skill of horse and rider increases.

Nowadays the mouthpiece of the curb bit is usually fixed immovably to the cheekpiece, although a few decades ago sliding cheeks were preferred. These passed through a hole in the end of the mouthpiece and could be moved very slightly up and down by the horse, should he wish. Also, as the curb was used, the mouthpiece would slide up a little, probably no more than 1/8in, so increasing the leverage and having the effect of very slightly lengthening the cheek. Nowadays this is felt undesirable: it certainly increases the severity of the bit, and some trainers and riders do not want the horse to be able to move the bit mouthpiece to that extent, seeming to regard it almost as an evasion. Having been brought up on sliding cheek curbs, I tend to feel these arguments are splitting hairs and consider it is worth trying both to see which the horse seems to prefer.

Types of curb chain

The type of curb chain used is yet another point of contention. There are several sorts, although the most important thing is that the chain must be comfortable to the horse if he is to accept it and co-operate with its action; it must also be attached correctly to the hooks to prevent chafing the very sensitive skin in this area. There are ordinary 'single link' chains which are most commonly available today; flat (shaped) links which are more comfortable; double, finer link chains which give the feel of a smooth mesh; and also leather and elastic curbs, as well as rubber guards for covering a metal chain. Probably the least comfortable is the ordinary single link chain, which you will undoubtedly be offered if you just ask for a curb chain. Reject it and insist on one of the other types, even if this means searching round a few shops or buying one mail-order.

Non-metal curb 'chains' may be elastic on leather, with links on the ends for attachment and adjustment, and must give a softer feel to the horse. Rubber guards are fine, although I always feel that since rubber is not absorbent it cannot feel very pleasant if wet with saliva or sweat. My favourite curb is felt-covered leather which never causes any trouble if kept clean and soft. Alternatively you might have a shorn sheepskin or cotton fleece fabric sleeve made up, to cover a metal chain, on the same principle as a fleecy girth sleeve.

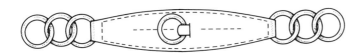

Although Western (and similar) riders break in horses in a bosal (hackamore) and put them straight into various types of curb bit, the process should not be rushed. When it is, problems can arise. Not all Western horses are light in hand and obedient, stopping and turning on the curb with their mouths closed, their jaws softly flexed and their heads flexed at the poll. Open mouths and wild eyes at the pain of a pull on the reins are not exceptional.

In military parades, horses selected for VIPs have to be very well schooled by the regimental riding masters. They will often be schooled to go on the curb, even though the VIPs concerned may not be able to ride them thus! The object is to have the horse responsive, well behaved, steady and reliable.

The rider's seat and saddle are also of crucial importance. Without a truly deep, independent and balanced seat the rider cannot be in full control of his or her hands and may easily pull on the reins or make involuntary movements which may hurt or confuse the horse. He or she may then reprimand the horse for responding to that 'aid' which the rider never knew was given.

It can be seen that riding on the curb is not a practice for the novice.

Curb chains
From top: a double link chain; single-link chain; jodphur curb chain which helps prevent the horse lowering his head too much and finally a leather curb

The lip-strap

The lip-strap is less and less used today. At one time we were taught that it prevented the bit cheek reversing or coming forward – both of which I find impossible to imagine and have certainly never experienced. If the curb chain is fitted too loosely (making the curb principle *in*effective), a lip-strap will stop it turning over and twisting in the chin groove. It also helps prevent losing the chain off the bridle when the double bridle is being carried correctly, with the nearside unhooked – although there is no reason why you shouldn't carry the bridle with both ends of the chain hooked up, or even with the chain in your hand or pocket! Obviously the chain should have the nearside, at least, unhooked before you put the bridle on.

It is possible for the curb chain to ride up out of the chin groove on horses with long jawbones and/or with curb bits that have rather long upper branches. The point should be carefully checked, and if this does happen, a bit with a short upper branch should be used instead; otherwise the chain will be operating on a much more sensitive, bony area. This is also one occasion where a lip-strap *is* helpful in keeping the chain down where it belongs: in the groove.

Pelhams

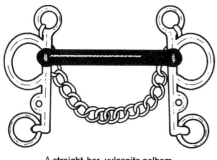

A straight-bar, vulcanite pelham

The pelham is effectively a compromise: it aspires to the effects of a double bridle while giving the horse only one mouthpiece to cope with. Purists seem to hate pelhams, maintaining that one mouthpiece cannot do both jobs (anyway not at the same time) and even that pelhams cannot be fitted properly – if the mouthpiece is fitted so that it wrinkles the corners of the mouth as would be correct for a bridoon, this is incorrect for the curb action; but if it is fitted lower, where a curb should go, it cannot act like a snaffle. The recommended positioning for a pelham is for it just to touch the corners of the mouth without wrinkling them – and this, says the purist, is a compromise which suits neither purpose (neither bridoon nor curb). The pelham, he continues, is imprecise in its action; which is probably why so many horses co-operate and go so kindly, not to mention correctly, in a pelham. Horses with a small mouth certainly seem more comfortable with 'only' a pelham rather than the mouthful presented by the two bits of a double bridle.

The pelham looks just like a curb bit at first glance (the letter H with the horizontal bar – the mouthpiece – displaced upwards) but with a ring on each end of the mouthpiece as well, to take the 'snaffle' or 'bridoon' reins (though there is, of course, no bridoon in this bitting arrangement). In other respects, it is just like a curb bit.

There are pelhams with ported or with mullen mouthpieces, and the best to use depends, as always, on the sort of bit your horse goes best in.

The problem of the curb chain rising up and acting on the jawbones instead of in the chin groove is even more likely with a pelham than with a curb due to its higher fitting; horses with long jawbones (usually Thoroughbred or nearly so) may therefore be unable to wear a pelham for this reason.

As with a curb, the pelham is also better with the upper parts of the cheek angled slightly outwards; a good loriner or saddler will be able to get this done for you. One bit, however, obviates the need for this: the *Scamperdale pelham*, because the ends of the mouthpiece, and therefore the cheeks attached to them, are set back an inch or so from the corners of the mouth. A possible disadvantage of this bit is its straight-bar mouthpiece, which many horses do not find very comfortable.

Another pelham with a straight-bar mouthpiece is the *Rugby pelham*. The Rugby has more the action of a curb, rather than the combined effect of curb and bridoon, largely because the bridoon rings are attached to the ends of the mouthpiece by means of a little link which lessens the bridoon effect.

There are also jointed mouthpiece pelhams, although it is difficult to see what these hope to achieve since the curb action will be largely negated by the joint.

As in the curb of the double bridle, the comparative length of the upper to the lower cheek (one third to two thirds) also applies to the pelham, although pelhams tend to have quite long upper cheeks because of the bridoon rings on the mouthpiece. This extra length will also cause a curb chain to rise up.

There is a good case for a young or inexperienced horse to have a curb or pelham with a fairly short lower cheek. To this end the *Tom Thumb curb*, which has a lower cheek no more than 2in long, is a good bit; and although there is officially no such thing as a Tom Thumb pelham, a good saddler will know exactly what is wanted and may well be able to come up with something.

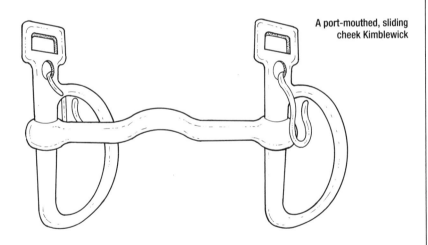

A port-mouthed, sliding cheek Kimblewick

The *Kimblewick* is a sort of pelham that looks rather like a snaffle. Its name is that of the place where it was introduced, although it is known as the Kimberwick in the USA; it is also sometimes known as the 'Spanish jumping bit', because it did actually originate in Spain but was introduced to Britain via Kimblewick by Phil Oliver, who lived there. It usually has a ported, sliding mouthpiece, although mullen types are also available, and the rings at each end are D-shaped with an oblong eye on the top of each to take the bridle cheekpieces. This produces a more direct feel on the poll, increasing the pressure there. The hooks for the curb chain are set below the eyes. When the rein is used normally the bit has more the effect of a snaffle; but if contact is released and the hand lowered, the reins slip down the bit-rings – when contact

Pelhams

Pelham bits were very fashionable from about the middle of the last century to the first quarter of this one. Named after the Pelham family, a seemingly never-ending number of pelham bit designs began sprouting from loriners and saddlers all over the country. It seemed that whatever new shape or form someone thought of somebody else would buy.

In the Neapolitan school of equitation during the Renaissance, a type of curb bit with rings at the ends of the mouthpiece as well is known to have been used, but curb bits proper were the norm until the mid-nineteenth century when pelhams made a sudden reappearance.

This outburst of popularity continued to about the 1940s when it began to wane. However, standards of riding began to drop at the same time, perhaps due to fewer instructors being produced by the military schools (which were cutting back or closing down) and the fact that the reduced economy caused by two fairly close world wars did not favour private training. The British Horse Society (initially called The Institute of The Horse) was a tiny organisation compared to the one we know today and, on the whole, the snaffle bit – less damaging and easier to use, it was thought – became the most common bit in use, and it still is.

The pelham bit and, of course, the double bridle, continued to be used. Old pelhams were unearthed in long-forgotten tack boxes, cleaned up and pressed into service, without their users having any real idea of how they were supposed to act on their horses' and ponies' mouths. I remember one small riding school in our locality when I was a child which bitted all its horses in pelhams *without* curb chains 'so that people can't do any damage with them and spoil the horses'. (continued on p 72)

I also remember several fascinating afternoons at a friend's place, rooting out old bits in the disused tack room and stables, most of which were peculiar pelhams which we cleaned up and tried out on other people's long-suffering ponies.

The large variety of pelhams has now disappeared and the simpler ones now available in tack shops certainly have a place in today's horse world.

The usual criteria of size, comfort and sound materials still apply, of course, and there must be many horses with shortish jaws (such as Arabs and cobs and many ponies) who would be far happier in a pelham than with the mouthful presented by double bridles, and I feel this is also true for many show ponies.

is taken up again, the cheeks of the D-rings are pulled back to a 45° angle and thus implement the curb chain and poll pressure effects; the combined action of which brings about a lowering of the head and more control for the rider.

Many pelham users like to fit the curb chain through the 'bridoon' ring on each side to help prevent chafing of the jawbones, and this can certainly help where chafing is a problem. The length and adjustment of the chain, though, should permit the same angle of the bit cheek as with a curb, however the chain is actually positioned.

Pelhams are often used for children not strong enough to control their ponies in a snaffle, though young children in particular are not always able to handle two reins. The solution to this problem is to use a short loop of leather – called a *rounding* – which fastens to the bridoon and to the curb rings, one loop on each side of the bit; a single rein is then fastened to the loop. This makes for a fairly even pressure on both bit-rings, and means the child cannot specifically use the bridoon or the curb for their separate effects (even if it were capable). The curb chain should be adjusted so that it comes into effect when the bit cheek, operated by the rounding, forms a 45° angle with the lips, which is quite adequate for children. In my opinion, however, it should be strongly emphasised to all child riders that even with a rounding, the pelham bit is considerably stronger than a snaffle, and they should not be lulled into a false sense of security by the single rein.

Pelham bit with roundings for the reins, curb chain and lip-strap. Some people like to pass the chain through the upper bit ring which helps prevent possible chafing of the jawbones with a pelham, where the chain may operate higher than in a conventional curb which is fitted slightly lower

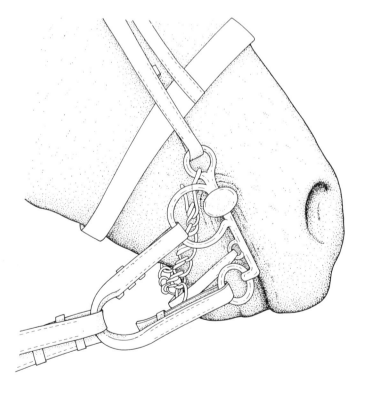

Gag snaffles

Gag snaffles have had rather a bad press over the years, as have the horses which wear them, invariably categorised as inveterate hard pullers who get their heads down and take off. The gag can certainly be severe if (as with most things) it is used harshly or incorrectly, but probably it is possible to inflict more pain and damage with a wrongly used curb than with a wrongly used gag.

The idea of the gag is to raise the head, and this can be a great relief on a horse which persistently goes along with his head down and too fast, not traits designed to inspire confidence in many riders! It also delivers a clear message to the horse to slow down, and is useful for horses which have discovered that if they go along with their chins on their breasts, the rider has very little control. Of course, the horse may go like this because the rider is also pretty useless, having probably created that response in the first place, either through heavy hands or by using an unsuitable bit in the past.

The gag snaffle has a cord or rounded leather strap which passes vertically up through the centre of the bit-ring, and buckles on to the upper part of the bridle cheekpiece (obviously the lower half is dispensed with). The other end of the cord or rounded strap continues in a rein to the rider's hand. The effect is such that when the rein is used, the bit-ring is drawn up the cord and creates pressure on the tongue, the corners of the lips and the poll. The action on the mouth tells the horse to raise his head but the poll pressure tells him, if less strongly, to lower it. Contradictory though this may sound, the gag does have a mainly raising effect – and quite a salutary one! – on most horses.

Most horses will probably go well enough with a rubber-covered or plain-mouthed gag, but the cherry roller gag is often used with very strong or over-enthusiastic horses that tend to be 'deaf' to the rider's aids. The gag should always be used with an additional rein going straight from the bit-ring to the hand, as with any ordinary snaffle, and the gag rein only used when the horse ignores the plain snaffle effect. Normally the gag rein is held between the little and fourth fingers, with the ordinary snaffle rein under the little finger.

A gag is often seen used with a flash noseband (see p81) or a drop noseband to prevent the horse opening his mouth too wide and trying to avoid the bit. However, if these are used, they should not be fitted too tightly, as opening the mouth with a gag is perfectly understandable and does not, in practice, nullify its effect very much. If the flash or drop noseband is fitted at all tightly, the horse may well stop too suddenly or produce some other undesirable reaction!

Using a martingale (see Chapter 3) with a gag is another moot point. A standing martingale is often used to stop the horse raising his head *too* far, and a running martingale might be fitted to keep the bit action on the bars of the mouth, where a gag hardly works when the gag rein is used. Much depends on the traits of the individual horse and the rider's abilities; though if any complicated side effects are provoked by the use of various nosebands and martingales, particularly with a bit like a gag, it is most important that the advice and assessment of a really knowledgeable instructor is first sought.

Correctly used gags are not a black mark in themselves against horse or rider, particularly when used with the second snaffle rein. Big, green horses

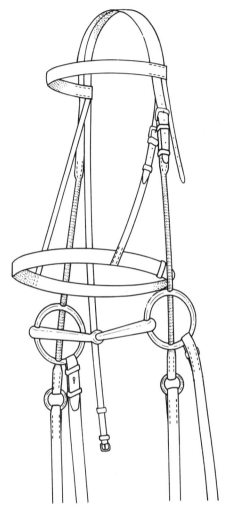

Gag snaffle bridle showing an extra pair of reins fitted directly, and correctly, to the bit-rings

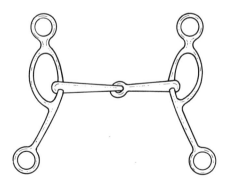

An **American gag** in which the gag rein is fitted to the bottom rings of the bit cheekpieces and the snaffle reins to the rings at the ends of the mouthpiece (the mouthpiece sliding up the sides of the rings when the gag reins are used)

Riding without a bit

Training a horse to go in a bitless bridle is surprisingly easy. It is usually the rider who needs to adapt most and alter his attitude. If you have attended a conventional riding school where cosiderable emphasis is placed on bit contact and getting the horse on the bit, you may find the lack of a bit disconcerting. However, bit contact and being on the bit are means to ends, ie to get the horse to accept the rider's aids, to go with impulsion with the neck and head relaxed (rather than stiff and resisting) and the poll flexed. All this is quite possible in any bitless bridle.

Your feelings still travel down the reins and if you pull or are tense and harsh, the horse will still resist or pull back accordingly.

A good start is to concentrate on your own seat. Relaxing down into the saddle, perhaps without stirrups, and with your toes hanging freely and being allowed to point wherever they wish (probably downwards). In this position, which some classical teachers use for lunge lessons, there is not tension at all in the leg muscles nor, provided the rider concentrates on relaxation, in the seat muscles. This enables the rider to really feel what the horse's legs, via the back are doing. A sensitive, balanced seat, which can be obtained through correct instruction on the lunge, helps give the rider not only confidence but also the facility to guide the horse more by means of seat, weight and legs — really riding the horse from the back end forwards rather than concentrating too much on what the bit would be doing with a conventional bridle.

Of course, you do still keep contact with the horse's head, and the type of contact depends upon what type of bitless bridle you are using.

(continued on p. 76)

going across country in any situation for the first few times, and which have a tendency to go with the head too low for comfort or safety, could well be ridden in a gag with no detriment to them. Also, riders who are not particularly fit or strong, who have to ride such a horse or one known to run on, can sensibly use the gag to help them stay in the saddle and to enable them to ride altogether better, instead of having to concentrate the whole time on keeping the horse to a sensible speed.

Ideally of course, as with any 'non-ordinary' bit, gags should not be needed, and would not be if all horses were correctly and expertly schooled, and riders too; but flesh and blood being what it is, perfection rarely exists – and if a horse is confirmed in his habits, the gag can make all the difference between him leading a useful life or ending up as pet food before his time.

Bitless bridles

A bitless (or 'nose') bridle is a very useful item of saddlery to have in a stable yard, and the fact that a horse wears one does not indicate that he is impossible to bit or that the rider is too incompetent to use a bridle with a bit. A bitless bridle can be the solution to various problems: it can be used on a youngster whose mouth is sore from teething; on a horse which has just had dental treatment or had his teeth rasped, as this can create a certain amount of soreness; on horses with any form of mouth injury or disease which makes having a bit in the mouth painful or uncomfortable; and certainly on those which are difficult to bit comfortably due to some unusual conformation, or even deformity, of the mouth, jaws or head. Many endurance riders like bitless bridles as they feel (not unreasonably) that it must be more comfortable and pleasant for the horse not to have a bit in his mouth during many hours of riding; furthermore these horses are encouraged to drink en route, and some riders allow the horse to graze or have a small feed at halts, which must be more pleasant and easier without a bit. Many endurance bridles can be made to convert quickly into headcollars, without having to fiddle about with a bit.

From the rider's point of view, not having a bit certainly need not mean less control, though this does depend on the horse and the bridle used. It does mean, however, that a horse can still be used when, for one of the above reasons, he otherwise perhaps could not be; and in the case of a mouth injury which is going to take some time to heal, a bitless bridle means that the horse's work and fitness régime can be continued uninterrupted.

Riders who are rather 'bit-orientated', as many seem to be these days, are often surprised at how little difference not having a bit makes to the horse's performance, and their own. Even so, they would do well to concentrate more on seat, weight, leg and voice aids, and perhaps teach the horse to neck-rein, something which was commonly taught in the past and regarded as a basic skill for a schooled horse, but which receives little attention these days except in Western riding and polo.

The Scawbrig

Probably the simplest and mildest bitless bridle is the Scawbrig: it consists of a headpiece with throatlatch and cheekpieces, as a conventional bridle, but these support a padded noseband (usually of chamois leather, sometimes sheepskin-lined leather) with a strong ring at each side. Another wide padded section rests in the chin groove, its ends tapering into reins which pass through the side rings to the rider's hands. There may also be a strap passing under the jawbones (not intended to be tight, but snug) which passes through a loop on the top of the chin-groove piece; this is simply to stabilise this piece and also to stop the nosepiece sliding around.

The nosepiece is fitted three or four fingers' width above the nostrils (it must not hamper breathing), and control is obtained by a tightening pressure round the nose and lower jaw when the reins are used. I should imagine it would take real brute force actually to hurt a horse with this bridle, and a lot of pressure is not needed. Horses respond very well and easily to it, and if they have been having mouth or bit problems, seem to acquire a new zest and enthusiasm for their work once they realise that guidance from the rider's hand will be without pain.

A **Scawbrig bitless bridle**: three different phases.
Left: The basic bridle. This example has a jowl strap fitted for extra stability
Middle: Here a sliphead has also been fitted to take a bit, but no reins
Right: In the final phase, reins have been attached to the bit so that the rider can gradually get the horse used to going from the bit instead of the nosepiece and chin-groove pad

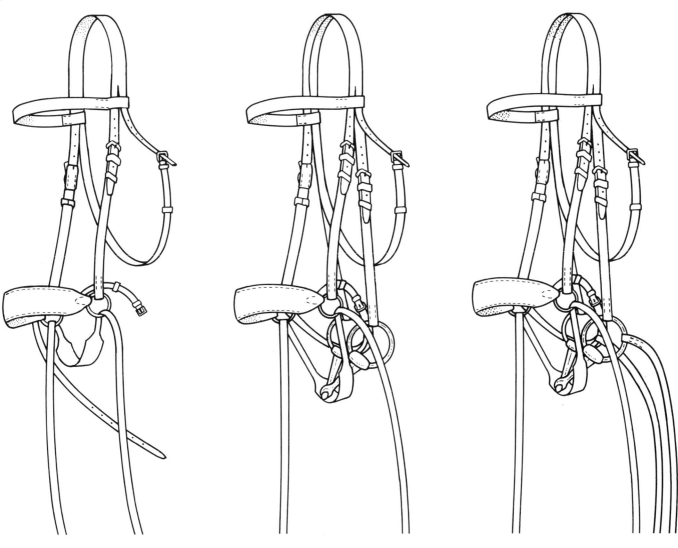

The basic Scawbrig bitless bridle

(continued from p 74)

In a simple Scawbrig you would take the same contact as with a snaffle operating on a leverage system you treat them more like a curb bit.

You may prefer to start off in an enclosed school of some kind if you are uncertain of your horse's response to having no bit, but few react adversely and many go better and more kindly depending on the kind of contact they have been used to via the reins.

Start off by just walking circles and figures of eight, plus other simple school figures such as serpentines, keeping a light contact on the reins and trying to guide the horse with your seat, and using it to feel where his feet are.

Use half halts to practise slowing down and changing gait, and also try lengthening the stride. Particularly when slowing down, don't hesitate to use the command 'whoa'. The horse should be familiar with this instruction so that he learns that he is getting tension on his nose to stop, rather than tension or slight resistance on the bit.

Increase speed and progress from gait to gait and keep the horse alert and listening to you, and keep using your weight and body position.

By the time you progress to canter the horse will be quite used to this new technique and you will feel sufficiently confident to jump from trot and canter, and hack out.

To summarise, it is mainly a case of riding more with seat and legs (if you have not been very used to this) and thinking less in terms of bit contact and more in terms of total contact, and mental communication, with the horse. This really works!

An additional sliphead is also available: this is a head-strap and cheekpiece/s which fits under the headpiece of the bridle proper and loops through the browband to keep it in place. A sliphead such as this is used to support the bridoon in a double bridle, and is an optional part of the Scawbrig; it is intended to support a bit in the horse's mouth during the mouthing process. Initially the bit just sits in the mouth to give the horse the feel of it, and the rider rides off the bitless rein. Later, reins are added to the bit-rings in the usual way, and, very gradually, the rider uses the bit more than the bitless reins until the Scawbrig can be dispensed with and the horse goes into a normal bridle.

The Scawbrig is also useful for novice riders not yet in control of their hands. It is quite acceptable, in fact, to use any snaffle mouthpiece or a Kimblewick with the Scawbrig, or even a curb without the bridoon for a horse which does not readily accept two bits in his mouth.

Blair's pattern

More familiarly, but incorrectly, called a hackamore, the Blair's pattern bitless bridle is quite different from the Scawbrig. It operates on a leverage system with cheeks of varying length, and can exert very strong pressure on the nose and jaw. These bridles need very sensitive, skilled handling from a rider of the standard required to use a double bridle properly.

There are a few types of Blair but they all work on the same principles: there is an ordinary headpiece with cheekpieces and throatlatch, and a normally padded nosepiece fitted to the lower halves of two cheekpieces, as a bit would be, with a backstrap or curbstrap and a fairly long metal cheek at each side up to about a foot or more in length (although many are shorter). The reins are fastened to the bottom of the cheeks, and when they are used a significant pressure is felt on the noseband, and also the curbstrap is drawn forward (like a curb chain on a double bridle) into the back of the jaw (higher than the chin groove). The same type of multiplying factor as described for the use of the curb bit comes into effect with the Blair, and it is easy to see that it would be quite possible to badly bruise the nose and jawbones (padding or no) or even injure the horse more seriously through excessive use of this bridle.

That said, it can also be appreciated that one sharp reminder to a recalcitrant horse from the reins would be enough to assure it that, despite the absence of a bit, the rider still expected to be obeyed. Obviously the Blair does have a stronger effect than the Scawbrig; and it seems to be preferred by show jumpers who can perform round twisting indoor tracks with no difficulty, using this bridle. Lack of control is not a problem!

Novice riders

I often feel that bitless bridles of the Scawbrig pattern could easily be used to great advantage in riding schools for novice riders, but I have never seen this done. They would save the horses and ponies many unintentional painful jabs in the mouth, until the riders learned better control of their hands.

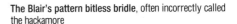

The Blair's pattern bitless bridle, often incorrectly called the hackamore

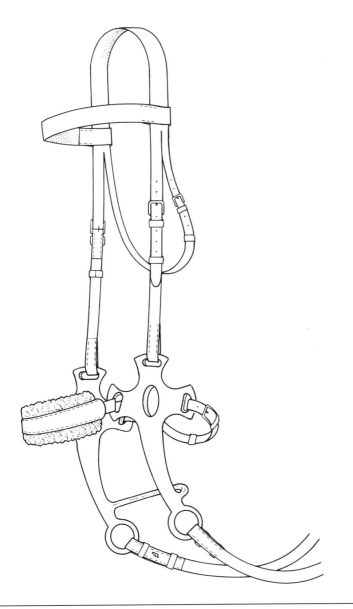

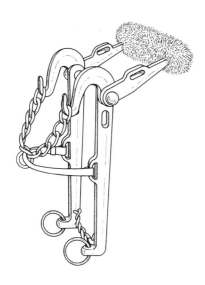

The WS bitless pelham or **Distas pelham**

The WS bitless pelham or Distas pelham

This bitless bridle has been known for generations, and may be described as kinder than the Blair as it is used with two pairs of reins: the 'snaffle' reins which exert a direct pressure on the nose, and the 'curb' reins which, in conjunction with a conventional curb chain, employ leverage on the chin groove and, again, the nose. The two reins can, of course, be used independently as with a double bridle. The nosepiece consists of a well padded bar or strap, and the metal cheeks are shorter than most Blair-pattern bitless bridles; moreover each cheek can move independently of its partner, so a fair amount of precision and individuality in use is possible. If you don't want to use a curb *chain*, a leather or elastic curb can, of course, be used instead.

This bridle is very versatile, and I should like to see it in wider use; in many instances it might well replace the Blair which I feel is often used rather as, in proportion, a sledgehammer might be used to bang in a drawing-pin.

The Jumping hackamore

The jumping hackamore is another mild type of bridle popular on the continent of Europe; it employs direct pressure on a slightly padded, rolled and stiffened noseband supported on cheekpieces forked at their ends. The two rear forks are linked under the lower jaw by a leather strap just above the chin groove,

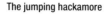

The jumping hackamore

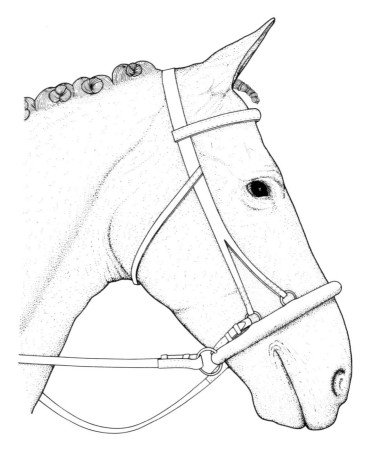

and the noseband itself is open under the jaw, each branch ending in a ring to which the reins fasten. Direct rein action produces pressure on the nose, while raising the hand tilts the noseband downwards a little and causes slight pressure under the lower jaw, resulting in the horse bringing his head up and in.

It is an effective, albeit quite mild bridle. The nosepiece should be fitted in the same position as for a Scawbrig.

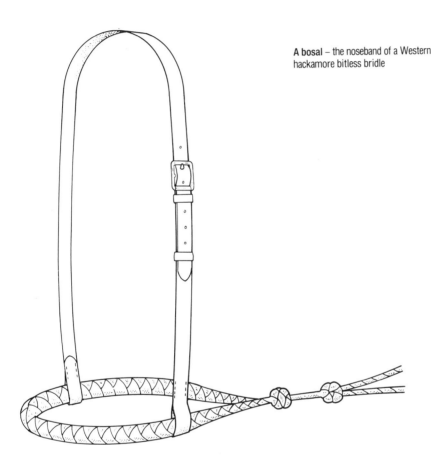

A bosal – the noseband of a Western hackamore bitless bridle

Nosebands

In many forms of equitation horses do not wear nosebands, the most well known probably being Western. Those following English-style riding, however, normally feel that a horse looks 'undressed' without a noseband, even if he only wears a simple *cavesson noseband* consisting of a sliphead and a horizontal band of leather round the nose and lower jaw, which buckles behind and on the nearside of the jaw. The cavesson is fitted quite loosely, so you can get two fingers' width between the band and the face, and it should lie about midway between the corners of the horse's lips and his sharp facial bones. This noseband has no physical effect whatsoever, but simply provides an attachment point for a standing martingale when necessary. It can be made decorative by being padded, rolled or having stitched designs or coloured borders on it (normally white) and it does 'set off' a head most effectively. You

The bosal

The bosal, or true hackamore, is an essential part of Western riding and training. It is normally made of plaited rawhide and is carefully balanced on the horse's head and fitted so as to prevent it rubbing the jaw raw.

It is kept up by means of a head-stall, and sometimes a browband is added. The headstall is often split to fit over one ear, a common arrangement in Western bridles.

A throatlatch is also usually used, consisting of a light cotton or horse-hair rope knotted under the throat and attached to a heavy knot — the heel knot — fastened round the back 'knob' of the bosal.

Horsehair, wool or cotton reins attach to the knot and the tilt of the bosal on the head can thus be controlled and finely balanced. The bosal should be so well balanced that when the rider's hand is not in use the bosal almost 'floats' around the head virtually without touching it. The front part of the bosal rests a good 4in above the nostrils and the rear arms do not touch the lower jaw (or should not). By this means, the bosal is a true nose-bridle.

There is a more closely fitted bosal which does actually work on the jaw resulting in a high-headed, flexed way of going, with the horse balanced on his hocks and really going from the back end, necessitating a sensitive and expert rider.

As well trained hackamore horses can perform the most intricate movements at high speed truly on the weight of the rein, this form of equitation, and the skill needed to use a bosal properly, have a respected place in the world of equestrianism.

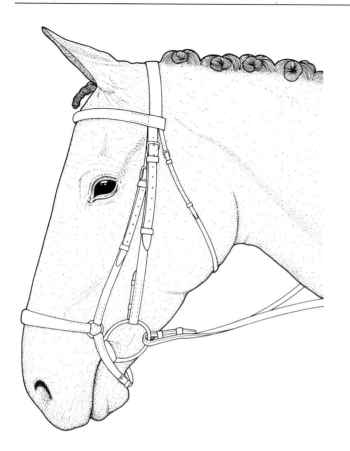

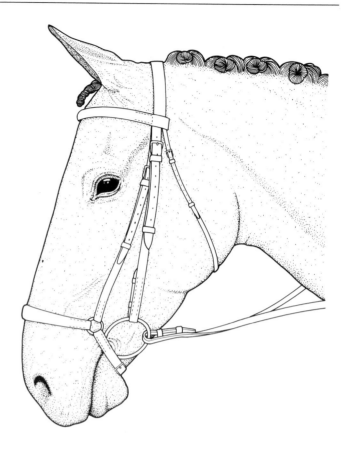

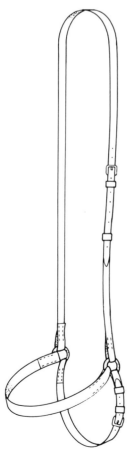

can adjust its height a little, up or down, to emphasise or flatter a head: for instance, a large head can be made to appear shorter by setting the noseband a hole or two lower than recommended; by using fairly broad leather, the head can be made to seem smaller; whereas finer, even rolled leather – as on Arab in-hand show bridles and headcollars – will flatter a small, elegant head but would look ridiculous on a heavyweight hunter.

If fitted fairly low and fastened tighter (enough to fit one finger between it and the front of the face), the cavesson may encourage the horse not to open his mouth to evade the bit. However, it should not, under any circumstances, be fastened any tighter.

Nosebands of all types always go under the bridle's headpiece, slotting through the end loops of the browband to keep them in place.

The Drop or dropped noseband

Despite everything that has been written about the correct fitting of this noseband over the few decades since it first became popular, it is still commonly seen fitted too low – too near the horse's nostrils – and too tight, restricting the breathing. The horse is an obligate nasal breather, in other words he must breathe through his nose, and cannot breathe through his mouth unless something is wrong with him. Therefore any noseband which restricts the airflow through the nostrils will at least partially suffocate him. Not only can this interfere with his oxygen supply and, therefore, his physical performance, it can cause great panic and correspondingly 'difficult' behaviour in the horse. It is not good horsemanship to try to dominate a horse by this means: it is counterproductive and can actually be classed as cruel.

The front strap of the drop noseband should be fitted only slightly lower than the cavesson, so that the bottom edge of the band is three fingers' width above the nostrils, on the end of the nasal bone. The back strap – which is often much too short even today – is fitted round the outside and below the bit, resting in the chin groove and buckling on the nearside just below the bit. If you buy a drop noseband and the backstrap does not allow the correct fitting of the front strap, get the saddler to alter it and explain why this is necessary, as some still do not seem to understand that it is the backstrap, not the front band, which is the 'dropped' part of the item, and this backstrap must be long enough to allow the front piece to lie where it belongs, out of harm's way.

The purpose of the drop noseband is to prevent the horse opening his mouth so wide that he evades the action of the bit. You should still be able to slide a finger all round the straps between the leather and the horse's head – like this it is effective whilst still being comfortable and *not* interfering with the breathing. Any other fitting is unacceptable.

Left: **A snaffle bridle with a drop noseband.** The front part of the noseband is correctly fitted – a little lower than a cavesson, but not so low as to interfere with the horse's breathing. However, this noseband is fastened too loosely for it to be effective. Too-tight drop nosebands are commonly seen. You should be able to slide a finger fairly easily all round under the noseband

The second part of the illustration shows the noseband correctly fitted

The Flash noseband

This has superseded the drop noseband in popularity, and must be slightly more comfortable for the horse to wear. It is simply a cavesson noseband (which is fitted normally or just slightly lower than an ordinary cavesson) with a second strap (or two, depending on the exact make) either joined to the cavesson at the front or run through a small loop sewn to its lower edge at the front; this strap then passes down below the bit, lying in the chin groove and buckling on the nearside just below the bit.

The flash discourages any opening of the mouth, and the cavesson part also provides an attachment for a standing martingale, which should never be fitted to a drop noseband.

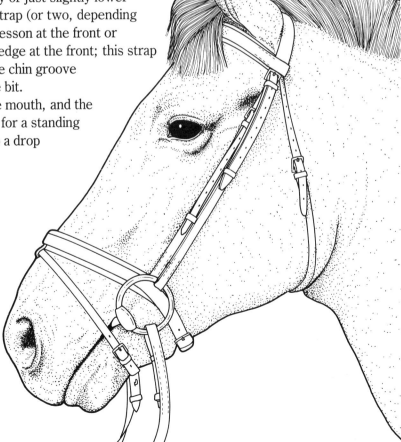

A flash noseband on an eggbutt snaffle bridle, correctly fitted

The Grakle noseband

This is also called the 'figure eight' and 'crossover' noseband. It consists of two diagonally-crossing straps with their crossover point – usually over a little pad of sheepskin or felt – on the front of the horse's nose. The top section of each strap passes under its relevant bridle cheekpiece, and they meet and fasten near the jaw; the lower sections pass under the bit on each side, resting in the chin groove again, and fasten on the nearside just below the bit (some people fasten them so the buckle lies between the bit and the crossover point).

The object of the Grakle is to prevent or at least discourage the horse from crossing his jaw and opening his mouth to evade the action of the bit. As with any noseband which passes along the chin groove, should the horse attempt to open his mouth, not only will he feel pressure in the chin groove but on the bridge of the nose, too, which has the subsidiary effect of bringing the nose in and maybe down. The Grakle and the flash are unlikely to interfere with breathing. They must be fitted snugly but comfortably, again allowing you to slide a finger under the straps all round – though if they are too loose, they will obviously be completely ineffective.

There should be a short vertical strap under the jaw linking the upper and lower halves of the Grakle; this keeps them in position and therefore more effective, and stops the top part from sliding up or twisting round.

Left: **A correctly fitted Grakle noseband**, but minus the desirable little circle of padding or fleece underneath the crossover point to prevent chafing

Right: **The commonly seen incorrect fitting** with the top strap too high and rubbing the face under the sharp facial bones. However, the padding is present

The Kineton

These are the four most common and useful nosebands in general use, but mention should be made of the Kineton which has a fairly irrefutable stopping effect on a strong horse. It consists of a sliphead and cheekpieces, with an adjustable strap over the nose fitted about level with the bit and the corners of the mouth, these two being joined by metal loops which fit next to the face (between it and the bit-rings) and under the bit. In this way, when the reins are used and pressure is put on the bit, it is transferred via the loops to the noseband and so you have both bit pressure and more or less strong nose pressure, too. It has no mouth-closing effect, of course, but it certainly stops a horse setting his head horizontally and so avoiding bar pressure from the bit. It is often maligned as being too strong, but in itself it is unlikely actually to hurt a horse and, like the gag snaffle, it does have a place in the humane control of horses with train-like tendencies.

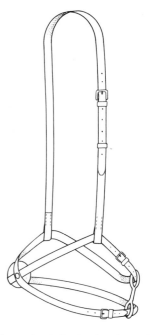

A **Grakle noseband** showing the often omitted short connecting strap between the two pieces of the noseband at the back, which lies behind the horse's jaw

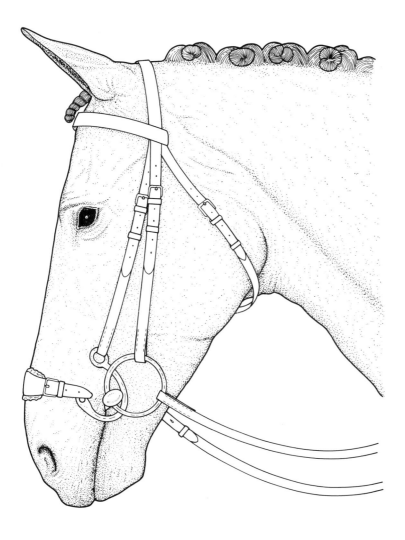

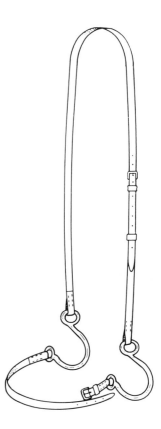

Left and above: **The Kineton noseband's** metal pieces fit underneath the bit-rings so that when rein pressure is used the bit itself pulls back the noseband, helping to bring the nose in and down, which discourages pulling

Bridles and Bits

Clockwise from top:
Rockwell bridle, a variation of the Norton but milder. The nosepiece, usually elasticated, is attached to the mouthpiece by special links and there are, again, central straps running from the nosepiece up the face so there is a combination of bit pressure, nose pressure and psychological persuasion to bring pullers to hand

Newmarket bridle, useful for young horses. It works in a similar way to the Kineton in that it places pressure on the nose via the rings on the ends of the noseband. Also, by fitting the reins to the noseband rings instead of the bit-rings, use of the bit itself can be avoided altogether. When reins are attached to both sets of rings the trainer can decide whether to use nose pressure, bit pressure or both

Norton bridle, used for a hard puller. The two thin mouthpieces bring pressure to bear on the poll (via the cheekpieces) and the nose (via the ends of the noseband) because of the positioning of the bits. In addition, the central facial straps have a psychological influence on a puller, and this combination of the physical and the mental is most effective in bringing one under control. A severe remedy

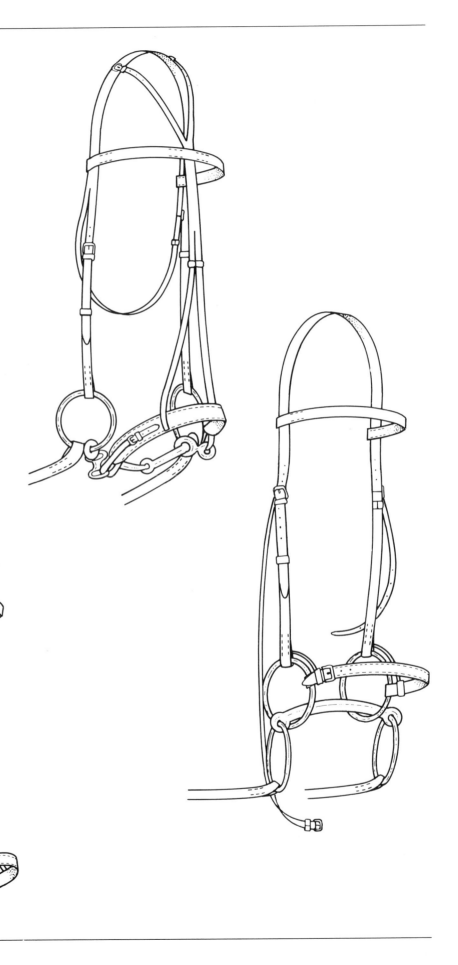

Bridle accessories

In cases where it is feared a bit might pinch the cheeks or lips, a temporary measure to prevent this is to fit **bit guards**, flat rubber circles with holes in the middle which fit round the mouthpiece (there is a slit to the centre so you can get them on) between the horse's face and the bit-cheek or ring.

Looking like an extension of the bit guard but not meant for the same thing is the **Australian noseband or cheeker**. This consists of rubber circles which fit round the bit in the same way as bit guards, but the circles have strap extensions which pass diagonally up the horse's face and meet on the bridge of the nose, continuing in a single strip of rubber which passes under the browband between the ears to the poll, where it fastens to the headpiece of the

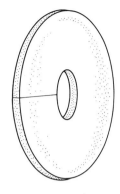

A bit-guard

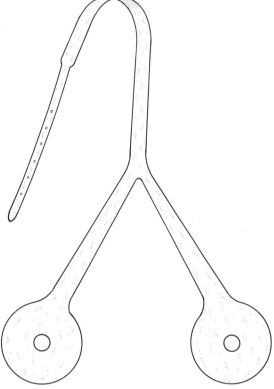

An Australian cheeker

bridle. Surprisingly this device really does help steady a hard-pulling horse; its effect seeming to be largely psychological. It also keeps the bit up in the mouth and is useful for horses in the habit of putting their tongue over the bit, thus evading control and creating injury to the tissues under the tongue. This device is used mainly in racing, but there is no reason why it could not be used in any circumstance where a hard-pulling horse needs to be restrained, out hunting or in eventing or hunter trials.

Tongue ports or grids are also used to stop a horse getting his tongue over the bit. A rubber port is used on a mullen mouthpiece and is illustrated. The tongue-shaped piece of rubber is passed round the mouthpiece and through the

Nose nets

The **nose net** is a useful small item of equipment which fastens around the muzzle to a cavesson noseband by means of loops. It is made of netting so does not in any way affect the horse's breathing, and as the loops which fasten it on are fitted at intervals round the the open top of the net, it can pass underneath the bit without interfering with it at all.

It works purely psychologically by resting lightly on the horse's muzzle, nostrils and feeler whiskers. This seems to inhibit his desire to pull and run on and has gently controlled many a hard-to-hold or excitable horse.

Left: **A rubber tongue port** to wrap round the bit mouthpiece

Right: **A tongue grid** which attaches to a separate headstall fitted into the bridle

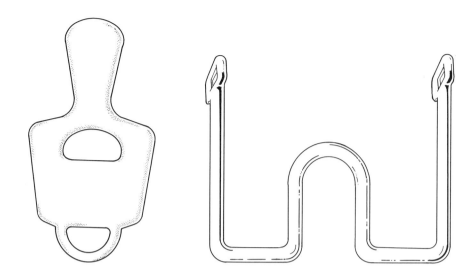

rubber loop at its other end, and then all is pulled tight and straightened out so that the tongue-shaped piece lies flat on the tongue pointing towards the throat. It cannot feel very pleasant but it certainly does its job.

A metal tongue grid (also illustrated) is suspended by a separate sliphead above the bit, well into the corners of the mouth but not pulling on them uncomfortably; it is also very effective.

Reins

People have many different preferences when it comes to reins, but the truth of the matter is that an unsuitable choice can noticeably affect the way a rider handles them and, therefore, the use and feel of the bit.

Reins are sold in pairs, joined at the rider's end with a buckle, and fastened to the bit at the other, normally with hook stud fastenings these days, although buckles and simple loop fastenings can be used. Hook studs are metal hooks set into the rein a little way down from the end: the end of each rein is passed

Rein fastenings
From left: hook stud (the most popular fastening currently in use), stitched fastening (not very practical as it makes cleaning less efficient and changing the bit a major job), loop fastening (quite good but less secure than hook studs) and buckle fastening (generally regarded as rather ugly but widely used on police and military bridles and also on driving bridles)

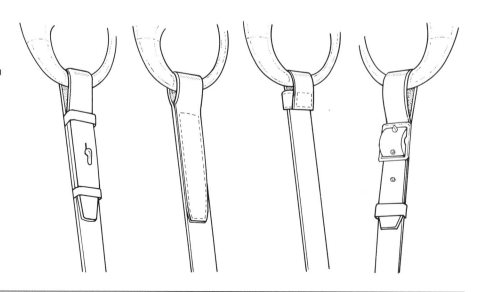

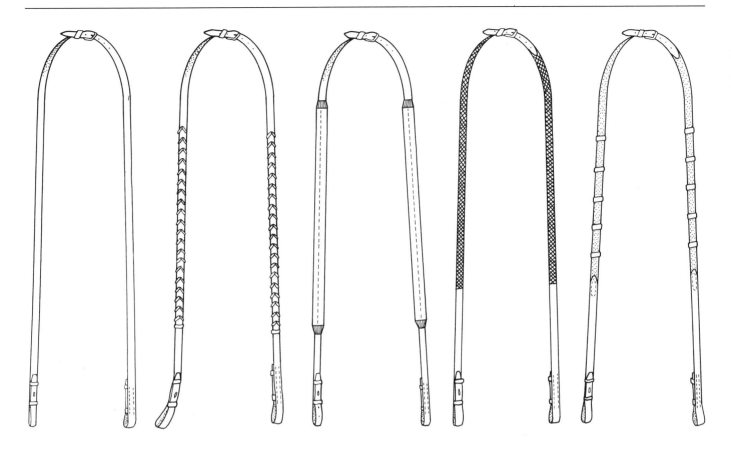

through the bit-rings and back through a small loop or 'keeper', pressed down on to the hook and pulled tight, then the very end is passed through another keeper for security and neatness. The hook fastenings are placed on the inside (the horse's side) so that the view from the outside, as it were, is of plain leather. Buckles are regarded as rather infra dig, although they are used almost exclusively on police and military bridles, and loop fastenings, where the reins simply slot through loops and go round the bit-rings, are not terribly secure. The buckle at the rider's end does no more than keep things together and help prevent a rein trailing should you let them slip or drop; it is hardly ever undone except when cleaning.

The width of the reins is as important as their texture. Curb reins and children's show pony bridle reins can be as narrow as ½in, otherwise reins can be as wide as 1in. Probably the most common widths are ⅝in and ¾in, but to be comfortable, the smaller your hands the narrower your reins will need to be, and vice versa. If the reins are too narrow for your hand size, it can lead to you clenching your fist in an effort to hold them, which makes for clumsy handling, in the same way as reins which are uncomfortably wide for your hands.

Reins can be plain leather (these are usual for showing, at least); laced leather, where separate leather strips are laced in a herringbone pattern down plain leather reins, usually only over the section of rein which is held; plaited leather, normally of five or seven strands; web with horizontal loops of leather at intervals down the 'hand' part; or rubber covered.

Plain leather reins very quickly become slippery when wet from sweat or rain, whereas all the other designs are aimed at preventing this. Laced reins

Various reins: (left to right) plain leather reins, laced leather reins, rubber-covered reins, plaited reins, webbing reins with handgrips

Decorated tack

Early civilisations used natural materials to make bridles and headstalls of various sorts, often with considerable ingenuity and trouble as they were not only well made but also decorative.

Initially, rawhide was used and also braided horsehair, wool and grasses and plaited straw, jute and flax. It all depended on what was easily available within the locality.

Decorations involved fancy plaiting and stitching and working strands around bone and horn where some rigidity was needed. As metals were discovered and their handling perfected, inset pieces of copper, bronze, brass, silver and even gold were also used.

It is still the habit to often decorate bridles. In Britain and other European countries coloured browbands of plastic or velvet are common, and fancy stitched brow and nosebands and browbands of brass or those of other metals are all familiar.

Perhaps today the 'top of the tree' as far as decoration goes is the heavily decorated, ornate Western saddle with its tooled leather work and silver insets and tassels, often with bridle to match.

can be good, as can the web and leather ones; plaited reins are fine when new but stretch in use, particularly if you or the horse habitually takes a firm contact. Many people like the rubber-covered ones, where pimple-rubber is sewn down the middle section of each rein (though some riders do find this design too thick and cumbersome). Any stitching weakens leather, however, so if you do choose rubber-covered reins, make sure they have just one line of not-too-fine stitching down the middle of the rein, rather than two lines down the sides. The parts near the bit and buckle ends are left plain because there is no need for rubber near the bit, and at the buckle end so the reins are more easily knotted; this is particularly helpful when riding across country when it may be necessary to slip the reins to the buckle end (which may not be able to take too much strain so the knot takes it instead), or to form a bridge over the lower neck if you fear you may be catapulted over the horse's head.

Non-leather reins include plaited cotton, which are very hard to get but can be made to order; plaited nylon (more or less out of fashion and harsh on the hands and the horse's neck); various acrylics and polyesters; and – awful in my experience! – plastic reins which crack and slip but still seem to sell!

At the present time, cotton or leather still seem to be the best.

Bridle materials

Most saddlers take a real pride in fine bridlework, and without doubt there is nothing so smart and attractive as a top-quality leather bridle, whether for showing or everyday use. Decorative stitching can be used on nosebands and browbands, and browbands can also be made up in colours, and patterns, often to your own choice; some people use their national, stable or team colours, or go for colours to complement their horse. Metal and alloy-covered browbands (such as the 'gold' continental ones) are fashionable in the show-jumping arena, and brass browbands have traditionally been used for generations on stallion and driving bridles, having little brass insets on leather.

Although synthetic saddles have taken hold in the market now, the same cannot yet be said for synthetic bridles. Nylon is usually too harsh, and other synthetics, apart from plastic, are quite rare. Plastic bridles do have their enthusiasts, but generally they are not particularly strong, the buckles are often of very poor quality and rust easily, and plastic is, of course, completely non-absorbent. In my opinion there is definitely a market for a strong, soft cotton web bridle with stainless steel buckles. This would be easily cleaned (warm, soapy water and a good rinse) with no danger of the buckles either breaking or rusting. As plaited cotton reins can be made to order by a good saddler, it should not be impossible for some enterprising firm to make a suitable range of cotton webbing bridlewear.

Whatever new synthetic materials come on to the market in future, the basic criteria should be that they are strong, either absorbent or permeable (and there are plenty of permeable textiles available now) and not harsh to the horse's skin. As the advantages of synthetics usually include ease of care and maintenance, these, too, are importants points.

You should be able to slide a finger easily all round a bridle under all the straps. The noseband here is too high and will rub the facial bones. The browband is a good length: it does not pull the headpiece into the base of the ears, causing discomfort and is itself fitted low enough to avoid rubbing the ears

You should be able to pull the noseband slightly away from the nose, like this – about two fingers' width is a good guide – otherwise it could chafe the jawbones at the back. However, if the cavesson is fitted a little lower and tighter than shown it does have the effect of slightly discouraging the horse from opening his mouth and evading the bit

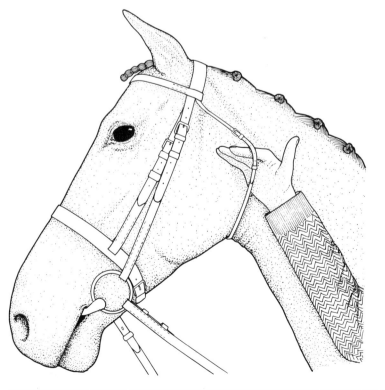

You must be able to fit the width of your fingers between the throat and the throatlatch so as not to cause pressure on the windpipe when the horse flexes to the bit

Putting on a Bridle

This sequence shows how to put on a bridle in the normal way. Some horses and ponies can be quite difficult over this essential operation.

Another method is to pass your right hand under the horse's head and hold the two cheekpieces together in it on the front of the horse's face. You then have control of his head as well as holding the bridle. Then just slip in the bit as usual.

When you cannot even get the reins over the head of the horse, simply unbuckle the reins at the hand end and pass one up each shoulder, buckling them again over the withers. Now bring the buckle up to the poll and you have effectively put the reins over the horse's head; by catching them together quickly under his throat should he move away, you have control of his head. If you pass the reins back to the withers (as is often taught when bridling) you do not have this essential control, which is needed with even the quietest horse.

You can also use the headpiece of the bridle to 'hook' down the head of a difficult horse. If he is standing with his nose well up on the air, just hold the bridle by the cheekpieces and hook the headpieces up over his nose, bringing it down within control.

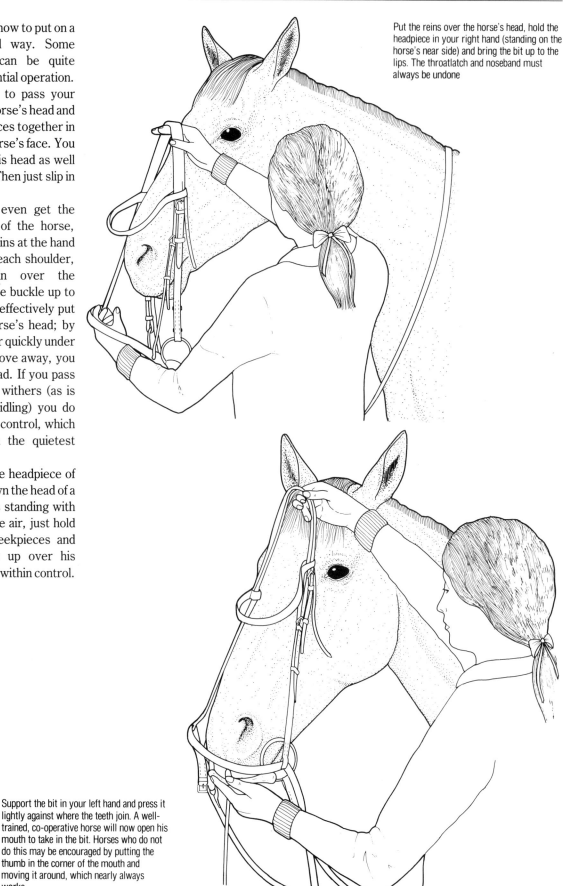

Put the reins over the horse's head, hold the headpiece in your right hand (standing on the horse's near side) and bring the bit up to the lips. The throatlatch and noseband must always be undone

Support the bit in your left hand and press it lightly against where the teeth join. A well-trained, co-operative horse will now open his mouth to take in the bit. Horses who do not do this may be encouraged by putting the thumb in the corner of the mouth and moving it around, which nearly always works

Ease the bit gently into the mouth and carefully put the headpiece over first one ear, then the other. Make the mane comfortably flat under it and pull out the forelock over the browband

Fasten the throatlatch first for security

Finally fasten the noseband. Make sure the browband is level and not rubbing the bottom of the ears, that all straps are in their keepers (the fixed loops immediately under the buckle) and runners (the loose ones which 'run' up and down the straps), and check that the noseband is also level, adjusting it from the poll underneath the headpiece if necessary

3
TRAINING EQUIPMENT

Lungeing and long-reining

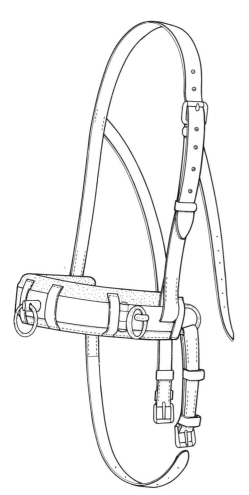

A well-made, useful lungeing cavesson with the necessary reinforced noseband, rings for the lunge- or long-reins, a sturdy throatlatch and also a jowl strap to help keep the cavesson in position

The horse's first experience of tack might well be a foal slip, fitted when he is one or two days old, depending on his owner's beliefs; otherwise the first significant item of training equipment used on him will probably be the lungeing cavesson. Lungeing and/or long-reining constitute the major part of any youngster's initial education, and the cavesson is crucial to their success. A well made, sturdy, well padded cavesson is a major asset to early training: one which is steady on the head, and which does not pull round under the weight of the lungeing rein or when force is brought to bear on it; which does not rub the horse's eye or face-bones, and which provides strong ring attachments on the front and sides of the padded nosepiece, and maybe on the back depending on the make.

Cavessons which have none of these good points can nullify all the trainer's efforts by irritating the horse or even hurting him; and if they do not enable sufficient control they risk interfering with the psychological as well as the physical effect the trainer is seeking.

There are various cavessons, but probably the best are the lightweight Wels type and suchlike patterns: these consist simply of a padded leather nosepiece with a metal band inside, and metal rings or dees (depending on the pattern) which are fixed to the band and protrude through the leather; the lunge rein or long-reins can be attached to these. It is supported by a simple strap which passes over the poll and buckles to its shorter partner on the near side (this allows for fit adjustment), with a throatlatch to help keep it steady and in place; the latter should be adjusted so it is snug but not so tight as to chafe the jawbones and hurt the horse. The nosepiece also has a buckle adjustment.

Some cavessons have a leather or metal band passing from the nosepiece to a browband or to the headpiece, and this does make for extra stability even if it means extra weight – the whole item is made of stouter leather than a bridle. A browband is a good idea anyway, as it helps stop the headpiece sliding down the neck; but it should be of the type used on police or military bridles, with a slit at one or both ends so that it can be positioned across the forehead and fastened into place by means of a stud or a slit over a metal fitting – thus you do not have to put it over the young horse's ears, and avoid the risk of frightening or irritating him.

Normally the lunge rein is attached to the ring on the front of the nosepiece by means of a buckle on a swivel which fits on the end of the rein. A nosepiece fitted just three or four inches above the nostrils, of the firm but comfortably padded sort, gives the trainer quite good control through pressure, when needed, on the nose from the rein. A few experts fasten the rein to the back of the nosepiece, as recommended by the late Henry Wynmalen, being of the opinion that the little jabs which may occur on the nose will inhibit the free, forward movement they are trying to encourage in the horse. However, this does not give anything like the control offered by the front ring position, which is the one nearly always used by most other trainers, amateurs and experts alike.

It is no use at all trying to lunge a horse effectively using the rear or side dees of an ordinary headcollar, as nothing like enough security or control can be obtained. It could even be described as 'a dangerous practice'.

The object of lungeing is to accustom the horse to working obediently – and preferably willingly – on command; to teach him the vocal aids as given by the trainer; and to develop his paces, encouraging him to go in a relaxed way with his head and neck more or less down (depending on your school of thought) – this will help 'stretch' his muscles and other tissues, relax and raise his back, and thus enable him to bring his hindlegs forward and under him, developing power and thrust from the hindquarters. Ideally he should swing along, particularly once he has progressed in his training and muscular development; his tail is a good indicator as to whether or not he is relaxed in his work – if he is, it will swing from side to side as he trots. Some trainers, I feel, go rather over the top when asking for the conventional 'long, low outline', insisting that the head is carried in almost the 'grazing position' (as described by one competitive dressage trainer). If the young horse continues in this position once he is working under saddle it can be most disconcerting for the rider, and is certainly taking things to unnecessary, even counter-productive extremes.

Once the horse understands the basic vocal aids, a suitably expert trainer might lunge him from a bit; either this is suspended by little attachments from

The use of side-reins in lungeing

If lungeing a horse in side-reins (discussed later) it is usual to fasten the right rein to the right side of the lungeing roller, and vice-versa.

However, there is another less widely used method which can be quite useful with difficult horses who develop a 'rubber neck' as an evasion, or whose headcarriage is not becoming steady as training progresses — although, as ever, expert opinions vary on the method's acceptability.

In this system, the left side-rein is fastened to the top right of the roller and vice versa, so that the reins cross over the withers.

Many trainers dislike this practice as it certainly does restrict the head-carriage and, being regarded as an 'old-fashioned' method, does not permit the horse to go 'long and low' as is the current practice.

However, I have seen it used in displays on highly schooled horses whose headcarriges are established and steady, and it is certainly effective at stilling the over-enthusiastic head movements of some other horses.

A lungeing cavesson showing the lunge-rein fastened to the front ring, which gives good control. This cavesson has a browband which is an advantage

the cavesson cheekpieces, or it is worn on a bridle which is fitted under the cavesson but with the bridle cheekpieces coming outside and over the cavesson nosepiece so that the latter will not interfere with the action and feel of the bit. This arrangement allows for the bit to be simply put in place so as to give the horse the feel of it (as it should be at first) and is *not* used to lunge from. Opinions vary on this point; some people never actually lunge their youngsters from the bit at all – the rider is put on board and gradually takes up the reins while the horse is still lunged on the cavesson, until eventually he takes over from the trainer.

Long-reining used to be a set part of every youngster's education at one time, and there are various methods usually designated by their country of origin. However, it is a technique used less often now. The side-rings of the cavesson are better fitted behind the cheekpieces for long-reining as this gives a more direct feel to the trainer's hands.

If lungeing has a disadvantage it is that the horse must go more or less constantly on a circle (up to about 35ft depending on the length of the lunge rein itself), and all work on circles is stressful. A 35ft circle equates to one of less than eleven metres which, under the weight of a rider, is quite a difficult size for a horse to accomplish. It is my contention that an unbacked youngster, still trying to co-ordinate his limbs and body to the physical constraints we impose

The Danish method of long-reining, preferred by Miss Sylvia Stanier, LVO. This illustration is taken from a photograph of her, and shows how the long-reins pass through terrets on a driving pad and then come direct to the trainer's hands, rather than the outside rein passing down the horse's far side and round the thighs to the hand, as in the traditional English method. Using this method, Miss Stanier has trained many horses to High School standard. Note the horse is wearing brushing boots as a precaution and is being worked directly from the bit, a practice which the expertise of his trainer permits

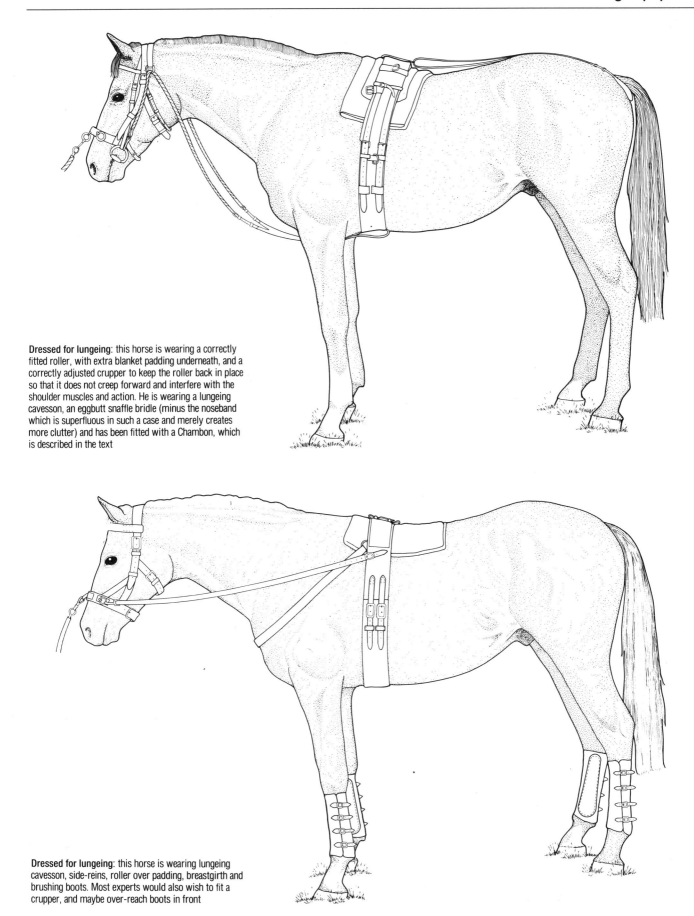

Dressed for lungeing: this horse is wearing a correctly fitted roller, with extra blanket padding underneath, and a correctly adjusted crupper to keep the roller back in place so that it does not creep forward and interfere with the shoulder muscles and action. He is wearing a lungeing cavesson, an eggbutt snaffle bridle (minus the noseband which is superfluous in such a case and merely creates more clutter) and has been fitted with a Chambon, which is described in the text

Dressed for lungeing: this horse is wearing lungeing cavesson, side-reins, roller over padding, breastgirth and brushing boots. Most experts would also wish to fit a crupper, and maybe over-reach boots in front

upon him when on the lunge, probably finds this size harder work than most of us realise.

The advantage of long-reining is that the trainer is not obliged to stand in the middle of a circle all the time, but can work the horse more on straight lines and from behind (depending on the type of long-reining used); this is harder work for the trainer but easier, physically, for the horse because of this. Changes of direction are more easily accomplished in long-reining, and when horses are long-reined from the bit, they can be taken right up to High School standard without ever having a rider on their backs, particularly when continental methods are followed. There are various continental forms of long-reining: the reins may pass through the rings or terrets on a special roller, across the horse's back to the trainer's hands, and the trainer will work the horse from the side or from behind; otherwise he may stay behind the horse, and sometimes very close behind as in the method used at the Spanish Riding School of Vienna, when the horse will be worked mainly from this position.

In the English method, a rein goes from the outside ring of the cavesson along the far side of the horse, round his thighs and to the trainer's hand; the other rein passes direct from the ring to the trainer's hand. This is said to give good control of the quarters (which it can, although some horses initially object to contact behind the thighs) which is impossible in lungeing.

The **lunge rein** itself is usually of rather heavy (in my opinion) tubular cotton webbing with a buckle on a swivel attachment on one end and a loop on the other, ostensibly for the trainer's hand; though horses are often lunged with the rein even shorter, its extra length held in loops in the hand. It is certainly dangerous actually to put your hand and wrist *through* the end loop, for fear of being pulled over and dragged by the horse.

The **roller** used for lungeing or long-reining is also designed for the fitting of side-reins, which should have a mainly psychological effect of control on the horse rather than a physical one of any significance; it is also to accustom the horse to the contact of equipment round his girth in readiness for being saddled and backed; though if he has been rugged up by means of the old-fashioned type of surcingle roller and rug he will be used to this anyway. The roller should be fitted snugly but not too tightly, sufficient to stay in place without causing discomfort.

Some of the rollers specially designed for lungeing and long-reining have rings fitted to the 'saddle' or padded part on the back of the horse; long-reins can then be passed through them or side-reins fitted to them. There are usually three sets of rings, or if a driving pad is used, 'terrets', which are rings on the end of short metal rods. The highest set is so the reins can be adjusted to approximately the level at which they would be held by a rider, and is for training at a fairly advanced level when the horse will have attained the higher head-carriage commensurate with better balance and steady self-carriage. The lower fittings are used for younger horses, for fitting the side-reins and to allow for the head carriage required by the trainer.

A ring may be fitted in the centre of the roller's back edge so that a crupper can be fitted. A crupper is a padded loop with adjustment buckles on both sides, with a strap to attach it to the back ring of the roller; its other common use is to attach to a pony saddle to stop it slipping forwards on a fat pony. If a roller is going to slip it will invariably do so forwards, unless the horse is in very poor

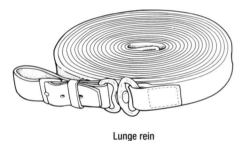

Lunge rein

13 At the top is an eggbutt snaffle, followed by a thick-mouthed German wire-ring snaffle and an ordinary wire-ring snaffle at the bottom, all jointed.

14 Left: D-ring snaffle with copper rollers. Middle: Vulcanite gag snaffle. Right: French snaffle.

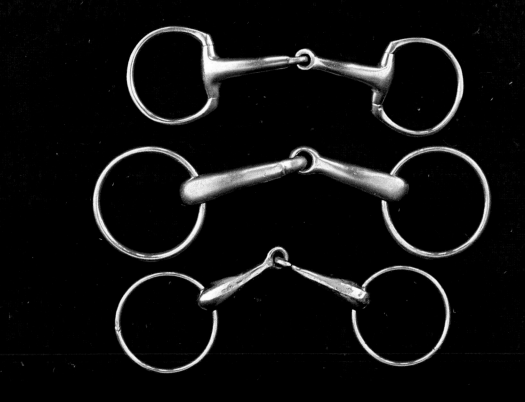

13

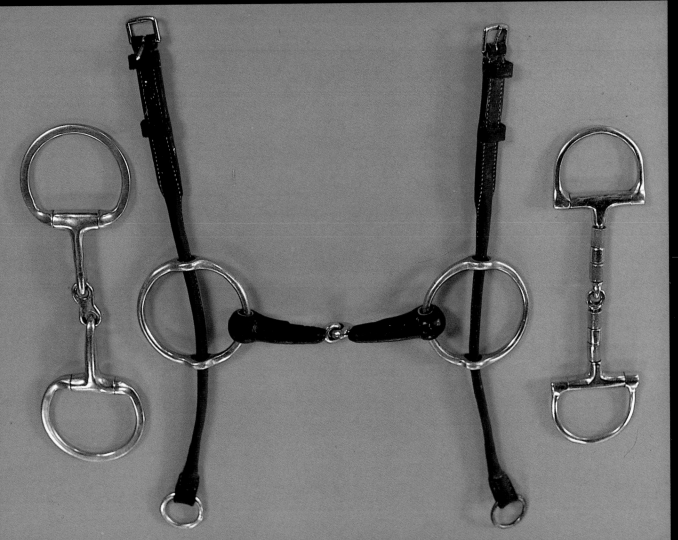

14

⑮ From top: jointed, vulcanite, wire-ring snaffle; wire-ring, tapered nylon snaffle; half-cheek vulcanite snaffle and a D-ring, rubber-covered jointed snaffle.

⑯ From top: Dressage bridoon; French loose-ring; French half-cheek and eggbutt snaffle.

⑰ From top: Dressage eggbutt bridoon; French loose-ring snaffle; French cheek snaffle and a Fulmer snaffle.

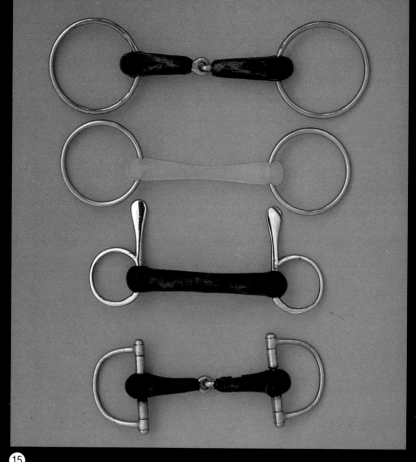

⑮

⑱ Right: Biothane bridlew is made from a tough nylon w bing coated with a thermopla polyurethane polymer which p duces a material claimed to many times stronger than leat The coating provides a tough and abrasion-resistant sur which is flexible in sub-z temperatures. It is rot and od proof and easily cleaned w water. There is a wide col range as well as the traditi leather look in black or bro The Combination Bridle quic transforms into a headcollar s ply by unclipping the reins fr the bit and attaching them to headcollar ring to act as a l rein. The bit can be quickly moved by unclipping it from headpiece. These two fact make the bridle popular in the durance world.

This endurance horse is we ing the popular combination b dle. He also wears both a coll type breastplate and a crupper help keep his saddle in place. saddle has a generous bear surface and is well padded extra comfort during long ho under saddle.

Biothane bridlewear can be tained through Yvonne Tys (address, p195).

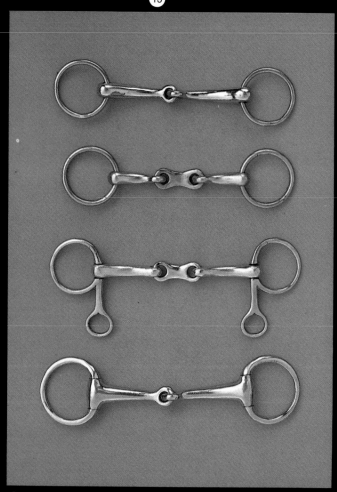

⑯

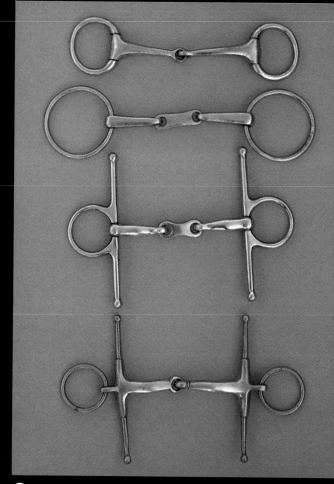

⑰

condition (in which case he should not be worked) or of bad conformation (so why train him anyway?). The crupper therefore keeps the roller back, and thus helps avoid the fairly common occurrence of the roller interfering with the horse's action because it digs into his flesh behind the shoulders. The shortened action and damaged mental attitude which can result from this can stay with the horse indefinitely, and a crupper is definitely a good idea. To put it on, put your hand and wrist through the loop, grasp the dock and bring it and the long tail hair up and out through the loop; this must be adjusted for fit so that it just touches the root of the tail snugly, and is neither tight nor loose. Some horses buck and kick at a crupper the first time it is used, but with tact and firmness they soon adapt to it.

The breast girth, which seems to be *de rigeur* these days when kitting a horse out for lungeing or long-reining, is less useful in my opinion. It is meant to keep the roller from slipping back, but as we have just discussed, this is far less likely to happen than it slipping forwards.

Side-reins are fitted from the bit-rings or the cavesson side-rings to the lower rings on the lungeing roller; they can also be fitted to the girth straps under the saddle flap. With a green horse they are fitted initially to the side-rings on the cavesson, although for the first few days of lungeing they are not usually used at all; they are then fitted to give the horse a preliminary suggestion of the contact he must come to expect from a rider's hand to his head. Side-reins are *not* meant to 'hold' the head in a certain position, although they do discourage a horse from throwing his head around – he soon learns that he can cause himself more (or less) discomfort should he position his head outside the area permitted by the side-reins.

(19) A well-cared-for double bridle with plain browband and noseband, a loose-ring bridoon and sliding-cheek Weymouth (curb) bit.

(20) Stephan van Ingelgem and Dante competing for Belgium at the Hermes International Dressage Festival at Goodwood in 1990. Dante is wearing a black double bridle, popular in dressage circles particularly on the continent of Europe, with an eggbutt bridoon and fixed-side curb bit. The lower parts of the reins are of rolled leather for elegance and to detract as little as possible from the horse's head and neck. He has a short belly girth on his dressage saddle with the buckles below the rider's knee. The saddle has the usual gusseted panel. The author would like to see the saddle cloth pulled well up into the pommel, the throatlatch a little looser and the noseband slightly lower so as not to touch the facial bones.

(21) A useful, everyday lungeing cavesson made of nylon webbing and manufactured by Cottage Craft. It is designed to come well away from the horse's eye: it is a common fault of lungeing cavessons to rub the eye.

(22) Rotherwood Sonata competing as a 3-year-old in riding pony youngstock classes, wearing an in-hand bridle with decorative velvet browband, brass fittings and being led from a leather leadrein attached to a coupling.

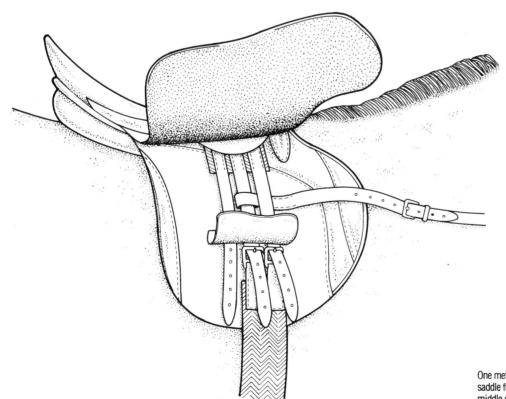

One method of attaching **side-reins** underneath the saddle flap. The side-rein loop has been slotted on to the middle girth and the first tab is holding it in place

Tight side-reins, like a harsh contact on the bit, have entirely the opposite effect to that which should be sought by the trainer, and actually create an aching neck, resistance and tenseness, and a horse which goes with a hollowed back, and stiff, shortened gaits. The ultimate aim, of course, is a horse willing to go calmly forward and straight, with a correctly achieved head carriage that comes from the horse working from back to front, using his back end to create impulsion and balance.

Side-reins are simply straps with buckle adjustments, with either loop, buckle or clip fittings for the bit- or cavesson rings; they can have elastic or rubber ring inserts or be of plain leather. Again, there are different schools of thought on this: for example elastic inserts are probably not helpful, because even when the horse does learn to 'give' and flex his jaw and poll in response to a contact, the elastic in fact keeps 'taking' and does not reward him with lessened contact. The same is true of rubber rings. Ordinary side-reins, carefully and expertly adjusted to create exactly the right amount of contact for a horse's stage of training, are probably the best.

Martingales

The Standing martingale

This martingale consists of a neckstrap which goes round the base of the neck, and another strap which goes through a slit in the neckstrap at the breast, buckling round the saddle girth at one end and to the back of a cavesson noseband at the other. It is much maligned these days, but has its uses with a horse confirmed in the habit of going with his head much too high, and which resists all the attempts of his connections to find out why. Some horses only occasionally put up their heads beyond the 'correct' height, but others may go like this permanently. Nowadays this martingale is seen more on the polo field than anywhere else.

A standing martingale is certainly a safety device to be recommended on a horse which, for whatever reason, has developed the habit of throwing his head up and back, maybe with a lift of the forehand, with the accompanying risk of hitting his rider in the face with his poll. Young horses, in particular, go through all sorts of phases even with highly expert trainers, and this trick is not uncommon, even when there is no apparent cause for such behaviour. A young horse of mine would swing his head up without warning even when just standing still, and if I had swallowed my pride and resorted to a standing martingale for the few months he enjoyed doing it, I should have saved myself a few black eyes and a bruised nose.

The correct fitting of a standing martingale allows you to fit almost the width of a hand between the throat and the strap passing to the noseband when this strap is pressed up the line of the gullet. If it is longer it will be useless; if shorter, the horse could learn to lean on it and possibly not only rely on it for balance, but also develop the wrong muscles in work. It could also dangerously restrict his action, particularly when jumping: a correctly fitted martingale

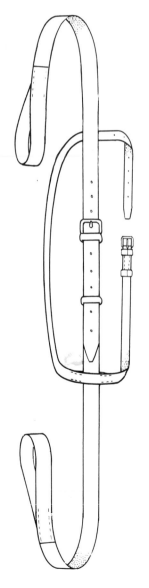

A standing martingale

A too-tight standing martingale. You should be able to press the strap which runs from the noseband down between the forelegs almost up into the horse's throat if the martingale is not to be too restrictive. This would be impossible with the martingale pictured

allows the horse complete freedom of head and neck when jumping.

The standing martingale must never be fitted to the backstrap of a drop noseband as it would be too severe, and would also hamper the action of the bit. Neither should leather or chain attachments be used to fit it to the bit-rings – an extremely severe and damaging way to use it. However, it can be made a little more effective, if thought desirable, by fitting the cavesson noseband a hole or two lower than normal.

The Running martingale

Running martingales are more common now than standing martingales, and operate rather differently. There is still a neckstrap and a strap passing to the girth, but a little way up from the breast it divides into two straps, each ending in a metal ring through which each rein is passed; the rings are thus free to 'run' along the rein to a certain extent when the horse is in action (hence the name). The object is to achieve a steadier feel on the bit in the horse's mouth: even if he raises or throws his head about, the rings keep the reins down and maintain the action of the bit on the bars of the mouth, preventing evasion. For green horses in particular which have still to progress to a steady head carriage, it produces a steadier feel on the bit in the mouth and helps prevent the reins being thrown around if the horse indulges in high jinks. The running martingale

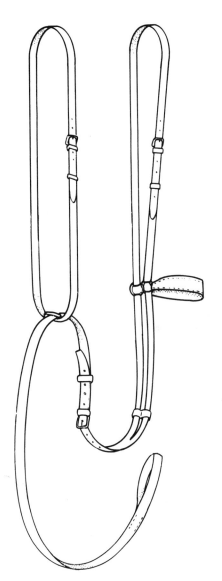

A **Grainger martingale** which, rather than being fitted directly to the back of a cavesson noseband, or sliding along the bridle reins, is attached to the ends of a noseband. As the latter is adjustable, it can be positioned like a cavesson, like a drop, or inbetween (although the difference should not be that great), the lower position giving more control but having the possibility of interfering with the horse's breathing if fitted *too* low. The breast buckle allows the two straps to be adjusted as desired, generally the same fitting as for a standing martingale, being both effective and safe

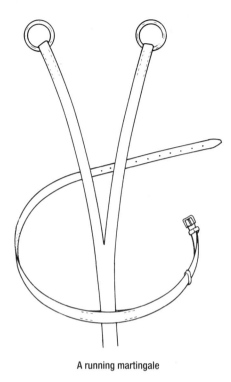

A running martingale

is also useful for novice riders who have not yet attained full control of their hand position, as the full result of their insecurity is not transmitted directly to the horse's mouth to the extent that it would be without the martingale.

This martingale should be fitted so that the straps, when not on the reins, can be passed up the shoulder more or less to the withers: when the reins are through the rings they should not come into play when the horse's head carriage is correct; however when the head is raised too high, the rings exert pressure on the reins. Again, if the straps are too long the martingale is useless; and if too short, so they exert constant pressure on the reins, they hamper communication between mouth and hand and are too restrictive. When correctly adjusted, the running martingale is quite safe to use when jumping.

It is important to use a 'stop' on each rein, a small piece of leather or rubber which slides onto each rein and is positioned between the bit end of the rein and the martingale rings; these prevent the rings running too far down the reins and getting caught on the rein fastenings, or even on the bit cheeks. On occasions when stops have not been used, horses with the habit of snatching at their reins have been known to get a strap or ring caught on a tooth, with very unpleasant consequences. This trick is less likely to happen if a **bib martingale** is used, where a bib of leather is fitted between the two running straps; this sort of martingale is quite common in racing circles.

A correctly adjusted running martingale, just coming into contact on the reins as the horse begins to lift his head too high. This picture does not show the little stops which should be fitted on the reins between the bit-rings and the martingale rings to prevent the latter becoming caught on the bit, or even on the horse's teeth, which can happen

The Pulley martingale

This is a variation of the running martingale, but instead of a simple divide of the strap at the breast there is a little pulley, and a cord with a ring at each end runs through it; the reins then pass through the rings in the normal way. It allows greater lateral movement of head and neck than a conventional running martingale and is useful in, for example, polo and gymkhana games.

The Combined martingale

As its name suggests, this is a combination of the running and standing martingales for horses who seem to need both effects. A somewhat 'belt and braces' piece of equipment, it is not seen very often.

Breastplates (for keeping the saddle forward) can have a buckle attachment at the breast, to which separate martingale fittings can be attached for either a running or a standing martingale; these are called martingale splits. A small rubber ring can also be fitted at the breast, to prevent the martingale strap which passes between the forelegs from hanging down too low – a potential

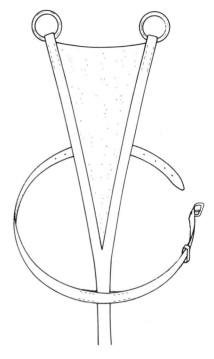

A bib martingale

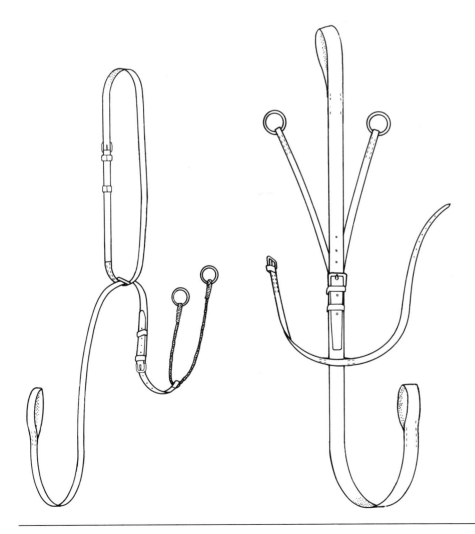

Left: **A pulley martingale**

Right: **A combination martingale**

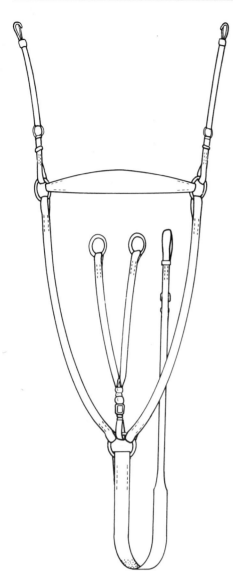

A breastplate with a running martingale attachment

An Irish martingale

source of danger if the forelegs were to get caught up in the course of an awkward movement or a fall. Such a ring is fitted where the chest strap passes through the neck strap, and tends to lie diagonally; it is called a martingale stop, (as opposed to a rein stop on the reins).

The Irish martingale

This is simply a short piece of leather the width of the distance between the reins under a horse's neck, with a metal ring on each end through which each rein passes; the martingale just sits on the reins under the neck. Its object is to stop the reins being thrown over the neck, and it is used in racing and on young horses when this sort of thing is more likely to happen. It is lightweight, but still interferes with contact and communication, although useful for its purpose. Surprisingly, it does seem to stop excitable horses throwing their heads about.

The Market Harborough

Sometimes called a martingale and sometimes a rein, the Market Harborough takes its name from the place where it is thought to have made its début. It consists of a neckstrap, and a strap passing under the breast to the girth at one end, and towards the other dividing, like a running martingale, into two thinner straps. However, these are longer than those on a running martingale; and each ends in a snap hook not a ring – these pass through each bit-ring, then are brought back to snap on to one of normally four pairs of metal dees sewn to each rein.

The influence of the Market Harborough directs the horse's head downwards should he raise it above the height at which control can reasonably be exerted. It has the feel of a running martingale to the horse, and can be fairly severe or quite ineffective according to which pair of dees it is attached to and how loosely or tightly it is adjusted.

Running reins

Running reins may be fitted in two ways: the least severe is to have the reins running from the rider's hands, through the bit-rings (usually from inside to outside) and back to the girth under the saddle flaps. The more severe fitting is for the reins to pass down from the bit-rings between the horse's forelegs, fastening round the girth at the breastbone. When fitted in the latter way running reins are often called draw reins, though I am assured this is incorrect.

Both fittings have the effect, even when not in actual use, of encouraging the horse to lower his head and neck and bring in his nose a little, so suggesting to him an easier way of going. The rider should differentiate between the two reins and hold them as he or she would double bridle reins, with the snaffle rein between the third and little finger as normal and the running rein outside the little finger (this is one method, at least), only using the running rein when the horse is going with his head up, nose poked, and with a hollow back and trailing

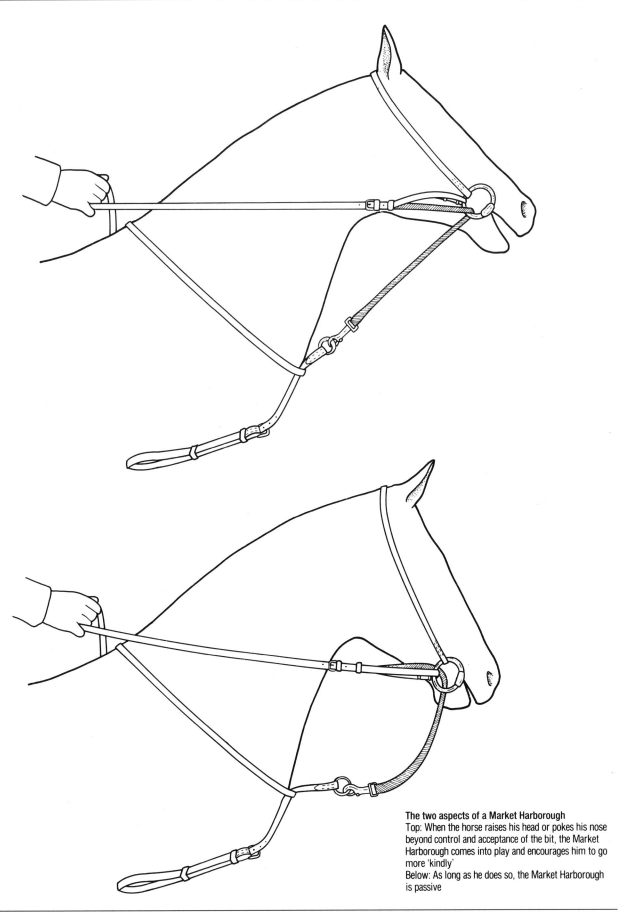

The two aspects of a Market Harborough
Top: When the horse raises his head or pokes his nose beyond control and acceptance of the bit, the Market Harborough comes into play and encourages him to go more 'kindly'
Below: As long as he does so, the Market Harborough is passive

Training Equipment

Running reins fitted in their least severe way, passing from the rider's hands, through the bit-rings, to the girth tabs under the saddle flap

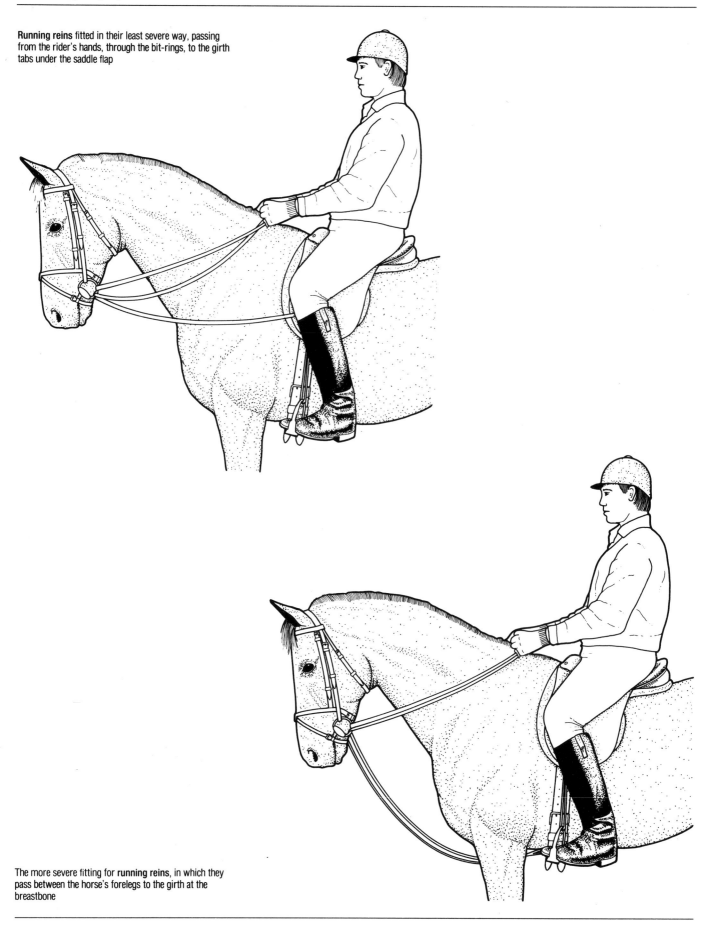

The more severe fitting for **running reins**, in which they pass between the horse's forelegs to the girth at the breastbone

hind legs (these four faults often go together). The rider must ride on the snaffle rein, not constantly on the running rein, of course.

In inexpert hands, running reins fitted either way can result in the rider trying to obtain a head carriage from manipulation of the head and neck only; in fact these reins should be used simply to suggest the desired way of going to the horse, whilst making sure that any *real* improvement is a result of the horse pushing forwards from the hindlegs and quarters and going with relaxed back and paces.

Running reins are sometimes mistakenly put on a horse which 'takes off', in the belief that they will provide additional control. In fact they will have the opposite effect, because horses which take off with serious intent put their heads down (albeit with their noses out), and the lowering effect of the running reins simply makes their task easier. Running reins can also make it easier for certain horses to buck, since bucking also needs the head to be down.

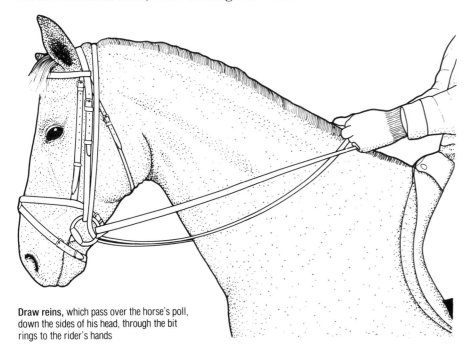

Draw reins, which pass over the horse's poll, down the sides of his head, through the bit rings to the rider's hands

Draw reins

In fact one continuous rein, a draw rein can be described as passing from the horse's poll, down the sides of his face, through the bit-rings from outside to inside, and then straight to the rider's hands. They have quite the opposite effect to running reins in that they raise the bit in the mouth and, therefore, encourage the horse to raise the head, although there is a lesser downward pressure on the poll – rather like the feel of a gag.

They are very useful when attempting to re-educate a horse which has adopted certain bad habits: the previously mentioned 'grazing position' may have been mistakenly instilled into him; he may like to get his head down and take off or buck, or to bore and lean on the bit; or perhaps he suddenly throws his head down, having learned that this is a fairly good way of unshipping some riders, particularly when done at speed.

Training aids

The title of this chapter is 'Training Equipment': it generally covers items other than saddles and bridles, from lungeing cavessons to 'gadgets' (to use their popular description) such as martingales, and sophisticated schooling aids old and new.

There is nothing new about the idea of training aids to give the normal equipment a boost. Old pictures and even carvings on archaeological finds depict any number of ropes, reins, hobbles, martingales and other items all obviously aimed at giving the trainer more control and restricting the horse.

The general idea of a training aid, schooling accessory or gadget is to get through to the horse an idea we are having difficulty explaining to him. As not all horses have the same problems or use their bodies in quite the same way, not all training equipment (other than the basics used for all horses) is useful for every horse. Damage can certainly be done if the wrong item is used where it is not needed, or if the right one is used incorrectly.

Aids are often used to speed up a process or quickly get through to a horse what we want him to do, or how we want him to go, even with a 'normal' horse who finds schooling easy. Aids can be a definite advantage in training more difficult horses, not only in getting a message through to the horse's brain but also to prevent the horse realising he can defeat the trainer if he has dreamed up some resistance that a properly applied aid or gadget will nip in the bud. Once a horse gets the better of a human he will always remember it, just as he remembers an injustice, an incorrectly applied punishment or, indeed, the reward of doing something right and being praised by his trainer.

(continued on p 112)

Specific training aids may also be used to help a horse whose action or conformation is not brilliant and who needs to be built up by working in a specific way.

Normally, aids or gadgets are best used by experts who know how to do so and understand their effects properly. It is quite common for inexperienced people to buy 'problem' horses or those which are young or only partly schooled, because such animals are cheaper than well-behaved, well-schooled ones. If such purchasers resort to some device or other to help them overcome their horse's deficiencies *without* expert supervision, at least initially, a great deal of harm can result and the horse can end up more difficult, more confused and more resentful than before.

Professional yards often use aids of various kinds because time is money and they certainly can help speed up the schooling process. Also, by being shown how to go properly a previously spoiled horse can be restored to good form and behaviour possibly more quickly than without the use of training aids.

The use of an appropriate training aid can make success by the trainer probable and domination by a difficult horse less likely.

It will probably always be the case that some experts will approve of one 'gadget' and others disapprove of it. The same can be said for any item of tack or method of training.

As far as training accessories are concerned, perhaps we could define the best as encouraging the horse, indeed helping him, to improve his natural, free paces and his mental attitude. Because of his mental nature as a prey animal, he finds force and restraint an anathema, so equipment which tries to restrict him in any way is less than useful, and maybe even dangerous.

The Chambon

This is not named after a place, but after the French cavalry officer who invented it: the Chambon (pronounced *shombon*) is used when lungeing or loose schooling to encourage the horse to lower the head and neck and – as ever – to help him realise that in this position he can go more comfortably with his back rounded and swinging, able to propel himself forward more easily from the hindquarters.

The equipment consists of a padded poll strap with rings or a little pulley on each end. A cord clips to the bit-ring on each side, each passing up the side of the head and through the ring on the poll strap, then down to the breast where they both buckle to two short pieces on a single strap passing between the forelegs and fastening round the girth. The horse 'works' the Chambon himself as it only comes into effect when he raises his head above a level acceptable to his trainer. The poll strap exerts downward pressure on the poll, and the bit is drawn rather uncomfortably upwards in the mouth (but with no backward pressure, as can be exerted from the saddle with draw reins); the theory is that in order to avoid this uncomfortable feel, the horse lowers his head again. Moreover it works in practice, too, many horses going with a lowered head and neck and rounded topline just from the feel of the Chambon in position.

Initially it is best fitted rather loosely so as to have little effect, but it can be increasingly shortened by an expert trainer as the training progresses and as he or she thinks fit. Some people feel the Chambon can and should be used from the beginning of a youngster's training as a standard part of lungeing equipment, whereas others only use it as a corrective device when re-training spoiled or mature horses which have never been taught to go in an effective manner.

The de Gogue

Another rein invented by another French cavalry officer, this time a Monsieur René de Gogue; the de Gogue is an extension of the Chambon but is used mainly during ridden work, although in one fitting it can also be used during lungeing and loose schooling. There are two ways to fit the de Gogue, known as the 'independent' and the 'command':

In the *independent* fitting, cords run from a strap at the breast (fastening round the girth and passing between the forelegs), up through a ring or pulley wheel on each end of a padded poll strap, down the sides of the head and through the bit-rings, and back down to the breaststrap again. As with the Chambon, the horse 'operates' this fitting himself and, depending on expert adjustment, it only comes into effect, with its bit-raising and poll-pressure technique, when the head is too high. It is used during lungeing and loose schooling in this position, although some trainers also use it during initial ridden schooling.

In the *command* fitting, the cords pass up through the rings or over the pulleys, down the face and through the bit-rings again, but thence back to the rider's hand, clipping to special short reins with rings to take the de Gogue clips. A pair of ordinary reins is also used on the bridle and the rider can use the

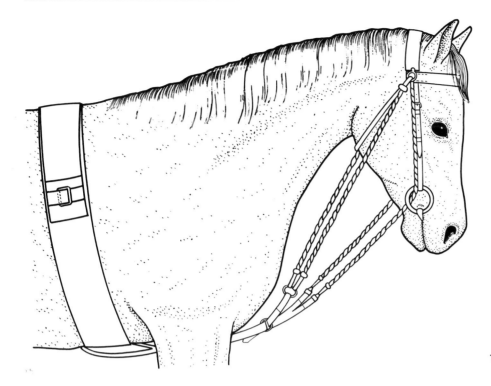

The de Gogue rein – independent fitting

ordinary reins and/or the de Gogue, as considered appropriate. Some experts, particularly on the continent of Europe and especially in France, use the command de Gogue without a direct rein; but this does take great finesse, knowledge and ability on the part of the trainer. Incidentally, the de Gogue can also be used when jumping and has been used in actual competition. Again, some consider it standard schooling equipment, and not an 'accessory' at all.

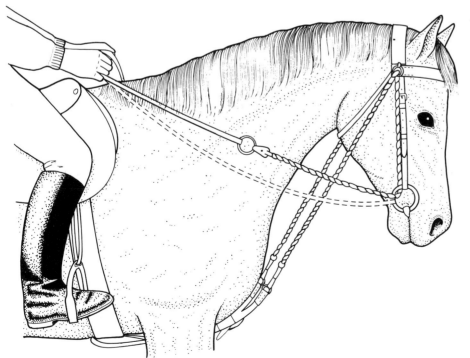

The de Gogue rein – command fitting

Domestication of the horse

The horse was the last of the most important animals to be domesticated, and this happened around the end of the New Stone Age. By that time man had had a good deal of experience in the handling and control of other animals; oxen were the main beasts of burden and draught.

Although the slow-moving ox was initially used with just a rope of sorts around the neck and the head free, ropes were eventually wound around the base of the horns. Reindeer were also ridden and used this way with ropes or straps around the base of the antlers, and sometimes still are today.

Before metal was available to early man bone and horn were used, and nose pegs, passing through the division between the nostrils (the septum) were used as forerunners of the metal nose ring used to control bulls in our own country and draught and pack oxen in others.

It seems that the ass may have been domesticated for work before the horse and there seem to have been early attempts to fit it with nose pegs or rings which, because of its anatomy, simply did not work.

The Asiatic wild ass was used as a work animal by the ancient Sumerians. According to historian Anthony Dent a means of control and protection against its habitual biting had to be devised. To this end, a muzzle was fitted with a ring on the end.

Once the horse itself was properly domesticated, the onager was abandoned as too much hassle. The horse was so much more pleasant to handle and was both stronger and faster than the onager and certainly the ox.

The technique of using horses, asses, onagers, reindeer and various cattle and oxen with nothing on the

Over recent years it has become fashionable to call anything other than basic riding and 'breaking' tackle (I wish someone would devise a more accurate and appropriate term than 'breaking in') as a 'gadget'. This word is defined as a 'useful device aimed at making a task easier', although in connection with equestrian equipment it has to come to be derogatory – yet so many of the items to which it refers are just what a gadget is: a useful item to make a task easier.

A horse is flesh and blood with an effective brain and is quite as capable of resisting our requests as he is of complying with them. He cannot speak our language and is not as easy to educate as, for example, a child who can be told what to do in a mutually understandable language and, furthermore, can understand a simple explanation of why he is being asked, or made, to do something. Obviously, no such basic communication is possible with horses, and training accessories can be a great help in getting our message through to the horse, whether as a polite request or a firm statement, *provided they are correctly and expertly used*. Most accessories should probably be used for only short periods at a time and as a temporary measure, although with some hardened cases they may be needed all the time – for example certain horses can only be ridden safely by certain riders in a gag. And for a certain type of horse, no amount of tactful schooling seems to succeed in reforming them totally, and permanent aids in the form of accessories, or gadgets, are needed to make the horse controllable. This may not be an ideal situation but then this is not an ideal world, and we do not all have the equestrian tact and expertise of the best, most talented and educated trainers.

So many accessories have undeservedly been given a bad name because they are used incorrectly and not at all as was intended – tight standing martingales combined with harshly used gag snaffles (with only one rein) and tight drop nosebands fitted too low (it sounds horrendous but is an outfit seen fairly regularly on the polo field, for instance) hardly create a favourable impression.

Used by an expert or under expert supervision, and used correctly and sympathetically, accessories can be a good thing – but like so many items, their implication and character change when they are used and fitted wrongly or inappropriately.

Bits

The process of educating and breaking in a young horse should be a smooth, continuous progression, each stage of handling and discipline following on easily from the one before: thus he gets used to being handled and led around, groomed and having his feet attended to, until he has a saddle on, and his trainer lies across and finally sits on his back; in short there is no big upset or panic when the horse is actually backed. Mouthing a horse is another thing altogether, and no amount of routine handling can prepare the horse for the undoubtedly unpleasant procedure of having a bit in his mouth, of getting used to the feel of the metal or whatever it is made of, plus the pressure and influence the rider will exert through the bit. And the experience is one he will be stuck with for the rest of his working life probably!

The object of mouthing is to get the horse to accept the bit to the extent that it does not bother him, and to encourage him to play with it sufficiently to encourage the formation of saliva to keep the mouth moist, but not to the extent that he constantly moves it around or tries to get his tongue over it in an effort to evade its pressure, or opens his mouth and draws his chin into his chest to try and get rid of it or avoid it. As schooling progresses he must learn to understand what a particular feel on the bit means when it is combined with other aids from the legs, seat, weight and voice. A properly 'mouthed' horse more or less completely accepts the bit, flexes to it once he has been taught, is not afraid of it and obeys its indications. However, it is debatable whether the horse actually likes having a bit in his mouth. Compare humans who have to wear dentures: many take a long time to get used to wearing them, and say that although they may not hurt, they feel like an alien presence in the mouth; and some complain of nausea if they keep them in for more than a very few hours, or caused by the material – plastic for example.

Even though horses normally these days only wear their bits for an hour or two at a time – except endurance horses, many of which wear bitless bridles – nonetheless they must surely consider the bit to be just as much an alien presence in their mouths as we regard dentures; and we should bear in mind, too, that they have no real say as to the material the bit is made from, nor its design, its fit, how long they must wear it, or the effect it will have on their mouth, head, even body.

When it comes to mouthing youngsters, a good deal more attention could be paid to this sort of thing. In my opinion it is a particularly unattractive practice to put a bit in the youngster's mouth, and then to leave him in the stable wearing it for maybe hours on end. During this time the horse has nothing else to do and must be preoccupied with this awful thing in his mouth which he cannot get hold of, cannot really manipulate, and cannot get rid of. Surely it must be better to follow the practice of giving the horse something else to do whilst being mouthed – lunge him, lead him around or at least groom him – anything to help take his mind off the bit somewhat, so that he may come to worry about it less and accept it more readily and quickly.

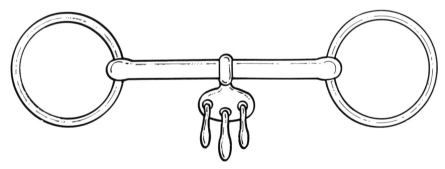

Mouthing bit, loose ring, straightbar, with keys

The mouthing bit

The traditional mouthing bit, of which there are a few variations, has little 'drops' of metal called keys suspended from the mouthpiece; the idea was that the horse played with the keys with his tongue, and this would encourage the

head at all was very common. A simple neck rope was used to stop the animal and a switch used on the neck and shoulders to control direction.

This technique does not seem to have been applied, however, to the usually nasty-tempered camel, which was/is led by a bitless headcollar-type of item for which the Arabic word is *haqma*, subsequently Anglicised to hackamore. When the Arab people first acquired horses (probably via Babylonia and Assyria — the old Fertile Crescent), they used a similar article and rode them in such bitless bridles.

The tendency towards using horrifically severe bits seems to have been developed in Spain and spread to Arabic countries, particularly the northern ones, after the Moorish conquest of Iberia.

The development of the bit itself was a major landmark as nothing like it had been used on other domesticated animals and it seems to have been invented by nomads living on the steppes in eastern Asia around Mongolia, who devised bits of rawhide, twisted between horn cheek- or sidepieces.

The earliest suitable metal for bits was bronze; copper, brass, silver and gold were far too soft for work, but not for decoration when necessary.

Although some early bits were jointed (and sometimes double-jointed), the basic design for both riding and driving bits (the mouthpieces were the same in early days) was the snaffle type.

It seems that horses have always suffered from mutton-fisted riders. Efforts were made to follow the still-common line of thought that a stronger bit must be needed to control the animal fighting those heavy hands. An early curb-type bit of

(continued on p 116)

Roman times was basically a snaffle mouthpiece with bars at each end joined under the jaw by a metal rod; when the reins were pulled the jaw was clamped between the straight bar mouthpiece and the rod below the jaw — a truly tortuous procedure which must surely have been entirely counter-productive due to the pain and injury caused.

Later bits had various ways of creating more tongue room, and the curb chain, believed to have been invented in Hungary, came to replace the rod.

For hundreds of years, snaffles and curbs seem to have been used, separately. The severity of some of the curb bits particularly in mediaeval and Neapolitan times, was absolutely dreadful.

In some cases, the curbs seem to have been used as a type of early pelham, the bit having two reins positioned as they are on a modern pelham, but used separately.

The double bridle as we know it is a comparatively recent invention of the late eighteenth century, and no significant improvements to its design have been incorporated since then.

The new synthetic bits on the market certainly seem to be a step in the right direction, although the basic shapes and thinking behind their operation offer nothing really new. Their lightness and comfort, however, must be a boon to the horses and ponies working in them.

production of saliva and familiarise him with the bit. Nowadays, although mouthing bits are still used in many yards, the prevailing view seems to be that an ordinary riding bit should be used for mouthing, as the keys encourage too much mouth movement and actually teach the horse to put his tongue over the bit. Moreover it seems that the results which can be obtained from an ordinary bit are just as good – people tend to use a half-moon or simple single-jointed snaffle suspended on an ordinary single headstall, without the use of a throatlatch or browband, under the cavesson headpiece but over its noseband. If the trainer feels the horse may get his tongue over the bit, he may choose the half-moon snaffle and position it fairly high (though not uncomfortably so) in the mouth, to discourage this. A jointed snaffle, whether it has one or two joints, naturally drops lower in the mouth and the horse will find it easier to get his tongue over it, even when fitted fairly high.

Mouthing bits are usually straight-bar bits, and these cannot be very comfortable as they allow no room for the tongue. Some may have a link or ring in the centre which acts like a joint when the horse plays with it, and gives a looser feel than either a straight-bar or mullen mouth. The keys will be suspended from the ring.

Some mouthing bits are made of wood in the belief that it is softer than metal and so possibly more acceptable to the young horse; the keys are suspended from a metal band round the middle of the mouthpiece. Another pattern has cheeks instead of rings so that if the trainer decides to ride the horse in the mouthing bit, as some do, the cheeks will help the horse understand the turning aids because they press his head towards the direction being asked for by the trainer.

Generally speaking therefore mouthing bits *are* still in use, but most experts these days prefer to use an ordinary snaffle.

The Tattersall bit

This bit is circular, and often has mouthing keys hanging from the side of the circle which goes in the mouth; it may have a dee or ring on the part of the circle below the jaw to which a leading rein can be clipped and the young horse (usually a colt) then led about; there are also dees on each side to which the bridle cheekpieces attach, obviously to keep the bit up in the mouth. These bits are used mainly in the racing world, but are also occasionally seen in colt-showing circles. The bit allows room for the tongue and also creates bar pressure (the section in the mouth being effectively a mullen mouth in feel), and the keys ostensibly persuade the young colt to play with the bit, as already described. However full of themselves, few colts would argue with the restraint possible via a Tattersall bit, but its excessive use would certainly not do anything to encourage a sensitive mouth – although racing folk don't always worry about this!

The Chifney

A Chifney lead or anti-rear bit again encircles the lower jaw, but the mouth-part has a downward curve in it which is designed actually to press into the tongue, and no keys as it is not particularly intended for mouthing or youngsters but for renegades who are very difficult to control in hand and are likely, or known, to rear. There are two rings for bridle cheekpieces, and one at the back for the lead-rein. The rings, unlike the rings or dees on the Tattersall, swivel on little shanks. The action is, therefore, pretty severe and the success of the bit very varied. I know of several professionals who would never lead a difficult animal, or attempt to load one into transport, without putting the horse in a Chifney bit, and swear by its effectiveness. Others maintain they are useless (this is my experience); and yet others that they actually *encourage* rearing in hand, as they can cause pain and a badly bruised tongue (again, my own conviction).

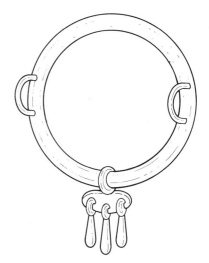

Tattersall's ring bit

The Nose net

Nose nets are an effective, harmless piece of equipment which seem to work on the horse's mind, rather than his body, to stop him pulling and getting 'strong'. They are currently rather out of fashion, which is a pity because they could well help some of those incompatible horse-and-rider combinations come to a happier understanding without the rider resorting to stronger and stronger bits, with a harder and harder mouth in the horse as a result. The net simply fastens to the noseband and covers the muzzle and mouth. The reins attach to bit-rings as usual and the net is suspended by loops which leave space for the bit-rings to lie outside it. It seems to work because the horse presumably doesn't like pushing his sensitive nostrils into the net, and so chooses not to pull. I cannot think of any other explanation. Furthermore my experience of the nose net is that it works even better on horses who have not been denuded of their antennae whiskers, than on those who have, though this is perhaps not surprising, as these whiskers are important in giving the horse information about his immediate surroundings, and they will be in more or less constant contact with the net; yet the horse does not appear to be irritated by it.

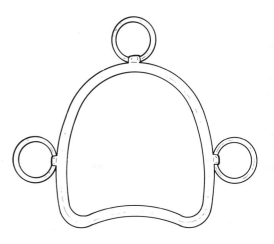

Chifney bit

4
HEADCOLLARS
AND HALTERS

Methods of restraint

Preventing a horse from moving freely in the way he wants is one of the most frightening things we can do to him. It is a minor miracle that it is possible to get horses to accept being led, tied up, ridden, held for various operations such as shoeing, injections, first-aid care and the like. Horses need to feel free to feel secure, and to be aware of space around them into which to escape should the need arise.

The horse often has to be restrained for various attentions, apart from everyday routines such as leading about, riding, driving, maybe tying up for grooming and so on. It is a sign of considerable trust of his handler when a horse allows what we might call 'care operations' to be carried out, particularly uncomfortable things such as having a cut dressed, without being tied up or held in any way. Once a horse does trust his human associates he will put up with a surprising number of attentions, many potentially worrying or even frightening, without showing much or any resistance.

When a horse has to be physically restrained, it should be done with as little strength and force as possible, taking into account the reason and the horse's character. The most simple form of restraint is holding the horse by a top lock of his mane to steady his head while, say, sponging his eyes, if he is not too keen of the job. Next comes the usual headcollar

A very good quality leather headcollar with adjustment buckles not only on the headpiece, as usual, but also on the throatlatch and the noseband. A beneficial addition would be a browband. The noseband on this headcollar is a good height (midway between the corners of the lips and the sharp face bones) but could be a little tighter

The Headcollar

A headcollar of whatever material is obviously a very useful item of equipment, but it is also misunderstood and does not offer anything like as much control as some people seem to think it does. It was intended not only for leading horses around, but also for securing them in stalls in 'the old days' (and some horses still live in stalls) and so its influence was only ever meant to be mild; therefore it is not surprising that it creates no real respect in unco-operative horses.

The headcollar is simply a stout, bitless version of a bridle, although most these days are used without a browband – surely a retrograde step, as a browband prevents the headpiece slipping uncomfortably down the neck, ruffling the mane and creating an indirect pull on the nose which can mark the hair and irritate the horse.

The very 'best' quality **Albert headcollars** have three rows of stitching down the cheekpieces (which are of double leather), rolled leather throatlatch, brass buckles and fittings (to which the different pieces of leather fit round the jaw area) and a brass dee at the back for attaching the leadrope. For this, brass is a foolish choice of metal because it is quite soft, and this dee has, in my

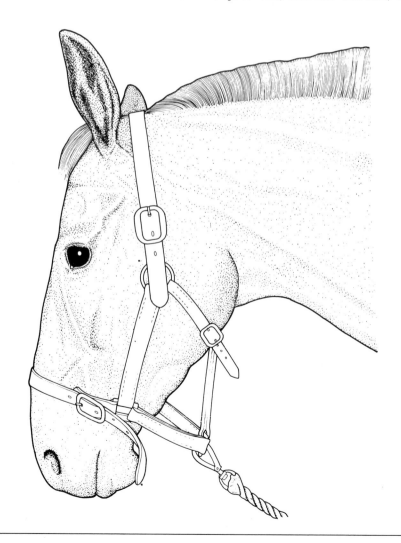

An everyday **nylon webbing headcollar**

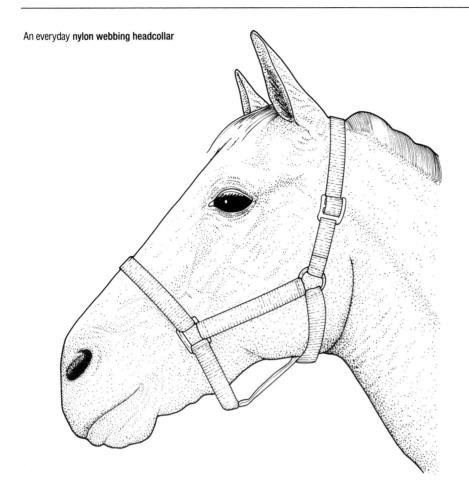

and rope equipment which is enough for most horses. It is always better to get someone to hold your horse while you work on him, to ensure that feeling of flexibility which the horse cannot have when tied to an immoveable object such as a post or tie ring. If this is not possible, the horse should be tied with a slip knot (half bow) which can easily be undone by a single pull on the free end should the need arise. Many people recommend tying the rope to a ring of binder twine through the metal tie ring so that the horse can break free if he panics. Others maintain that this actually teaches him he can break free and so he is never reliable about being tied up in future.

If you do tie your horse to a twine ring around a metal one, make sure you do *not* use binder twine, especially the synthetic sort, as it is far too strong. Use ordinary string which will break immediately.

Even with a seemingly trustworthy horse it is never a good idea to leave him tied up unattended, even for just a few moments. If anything happens to frighten him and there is no one about to calm him or untie him a nasty accident can occur.

experience, been regularly badly bent or even broken by a horse with the determined, inveterate habit of pulling back. The idea of brass is that, when cleaned and polished (if anyone has time for that these days), it does make a headcollar look very smart and impressive, particularly those that are fitted with a brass nameplate down the nearside cheekpiece engraved with the horse's name. I myself must admit a soft spot for these headcollars and tend to overlook the failings of brass, at least when the headcollars are intended for well-behaved horses; clean brass has a soft, warm glow about it that tones beautifully with clean brown leather with its saddle-soaped sheen. Fortunately they are still in regular use.

Probably the more practical **everyday headcollar** is the good quality, stout leather one with strong galvanised metal fittings – not so attractive to look at, but more serviceable for a difficult horse. Cheaper than Albert headcollars, they are in wider use. They may be stitched or rivetted together.

Most **leather** is vegetable tanned, but chrome-tanned leather – usually pale green – stretches more before breaking and so is stronger (although it is certainly not as strong as buffalo hide). Even the best-kept vegetable-tanned leather will break under not that much pressure (and a horse is capable of exerting a pull of two-and-a-half times his own weight) and so chrome leather is often used for items required to be strong such as field-quality headcollars (cheaper, in fact, than vegetable-tanned ones) and new Zealand rug leg-straps.

It is arguable whether or not a **field headcollar** should be strong or weak. If

Speak to your horse

Every effort should be made to keep a restrained horse calm. The human voice has a tremendous effect on a horse. Speaking calmly and confidently in a reassuring tone is often enough to quieten down a horse who is beginning to get really worried by something. The touch of our hands reinforces this effect. Again, a confident (neither too light nor too heavy) stroking is calming, and more relaxing than patting.

If a fairly mild form of restraint is not having the desired effect, it may be tempting to try a stronger method, but remember that this may have the opposite effect from the one wanted. The horse may get more and more worked up; this means more physical resistance, fear and panic, and against the physical strength of a horse we become powerless and everyone, human and equine, is in danger of injury. The horse also comes to expect trouble and resistance may then become a habit as the horse's instinct to preserve himself takes precedence over his conditioning to obey.

The method of restraint should suit the character of the horse as individual horses respond differently to situations. However, discipline is also necessary with such a large, strong animal.

it is strong and for any reason the horse gets caught up – in a hedge, or on one of those vertically-protruding hunting-latches on gates meant to be openable from the saddle (and which should *never* be used on the gates of horse pastures), or a tree branch; or gets his hind hoof caught in the headcollar whilst scratching his head – it is less likely that he will be able to break the leather and get free. Similarly, if he gets both legs inside one leg strap on a New Zealand rug after lying down or rolling (usually only possible because the straps have been adjusted too long), the strap will be that much more difficult to break and the horse's leg might break instead. However, some people believe that the headcollar (if not the leg straps) should be strong because once a horse realises he can break his headcollar by pulling on it, he will do so for ever more and in this respect becomes a menace to deal with. This also applies if you tie him up to a string ring, in turn tied to the tie ring or bracket – it will only take him one half-hearted pull back and he is free, and he will persist in this trick for ever after.

Nylon web headcollars are immensely strong and because of this are too dangerous, in my view, to be left on in the field. I am not in favour of leaving headcollars on in the field anyway, unless it is essential for identification purposes, for instance a mare sent to a large public stud, or if it is essential to fit a catching strap (usually about 6in/15cm long) to the back dee for a horse which is difficult to catch. Nylon web headcollars are ubiquitous now and, being cheap and easily washed, are popular. It should be realised though, that if they *are* left on for any length of time they can rub, as nylon is harsh as well as strong.

Fitting a headcollar

The best designs of headcollar, whatever the material, have the usual adjustment buckle on the cheekpiece but also one on the noseband (which is almost always too loose in other sorts) and on the throatlatch as well.

The fitting for a headcollar is as follows: if a browband is present, you should be able to slide a finger quite easily under it and also under the headpiece, all round. The browband, as on a bridle, should be long enough so there is no chance of it pulling the headpiece into the back of the base of the ears, nor of the browband itself rubbing round the base of the ears; though it should not be so long that it gapes out or flops around. You should be able to fit the width of your hand between the throatlatch and the round jawbones, but no more. The height of the noseband should be adjusted by means of the cheekpiece buckle and headstrap so that it is 2in (5cm) below the sharp face bones (perhaps a little more if the horse has a large head): the most common fault is for the noseband to be too high and to rub the horse raw here. If it is much lower, however, the horse may well rub the noseband down over the muzzle until eventually the entire headcollar comes off, or is left dangling dangerously round the neck. Adjust the noseband so there is ample room for the horse to move his jaws when eating: the width of four fingers should fit between the noseband and the front of the face – if it is looser than this, it is more likely to catch on things and to swing round annoyingly as the horse moves his head.

The Foal slip

This is a simple, lightweight headcollar for a foal consisting of a headpiece and noseband, both joined to a ring under the jaw and linked by a diagonal strip of leather at the side of the face. Integral to the design is a short leading-strap on the jaw ring, and a leadrope can also be clipped to or threaded through this ring. Note, however, that when a foal is first taught to lead, two or even three people are needed initially: one guides the foal with just a stable rubber round its neck whilst the other puts his arms around its quarters and breast; the third is needed to lead the mare.

One of the advantages of the short strap on the slip is that the foal can be caught with very little trouble, and this helps to instil the habit of obedience right from the start – you cannot expect a young foal to stand still while you try to put a foal slip on in the field, and it only needs to get away once or twice to learn the art of being difficult to catch. If you have help and a very co-operative mare, you could probably get the slip on, but on your own you are more likely to teach the foal that humans are not invincible – fatal!

Foal slips should be made of leather, for the very reason that nylon is too strong. Again, opinions vary as to whether it is advisable to leave slips on foals at pasture – some studs do, others don't; the better establishment will have plenty of help to catch mares and foals anyway. Whatever your view, foals should be watched carefully as they grow amazingly quickly, and slips will need regular readjustment by means of the buckles on the noseband and headpiece.

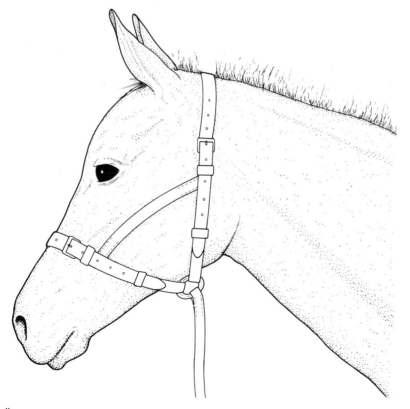

A foal slip

Early lessons

When observing a well-schooled horse being led about and gently handled in a simple headcollar and lead rope, it is easy to forget that he had to be taught to accept this simple form of restraint. Most domesticated horses are taught from foalhood to accept wearing foal slips and to being led with their dams. The sooner a foal is used to wearing a slip and to being guided alongside the mare, the better he will learn his lesson. The longer it is left and the more he is allowed to run free around the mare while she is being led, the more undisciplined he will become and the more difficult it will be for his attendants to school him later on. It is always better to begin handling, and get over any minor differences of opinion and willpower while the foal is still physically weaker than you so that you really can exert physical strength in teaching and restraining him (although never brutally, of course), and any arguments will not become major ones.

A foal can be taught to tie up by fastening a lunge-rein to the back of the slip, passing it through the tie-ring in a well-bedded loose box, and the loop end held coiled up by the trainer. In this way the handler can let out some line and play it like a fish when the foal pulls back (as it will do eventually). This gives the foal the impression he is not tied down but still cannot get free. He will soon learn that he must stand still and put up with being tied.

Dealing with pullers

Pulling back when tied up is a most annoying habit but even die-hard pullers can be improved and even cured by this method.

Instead of a normal leadrope, fasten a lunge rein or similar long rope to the nearside dee of the head-collar, up over the horse's neck, down through the offside dee and to the tie ring on the wall. The horse, if and when he pulls, will pull against himself in a way he finds hard to re-sist. A doubled rope can be used, if long enough, the middle then being placed on the neck, each free end passed through the side dees and from there to the ring in a slip-knot.

It may be more effective to fit a broad neckstrap rather than an ordi-nary headcollar, as horses do not seem to pull so hard against wide pressure on their necks.

The following method can be used with either a neckstrap or a head-collar. Fasten one end of a long rope or lunge rein to the ring on the under-neath of the neckstrap or to the head-collar's rear dee with a slip-knot. Pass the rope behind the horse's quarters (like a fillet string) and thread it back through the ring or dee, then tie it with another slip-knot to the ring in the wall.

Halters

A halter is an all-in-one design of headgear and leadrope, and is made of cotton or jute webbing or of rope. Normally it consists of a section of rope or webbing over the head and one round the nose and jaw, with a bound loop where they join on the nearside. Some people simply thread the leadrope through this loop – as there is nothing to stop it pulling tight, they feel that this in itself will provide sufficient restraint with a difficult animal; though awkward horses really should not be led in a halter, or even a headcollar, at all. Be that as it may, the safest way to fit a halter is to make sure it is comfortable, then tie a knot at the loop by passing the leadrope round the noseband behind the loop and then back through it – this will secure it without permitting it to be pulled tighter and tighter.

Halters are very much cheaper than headcollars and separate leadropes, of course, but not as widely used. Whitened halters are used in the show-ring to show foals, usually heavy breeds. As the leadrope is an integral part of a halter's design, obviously it cannot be left on when the horse is at grass or untied in the stable.

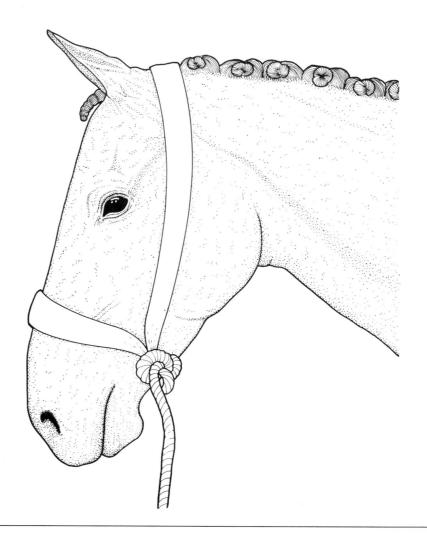

A webbing halter with a close-up of the all-important knot

Leadropes

Today, leadropes usually come in a fairly standard length of about 6ft (almost 2m), although some saddlers sell shorter ones for ponies. They have either spring or trigger clips fitted to one end, which fasten to the back dee of the headcollar. It is safest to fix them with the opening facing away from the horse's head as – unlikely though this may seem – horses have occasionally been known to injure their heads on this. Most people feel the trigger clips are safer than the spring clips.

Ropes can be made of jute which is hardwearing and strong although rather rough on the hands. Softer cotton, usually coloured or white, is widely used now, but it is not so hardwearing and can even snap; there is also nylon which is very strong but can also be rough on the hands. Moreover nylon seems to fray more easily in use than natural materials, and then becomes unsafe.

Instead of clips some leadropes have an eye or bound ring on the end: pass the rope through the headcollar dee, then thread the other end of the rope through the eye or ring. This is much less convenient than a clip, of course.

Although probably impractical for everyday use, it is best always to wear gloves when leading a horse as a sudden head movement or a determined pull to get away can tear the rope through your hands and badly burn them; gloves not only give a firmer grip but will also help prevent friction burn. Another idea is to tie a knot in the end of the rope so it will be less easily pulled right out of the hand.

Another type of leadrope but one fairly hard to find these days is the double-length leadrope: this simply threads through the headcollar dee so you are leading with two thicknesses of rope. There are no clips attached or eyes on the end of these ropes, the idea being that should a horse break away whilst being led and tread on the rope, he is more than likely to tread on only one of the two ends and the rope will thus be pulled harmlessly through the dee. Whereas if he were to tread on the end of a clipped-on rope, this will exert considerable force on his head and could very well bring him down. Some authorities advise that the rope should not be long enough for him to tread on, but this is quite ridiculous and impractical because if it is *that* short, it will be of no effective use for leading and tying up. Obviously, a knot should not be tied in either of the ends of a double-length rope, as this could easily prevent it being pulled through the dee, the whole point of the long rope.

This whole matter is one of significance as it is fairly easy for a horse in a headcollar and leadrope to break away from his handler – this may be simply out of badness of character, or because something genuinely frightens him and his instincts take over. And of course the risk that he may bring himself down is just as much present with halters and integral ropes: for this reason alone I am much in favour of leading with a doubled rope. However, I would only ever recommend leading a horse in a headcollar and rope arrangement if he were in an enclosed, secure area where, even if he did break free, he could not get into a dangerous area such as a public road. At all other times he should be led in a bridle, or at least a cavesson with the leadrope clipped to the front ring.

The matter of tying horses up is also the subject of two different opinions.

The horse should be tied so he is a normal distance away from the wall. Although the rope should not slip down when he is in this position, it must not exert any pressure on the backs of his thighs unless he pulls back. When he does, he will be pulling against himself; the harder he pulls the harder the rope presses on his thighs. If he resists this pressure (and few do) and decides to rear, the rope passing through the ring on the neckstrap or headcollar exerts a downwards pressure and firmly discourages this, too. The beauty of this method is that it takes only one person who does not even need to touch the horse but simply command him to stand and let him realise that not only can he not break away but also that it is much more comfortable to stand quietly.

An alternative method is to tie the rope round the horse's girth, securing it with a non-slip bowline knot, passing it through the headcollar or neckstrap ring and to the ring in the wall. Again, the horse is pulling against himself all the time and usually learns to stand quietly.

With both these methods there is no danger of the horse being swung, as there is plenty of length in the rope for him to get to his feet if he does fall: in practice, I have not known horses lose their feet. However, use these procedures only where there is soft footing and never to train a youngster, only to retrain a confirmed halter puller, and with expert help present.

One way to obtain slightly more restraint from an ordinary headcollar and leadrope is to pass the rope through one side dee, under the jaw and out through the dee on the other side. This exerts all-round pressure on the nose and jaw. The effect can be increased by fitting the headcollar with its noseband lower than usual if, for example, leading or holding a difficult horse. (continued on p 126)

The headcollar leadrope, in another method, can be clipped to the rear dee as usual, brought round over the nose about 3in above the nostrils and held together with your hand under the jaw. This can effectively restrain quite difficult horses, but do not have the rope so low that it will come off should the horse shake his head. You have to hold it firmly but not so as to interfere with his breathing.

Most teaching bodies recommend that horses are tied to a string loop which is itself tied to the tying ring or bracket – if the horse pulls back for any reason he will break the string and set himself free, and so avoid injuring himself in his struggles. Unfortunately a conventional leadrope is just as likely to bring him down since it will be left dangling under his chin in the way of his front hooves. Nevertheless, there is a little item which virtually removes the danger from this situation, although nowadays it is very hard to find: a *metal safety clip* which can be used to fasten the rope to the headcollar. It is made in such a way that if the horse pulls back determinedly the clip opens, dropping the rope which is left hanging harmlessly down the wall, whilst the horse is left to cavort around wearing just a headcollar. If the horse has been tied in an enclosed area such as a field or yard with the gates closed, this is relatively harmless: there is no rope hanging down, and he cannot escape on to a road unless he is prone to jumping the gates or fencing.

One final word: if you *do* belong to the school of thought which favours the string loop, at least use string and not binder twine which is very strong, especially the modern polyethylene type, and won't break easily. Otherwise binder twine has many uses around the stable yard – not least that of being good material for plaiting into leadropes, double length or otherwise.

Showing in-hand

The variety of bridles, headcollars and halters for in-hand showing classes can be confusing and seemingly illogical to the uninitiated, and not all breed and showing organisations are very helpful when it comes to advice as to what is most suitable. If you cannot get the information you need, the best solution is to go to an important show – at least County standard – and study what the winners are wearing. You will notice, for example, that hacks and children's ponies often wear coloured, patterned browbands but hunters have plain leather. Stallions are led in bridles that no one would ever put on to ride in; and broodmares, who are probably never ridden in their lives, are shown in-hand in ordinary 'riding' double bridles!

To begin at the beginning: foals should be shown in a smart leather or white cotton webbing slip, with a leather or webbing leadrein. Older but unbroken youngstock wear smart leather headcollars of narrow, stitched leather with brass fittings and maybe a white browband, with a leather or webbing lead, possibly with a short chain section at the 'head' end. Pure-bred Arabs and Arab crosses in particular, but also youngstock of other breeds as long as they have 'refined' heads, often wear a showing headstall of fine, maybe rolled leather, sometimes decorated with metal or coloured inserts, and with no backstrap under the jaw. At the junction of the noseband and cheekpiece on each side is a ring, through which a chain is passed; this chain also has small rings on each end, and these are caught together under the chin by a clip on the end of the leadrein. When pressure is put on the leadrein the chain tightens under the jaw and the noseband across the nose, giving a certain amount of control.

Unfortunately, many of these showing headstalls are not at all strong and can be easily broken by a robust, unschooled youngster excited by the sights and

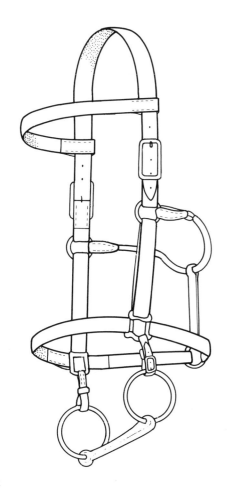

A showing headcollar with bit attachments and straight-bar snaffle bit.

Fine leather **Arab-type showing headstall**

Leading difficult horses

Horses who are difficult to lead in hand can also be improved. Extra control can be obtained by using a bridle but the bit should be used carefully and never roughly. It has a psychological effect on the horse as much as anything else but can come into play when the need arises.

In cases where a difficult or green horse has to be led on a road or somewhere he may play up, such as passing his friends or through a crowd of people, a well-fitting lungeing cavesson should be used, maybe on top of a bridle, with a lead rope attached to the front ring. The bridle reins, if present, should be passed over the head as usual and used for leading, maybe in addition to the rope on the front ring, and don't hesitate to use two people in such a case.

The handlers can use schooling whips in their outside hands (one on each side of the horse) to control the quarters when needed.

Another method is to take a long, soft rope or lunge rein, place the middle under the tail, knot the two pieces over the quarters to stop the loop you have formed falling down, and again over the withers for the same reason, then pass both free ends through the back dee of the headcollar. At the instant you give the command 'walk on' pull firmly on the rope which will jerk the horse under the tail without hurting him, and usually result in his springing forward in surprise and distaste!

A few horses will baulk and may even try to sit down, run backwards or half-rear, but they are in the minority. In any case, to be ready for this, start the horse off in a corner such as that made by two meeting lines of fencing, a corner of a building

(continued on p 128)

sounds of the show – how often have you seen some young Arab careering around a showground, having broken loose from one of these?

Although it is not essential to show youngstock in a bit, it is considered to look more impressive for three-year-olds. A simple mullen-mouthed snaffle can be used, vulcanite maybe or rubber, attached to a showing headcollar (though not the very fine variety just discussed) by means of a little bit-strap on the bottom of each cheekpiece. However, most sensible handlers will not wish to risk ruining the mouth of a virtually unbroken youngster by leading directly from a coupling attached to the bit-rings and thence to the leadrein; they will therefore buy special couplings which attach to the bit-rings as before, but they also attach to the neck of the headcollar dee and are adjusted in such a way that the dee, and therefore the headcollar noseband, takes most of the pressure before the bit comes into action. Young horses which are broken in can wear a showing snaffle bridle with the coupling attached to the bit-rings – but should only do so if the handler can be relied on to use this very sensitively, and if the animal has been well handled and thoroughly taught to lead in-hand and behave at home.

In-hand hunter youngstock, or indeed any riding youngstock, can wear this arrangement, or a smart show bridle with coupling and leadrein. In cases where a double bridle is the norm for in-hand showing, the reins are brought over the head and used as a leadrein: it is advisable to buy long-length reins for this purpose.

Pony youngstock is usually shown in a snaffle bridle with a coloured

or, ideally, a holly or hawthorn bush. When the horse tries his usual backward rush he will be met by either solid resistance or very uncomfortable prickles. Interestingly, a horse will always learn best a lesson he seems to have taught himself rather than had inflicted on him by humans.

Keep repeating the procedure and the command at exactly the same time so the horse is sure to associate the two, and a vast improvement will become apparent in no time.

browband, but a headcollar with or without a bit could also be used. Native pony and cob breeds are often shown in whitened cotton web halters, as is heavy horse youngstock.

A stallion is normally defined as an entire from three years old, and will wear a special stallion bridle with a bit. The bridle is strong but not over-heavy, often of stitched, padded leather and usually with a brass browband with a brass disc or boss at each end, depending on breed, fashion and preference. He will wear a straight-bar (usually) bit (although he would be more comfortable and probably controllable in a mullen mouth) with brass horseshoe cheeks, to which is attached a brass chain coupling on a leather or webbing leadrein; this is often longer for stallions in case they rear.

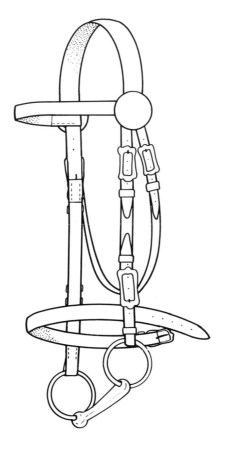

Stallion in-hand bridle with an ordinary bit. Most stallion bridles have bits with horseshoe-shaped cheeks (Below) **Chain coupling** which clips to each bit-ring, the central ring taking the lead-rein clip

Some people accept this sort of disobedience in stallions, but it should be severely frowned upon: a stallion brought out in public should be very well-mannered even in the presence of other stallions. Behaviour in horses is so often related to feed, and many people still misunderstand the correct feeding of stallions: they should not be corned up to the extent that they misbehave and cause a nuisance, and possibly a danger, to other people and animals near them. Further, they should be worked (exercised) hard enough to prevent this, not simply led out in hand as is the usual practice with British stallions, and fed appropriately *as well* as being regularly turned out.

Rollers and side-reins are often used on stallions, partly for appearance but also because they do facilitate control: they should be attached to the bit-rings and there should be a crupper attached to the roller. A roller on its own, without side-reins or crupper, looks ridiculous and is obviously pointless.

5
CLOTHING

Colours in clothing

As the range of horse clothing has become more and more updated and varied so have the colours and patterns which are becoming acceptable. From flamboyant colours in previous centuries to duller and more subdued ones in Victorian times and early this century, we now have every colour of the rainbow on not only bandages but numnahs and rugs, too, not to mention nylon headcollars.

Some like to have 'stable colours' in which scheme every horse has the same colour rugs, bandages and browbands. Others prefer the more personal and individual approach and do not like their horses in 'uniform' but key his clothing and equipment colours to his coat colour.

Many people feel that chestnuts look good in green, but if you feel this colour combination is a little hackneyed blue and pillar-box red looks really good on chestnuts, but avoid orange or burgundy-type colours.

Grey horses, look good in a rich blue and also in maroon but I feel green does not really suit them. Bay and brown horses look particularly good in maroon. However, they do look good in any colour as do true blacks; black horses with a blue sheen to their coats looking particularly good in navy or royal blue.

Tartan patterns are universally popular, not necessarily formal clan weaves but 'bastard' tartans, sometimes with a predominant colour and sometimes mixed. Make sure the main colour is the one which most compliments your horse's coat.

Bindings can be matching, toning or contrasting according to taste. Navy blue can look good with a contrasting yellow binding, although it is often seen with pale blue and sometimes red. The binding on a tartan rug will look good in any colour from

The horse's coat growth and hair 'patterns' are often quite adequate to keep him warm enough and to protect him from the weather if he has reasonable shelter facilities, but there is no doubt that a good wardrobe of well designed, properly fitting clothing is a definite advantage to horse management, particularly when looking after, for example, hot-blooded animals not evolved to live in colder climates. The range of clothing now available is vast, and a good rug can cost more than a saddle (albeit a cheap one).

A couple of generations ago choosing a rug was simple – there were night rugs, day rugs, summer sheets and New Zealand rugs and, with minor variations of colour and fabric pattern, that was it. Now, in spite of the revolution in the textiles used for horse clothing, traditional rugs and fabrics are still available and in use, and still have good points even though they have been updated. There is probably nothing so smart and luxurious as a top quality woollen day rug, bound in a toning or contrasting colour, with the owner's initials set diagonally across the back near-side corner – or the family crest, or even the horse's name, to make a nice change. For night-wear the woollen day rug is too good to risk getting heavily soiled, and the sturdy, cheap jute rug used heretofore, usually wool-lined and bound in cotton, is still serviceable. Not so long ago, better-class night rugs were made of sailcloth or even lightweight canvas and had smart checked wool linings instead of the plain grey; indeed these are still readily available and used today.

The summer sheet was designed with the intention of keeping dust and flies off groomed, stabled horses; they still come in cotton, and the better quality linen ones in houndstooth check, Prince of Wales check or tartan patterns; again, they can be bound and initialled. And as regards turnout rugs (usually called 'New Zealand' but rarely of the true New Zealand pattern), it is probably true to say that the traditional style rugs are, even now, more common than the new synthetic ones.

However, traditional fabrics have their drawbacks. They are a good deal heavier than most modern textiles and are certainly much more difficult to launder. For example, it was always considered *de rigeur* to have woollen day rugs dry cleaned, a process which involved having all leather fittings (usually the breast strap and possibly wither reinforcing strips) removed by the saddler so that the dry cleaning fluid did not ruin them, and resewn in place after cleaning. This is not common practice today, I am sure!

Night rugs constructed of traditional fabrics have always brought certain problems. Again they have leather fittings, but the main difficulty concerns the two main fabrics used – jute (or sailcloth) and pure wool. These materials require quite different washing methods if they are to be rendered clean but also maintained in good condition: namely, if you wash jute in water hot enough to clean it of 'biological stains' like droppings and urine, the wool lining will mat and shrink disastrously, this will affect the lie of the rug, and it may go into holes. On the other hand, warm water which suits the wool will never get the outer fabric clean, or at least stain-free. Furthermore when wet, these rugs are very heavy and cumbersome and take a long time to dry, particularly if your washing machine isn't big enough to spin them in first. The old way of washing them was in the bath or tub – with washing soda, too – which also meant that to dry them, you first had to let them drip over a fence, gate or wall (weather permitting and if you had nowhere under cover), and then progress to, hopefully, a rack high up in a warm tack room or kitchen.

To provide extra warmth, woollen blankets of various qualities were worn under day and night rugs, two thin ones being warmer than one thick one. This is still common practice, and the thinner type of blanket used is usually of grey, sometimes beige wool, whilst the top quality ones are of the Witney style, rich, mid-yellow with black and red stripes, and of very thick luxurious wool. Blankets come in various sizes: when buying, simply give the size of the rug the blanket is to go under, and you should get one to fit. They are just like household blankets – rectangular wool pieces with blanket-stitching along the short edges to prevent fraying. It is therefore useful to remember how to do blanket stitch for small running repairs, as continuing use will nearly always result in the stitching coming undone!

Summer sheets have always been easier to deal with, but many still have leather fittings which, again, are supposed to be removed before washing or cleaning; though most people don't bother these days, particularly if they have been able to get a rug with washable leather, like the washable suede patches on modern breeches and jodhpurs. Whilst on the subject of maintenance, I remember one old house I used to visit as a child where there was a regular and continuing dispute between the stud groom and the housekeeper throughout the summer and autumn over whose job it was to iron (immaculately) the horses' linen summer sheets. The housekeeper usually won, and the stud groom was obliged to do this 'cissy' job.

the tartan. For example, a green tartan with the occasional yellow or red line running through will look good with either matching green, black (present in most tartans), yellow or red for the binding.

Prince of Wales check patterns also look good in horse rugs but here your colour choice is much more limited; grey or muted brown are the most common colours used, with darker grey or dark brown binding.

It is usual to have the owner's initials or even the horse's name in lettering to match the binding.

In these days of sponsorship, it is common for sponsored horses to bear their sponsor's logos or team name and copyrighted trade marks on their rugs or exercise sheets. This is understandable but, again, smacks of 'uniform' and I should like to see some system whereby the horse's individuality could also be taken into account.

Modern textiles

Probably the biggest revolution in horse clothing has concerned the vast and undreamed of improvements in the textiles used, a revolution which is also now affecting numnahs, saddle pads and cloths, and girths. When the Lavenham Rug Company first introduced their quilted nylon rug in the 1960s many people threw up their hands in horror (just as they did later over rubber riding boots) and swore the horses would sweat to death in them, despite the claims of the company and the results of its private trials. Of course it was a fairly reasonable criticism, nylon being non-absorbent and 'non-breatheable', as anyone who used to wear Bri-Nylon shirts or blouses would confirm; but in practice the new rugs have never caused sweating – or rather, prevented its evaporation – and, very gradually, have gained acceptance: today they are still among the best sellers, along with various improvements.

The most significant of today's horse-rug textiles are the permeable ('breatheable') sort, and the heat-retaining ones; both of these are catching on, although they are still not properly understood. In all truth, anyone who launches anything new into the horse world, particularly the British horse world, is very brave, as it takes a long time to become accepted, let alone established; there are so many people of conservative, even purist belief who seem automatically to 'knock' anything new. However, those who have tried the better modern rugs cannot possibly knock them, with their improved horse-friendly designs and owner/groom-friendly textiles. Turn-out rugs – otherwise known as New Zealand rugs – are the last in the process of being converted to modern synthetic textiles, although there have been many difficulties with these: rugs that have 'leaked' and have had to be sent back to the retailer or manufacturer time and again, problems concerning reproofing them after laundering – even in developing synthetic textiles which would stand up to the very rough treatment that turn-out rugs are habitually given by their wearers. All these are being largely overcome, however, so this last remaining bastion of traditionalism will probably soon be breached.

As regards turn-out rugs, there can be no doubt at all that a soaking wet 'traditional' canvas rug is an extremely uncomfortable, stiff, heavy thing for a horse to have to tolerate for maybe twenty-four hours a day, week after week, in the course of a typically wet, windy, cold British winter. True, such a rug is probably changed, and dried and cleaned up at least partially whilst its replacement undergoes the same treatment on the horse: but a canvas rug is what it is, and the horse gets no real relief, particularly in wet weather. This is where the lightweight, tough synthetics will come into their own, once fully accepted. Even when wet (and some of them shrug off the water so they never actually become soaked) they are a fraction of the weight of the canvas ones, and laundering them is so easy. Even when thoroughly mud-coated and soaking wet, a synthetic turn-out rug can be removed at tea-time yet is ready to put back on next morning if there is somewhere reasonably warm to dry it overnight – a boon for horses who spend every day in the field.

Nowadays indoor rugs are defined as 'stable' rugs, rather than as 'day' or 'night' rugs, because the modern textiles are so easy to launder – a night spent rolling around in fresh manure and urine doesn't matter. These permeable fabrics mean that the 'body atmosphere' (in the words of one manufacturer) can be more healthily maintained: in other words, the sweat which the horse is

Quilted nylon stable rug with wide self-fabric girth for extra warmth, attached on elasticated straps which do make for extra comfort. The fillet string attachment can be seen. The rug is correctly shaped along the back seam and in practice these rugs work well

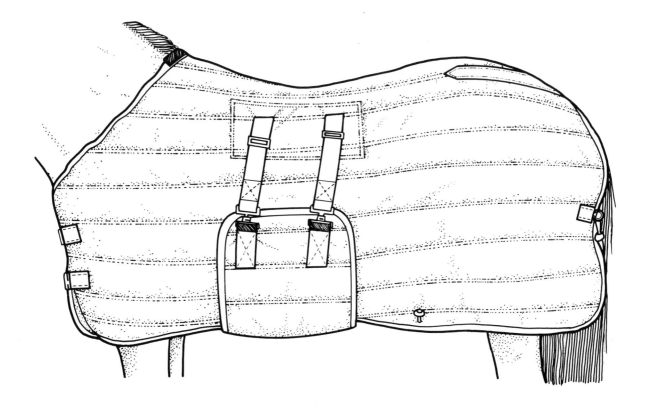

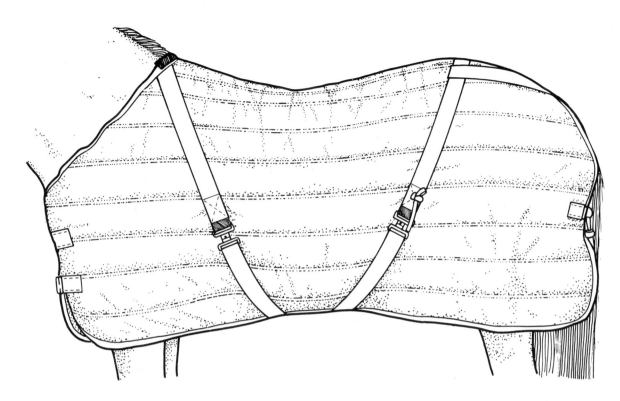

Quilted nylon stable rug with crossing surcingles. Well shaped, these rugs are light, warm, comfortable and normally stay well in place

giving off all the time (even though we don't notice it) can rise up through the rug, and maybe its under-rug if worn, and evaporate into the outside environment much more easily than if the horse were enveloped in woollen clothing and, in particular, close-woven sailcloth. Jute is not so bad because at least it has a looser weave; but it still has a woollen lining.

A horse which 'breaks out' in a cold sweat, usually after work, can be a problem. Sometimes this is a sign of bad management, in that insufficient time has been spent walking him round and cooling him off after work. Now, these horses can have a permeable fabric rug put on, and however much they break out they will not become cold and clammy if their human connections have failed to check them and walk them round till they were dry. Of course, these rugs are not intended to make up for poor care, but the fact is that such things can, and do happen.

These rugs are also very useful when horses come home wet with rain, or have been shampooed, as they can be put straight on and there is no need for thatching – the horse will dry off well and safely underneath without risk of clamminess or retention of moisture; his own body temperature will keep him warm, and will dry off any moisture present in the rug. In practice they work wonderfully well.

Heat-retaining textiles are not always permeable as well, although some are. Their biggest boon is that even a real cold fish of a horse no longer has to be swathed in numerous woollen blankets under his rug to keep him warm. Just one of the better heat-retaining rugs will keep him as warm as a 'traditional' rug and two thin conventional blankets; and if further warmth is needed, under-rugs are available which clip into the top rug or fasten in with Velcro. Indeed, some rugs have inter-changeable linings of various synthetic fabrics, most of them acrylic or polyester-based, which can be changed to suit different

㉓ A polo pony wearing the type of equipment typical in this discipline today – a breastgirth, a standing martingale attached to a cavesson noseband, a drop noseband and a gag snaffle bridle. The pony is also wearing running reins for extra control. The legs are protected by bandages.

extremes of temperature: as the temperature rises or drops, a lining of a different type or weight can be simply clipped in, to cater for the horse's changing requirements.

Many synthetic rugs are advertised as being able to 'wick' away moisture from the horse's coat. To date there does not seem to be an 'official' definition of the word 'wick'; nevertheless, the meaning is that the fabric draws moisture away from the coat and through the rug to the surrounding air, where it evaporates – the same system, in fact, as rugless sweating: the fabrics apparently do not simply absorb and hold the moisture, they actually get rid of it. Again, they do work in practice; and as might be expected of a textile with these qualities, they are much easier to launder (see Chapter 8, p191).

A problem can occur with some heat-retaining fabrics, however, and not all manufacturers warn purchasers of it: if you stand a horse in a heat-retaining rug in a box with an infra-red heater on, you can virtually cook him! As the horse warms up, the heat cannot escape and the skin can become badly burned under the rug – it is certainly a point to watch. If there is any doubt as to the exact qualities of the textile from which a rug is made, contact the maker, not simply the retailer who may not be equipped to advise you correctly. It is not worth taking chances when the horse's health may be at risk.

Rug designs

Most of the rugs which come in the new textiles seem to have good design qualities, unlike many of those in traditional, natural fabrics, although there are exceptions. Should the chance arise to study horse clothing of forty or fifty years ago or more (and some does still exist, even if it is not in regular use), you may notice that there is only the occasional concession for the shape of the horse's back – a slight upturn at the withers and a downturn towards the root of the tail, but this is usually all. Even today, many items of traditional character are cut with no regard whatsoever for the horse's shape. When a rug is folded lengthways in two and laid out, it can be seen that the seam running down the back is cut in a straight line. Also, the seams and the neckline are reinforced with firmly stitched-on binding and have no give in them whatsoever. This means that when these rugs are put on the horse they inevitably cause considerable pressure on the withers and, to a lesser extent, the points of hip and croup. The point of the shoulder, too, comes in for a good deal of rubbing: towards the end of the winter, the shoulders of horses who have spent months in such clothing are usually almost or completely bare. The quality of the cloth, too, is generally not as good nowadays.

Another drawback with all traditional-style clothing (except some of that made very recently) is the method of securing it on the horse's body. Invariably either a separate rug roller is needed which goes round the horse's girth like a belt round his ribcage, or there will be a relatively narrow web surcingle sewn on to the rug. The roller sometimes has a breastgirth in an attempt to stop it slipping backwards with the rug; it is certainly the better of two unsatisfactory methods. The roller will have a padded section on the part which touches the horse's back, with a space between the two pads intended to accommodate the

24 A quilted synthetic stable rug, well shaped and with surcingles crossing under the horse's belly. Their points of attachment to the rug ensure even tension and, together with the rug's shaping, will ensure that it stays on and in place well. Details from Hydrophane Laboratories Limited (address, p195).

25 This is a good example of a well-designed traditional-type turn-out rug. Although marketed as the Lansdown New Zealand (and an 'All Season' version with detachable synthetic or woollen extra lining), it actually uses the Australian type of foreleg straps passing from the breast, between the forelegs and passing up the sides of the rug to clip on just below the hip. There is a fillet strap behind the thighs. The rug is well shaped with pleats below the shoulders for freedom of movement. It is made of rip-stop polyester cotton with a 'weather-guard' strip along the back seam, and also has quarter darting, with an overlapping front with woollen fleece lining. The rest of the rug can be lined with a synthetic Flectalon or woollen fabric.

26 An extra-deep New Zealand canvas rug with co-ordinating neck hood overlapping the neckline of the rug, preventing water seeping underneath it and causing discomfort and rubbing; wet skin being more prone to friction and pressure injuries than dry skin.

The extra depth makes the rug useful in windy weather and for horses who are particularly susceptible to the cold.

27 Lansdown also make this ingeniously designed quarter rug which can be fitted and removed without having to remove the saddle. The rug fits behind the saddle and covers the quarters. There is a cut-out shape which enables it to fit just underneath the rear edges of the saddle and there are loop fastenings which go round the girth on both sides to keep the rug in place.

There are two types of quarter rug in this design – one is filled with the thermal material Flectalon and has an outer cover of showerproof polycotton. The second is of waterproof rubberised cotton with a cellular cotton lining. Because the rug is so easy to put on and remove, it is convenient both for use during exercise and as a throwover to keep the quarters warm with no danger of it slipping off.

28

29

Training aids

From time to time something apparently revolutionary comes on to the equine market and undergoes all the usual criticism common to most new inventions. Although a book cannot hope to be newsworthy in the same way as a magazine, we are pleased to give details here of two new developments in the schooling aids field which seem to be successful in practice as well as sounding good in theory.

Any schooling aid, of course, should be used as a means to an end, and if it helps the horse understand what we want, and encourages him to go in a way which is ultimately easier for him and enables him to do the work we ask in a correct way, the aid can surely only be beneficial.

Time will tell whether any particular piece of equipment will be given a permanent place in a humane horseman's repertoire: the two items detailed here seem worthy of consideration.

---

(28) The Schoolmasta training aid. It comprises a cotton numnah with a little pulley wheel at the withers on each side and a cord running through which is attached to reins clipped to each bit ring. It is recommended for strong or green horses or ponies inclined to lean on the bit or pull. When the horse is working in a correct outline, giving to the bit, the device takes no effect but if he starts to lean or pull, to take hold or poke his nose, the Schoolmasta's effect is felt and the horse, realising he is only pulling against himself, quickly stops pulling. The rider does not have to cope with the horse's actions and can maintain a light, sensitive contact on the bridle reins. Depending on the rider's skill, this helps him or her to maintain a balanced seat in the saddle and to concentrate on effective sympathetic riding.

The Schoolmasta is 'designed to assist the rider in improving the control, obedience and general way of going of all horses and ponies starting from initial breaking through all levels of training to top competition standard'. It is completely independent of the rider's hands and is said to induce a good head carriage, correct outline and to lighten and 'lift' the horse's forehand which helps improve collection, balance and movement whilst still maintaining suppleness and the ability to bend. Although looking rather like side-reins, the device is less restricting and is also available as a breaking roller. Details from Masta Horse Clothing Co, Ltd. (address, p195).

(29) In these days of increasing interest in true classical equitation with its emphasis on lightness and an ultimate weight-of-the-rein contact, a schooling aid which appears deliberately to put weight on the bit may seem a little incongruous at first sight, but users report that on careful study of the principles behind it and having regard of the 'proof of the pudding' – the way the horse goes wearing the device – this device teaches lightness and acceptance of the bit, plus correctly developing the horse's way of going and his physique and topline.

The Equi-Weight consists of a weight (three different weights are available) which clips to the bit rings and is used when the horse is lunged, long-reined or loose-schooled. It has no direct attachment to the trainer and was particularly designed to aid less-than-expert trainers get correct results from their horses more quickly. To quote from the detailed instruction booklet supplied with Equi-Weight:

'Equi-Weight is a scientifically designed device that is attached to the horse's bit and substitutes for the weight of a rider's hands transmitted through the reins to the bit. It has a calming effect, making the horse easier to handle; but just as importantly, its influence through the neck and spinal vertebrae and the horse's musculature is to encourage the correct movement of the rear legs, to build up the topline, to reduce unnecessary muscle below the neck and to open the shoulder blades – all of which considerably improve the horse's going and carrying capacity when ridden. Hitherto, dramatic improvements in these areas could result only from very skilled riding by professionals. Now, Equi-Weight gives all horse owners the potential means to achieve excellent results, very safely, and in a much shorter time.'

Poll pressure is created which requests the horse to lower his head and neck, thus making it easier and more comfortable for him to swing his back and thrust forward from his hind legs. The horse quickly learns that by going in this manner and giving his lower jaw to the steady bit contact he relieves himself of bit pressure and accepts and carries the bit easily. Because there is no backward force on reins and no erratic contact from a rider, the horse trusts the bit and the contact and learns to go confidently and freely in a calm state of mind wearing the Equi-Weight during non-ridden work. No resistances are produced as the weight does not restrict the use of the horse's head and neck for balance. Use of the device enables the trainer to build up the horse's physique and to further his training considerably before mounted work is undertaken.

Any fears that the weight will teach the horse to go on the forehand seem to be unfounded in practice as horses seem to learn quickly that they cannot try to lean on the bit as they might where reins were used: leaning creates an imbalance which the horse has to correct by bringing his hind legs further forward beneath his body.

The horse is prepared for lungeing in the normal way and has his lungeing cavesson fitted over a snaffle bridle with a German Nathe bit or a vulcanite or rubber snaffle. The retaining clips and chain on the weight are adjusted so that it fits as closely to the jaw bone as possible. Initially, as with any new piece of equipment, the horse has to get used to the feel of the weight and may raise his head or shake it or carry it in unusual ways until he works out what the weight does and what he can do with it. This stage soon passes as the horse becomes accustomed to it and learns that what we term the correct position of head and neck is the most comfortable for him.

Once the horse has become established in his work side-reins can be fitted, if desired, during lunge work. If the horse is to be loose-schooled in his Equi-Weight he wears a normal bridle and noseband with Equi-Weight clipped to the bit rings, although it is quite permissible to work him in a lungeing cavesson if the two types of work are being combined in one lesson. Experienced horses can be safely jumped loose wearing the Equi-Weight.

Equi-Weight comes in three weight sizes according to the type and stage of training of the animal involved. Size 1 is for general use with horses and ponies up to 14.2hh and for the aerobic exercise of horses over that height. Size 2 is for general use with animals from 14.2hh to 17hh and Size 3 is for very large and particularly difficult horses. Sizes 1 and 2 comprise the Standard Equi-Weight Pack A for horses between 14.2hh and 17hh and Sizes 2 and 3 comprise Standard Pack B for horses over 17hh. All sizes can be purchased separately. The need for different sizes is explained in the detailed instruction booklet supplied with Equi-Weight which says:

'The different sizes correspond broadly to how much weight in the hand a rider would have. A child would take a contact of around 2 to 2.5lb in each hand and a man on a large horse 3.5 to 4lb in each hand. This, of course, only until a horse carries himself in balance and becomes light to the rider's aids, which will happen when the horse has learned to carry Equi-Weight correctly. This improvement will then be found to exist when the horse is ridden.'

Full details of Equi-Weight can be obtained from Carin Newman (address, p195).

spine and keep it free of pressure from the roller. Often, however, the pads are too close together and the spine is subjected to a certain degree of pressure. There is also the anti-cast roller, designed along similar lines but made in two completely separate parts joined together with a leather-covered and very strong metal arch over the spine. This does remove pressure altogether from the spine itself, but it is often overlooked that every time the horse rolls wearing such a roller he inevitably jabs himself in the back, bruising the very muscles which bear the saddle and weight of the rider.

The sewn-on surcingle is an even less satisfactory method, often completely ineffective because it allows the rug to slip back and round, and more significantly, because it *does* cause considerable and direct pressure on the spine. Some manufacturers try to mollify customers by sewing a length of sheepskin under the surcingle inside the rug, a practice which in fact does not reduce pressure one iota!

Both roller and surcingle, and particularly the surcingle, have to be fastened fairly tightly to keep the clothing in place, although certainly not as tight as a saddle girth. It should be fairly easy to slide the flat of the fingers down the horse's side under the roller or surcingle, and pull it away from the ribcage a little. Even so, when the horse lies down his trunk will inevitably expand somewhat, and it is not always appreciated that the roller/surcingle will then

A traditional rug with simply a surcingle, not even a padded roller, 'securing' it. This type of fastening is uncomfortable for the horse; it causes direct pressure on the spine and is very ineffective at keeping the rug in place. The rug itself fits well and is shaped along the spine

almost certainly become uncomfortably tight. Furthermore, because the rugs have no real shaping, they still tend to slip round and slide backwards and this creates another damaging and extremely uncomfortable situation for the horse: pressure on the sensitive withers. I have seen horses with withers bruised by their rugs to the extent that they could not wear a saddle (even though the saddle did not touch the withers). Again, sheepskin sewn inside the withers does nothing to lessen pressure. Sometimes the horse suffers no more than rubbed hair and seems to escape withers actually rubbed sore – but this is still a sign of friction and pressure where it simply should not be, and indicates the sort of outfit which must be significantly uncomfortable for the horse. Bear in mind that he will be wearing it for about twenty-two hours of each day for several months; also that he may have to wear a similarly designed summer sheet at other times, and maybe an equally badly designed turn-out rug in the field, and you will appreciate that he will be in constant discomfort: hardly good horse management. So many people simply do not equate rug friction and pressure with that from a saddle under the weight of a rider, but the effect on the horse is the same: a saddle is worn for a much shorter period of time, but the pressure, where it exists, is much more intense than that caused by a roller; but a rug which has slipped out of position and is held tightly there by a roller or surcingle can do just as much damage by being present over a longer period.

Modern rug shaping

Nowadays, however, a horse should not have to put up with this sort of thing at all: modern, well-designed rugs have virtually none of these problems – but how do they differ? For a start, the textiles from which they are made are very much lighter in weight; but probably the most significant improvements are that they are 'horse-shaped', designed to fit the shape of the horse's body in the same way as tailored human clothing; and also their fastening methods avoid the round-the-girth tightness and pressure altogether.

Take a well-designed, modern rug, and as before, fold it lengthways (along the back seam) and lay it out on the floor: you will see that the back seam follows the shape of a horse's back very well. It rises in line with the withers, dips for the back, rises again to allow for the croup, and dips again towards the root of the tail. In addition, the darts or tucks on the bottom edge at elbow and stifle create shape and room for the protrusions of shoulder and hip. There should be more darts round the neckline to create additional shape and room for the shoulders; also round the back edge to define the room needed for the hip and rounded shape of the quarters. These are the essential design elements of a good, modern horse rug as regards shaping. Horses are not flat!

Modern rug fastenings

The improvement in the method of keeping that rug on the horse is just as significant. The old-fashioned, uncomfortable and restrictive roller/surcingle

Improving badly designed rugs

You can improve a badly designed rug with a surcingle (girth-type). Taking care not to pierce the outer covering if it is a turn-out rug, sew four pieces of thick, old-fashioned numnah felt (obtainable from similarly good old-fashioned saddlers) to the lining.

Position these on either side of the back seam where the highest point of the withers goes, and also on either side at the back area directly under the surcingle. Leave about a couple of inches (4cm) between them to create a channel of space. The felt should be at least an inch (2cm) thick and will raise the rug off withers and spine and 'wedge' the rug in place, greatly improving its effectiveness and the horse's comfort. A saddler would probably add elbow and stifle darts for you, in which case you could probably remove the surcingle.

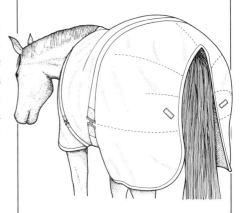

Back view of a modern rug, showing shaping seams and darts round the buttocks for a cosy fit

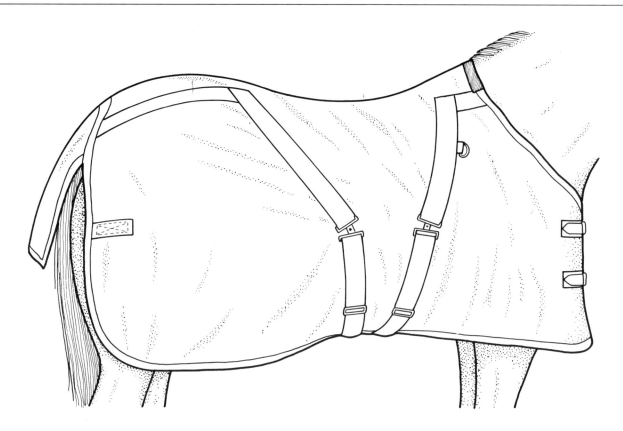

This **turn-out rug** has a tail flap at the back which helps protect the sensitive rear end against heat loss from wind and weather. This is a definite advantage for horses which are extensively clipped and/or have pulled tails. It has clip on, crossing surcingles and two breast straps to allow for finer fit adjustments

has been abandoned and in its place are leg straps or a complete under-harness which help to keep the rug in place and – just as important – do not prevent its returning to the correct position after the horse has rolled or been lying down and gets up. The main point about the shaping is that because the rug conforms to the horse's body, it has a self-righting or self-correcting quality the old rugs could not have. The rug is designed to position itself in the correct place on the horse, and when he shakes and moves it automatically settles in the right place – as long as it is fastened on loosely enough to permit this. This is the key: the new-style fastenings must be fitted closely but loosely so that the rug is free to move back where it belongs. You should be able to fit the width of your hand between the surcingle, strap or harness and the horse.

A very common method is to use surcingles perhaps just two or three inches wide (depending on the make) which criss-cross under the belly. These may be sewn to the rug at one end and clip on further back to an integral dee, or they may have dees front and back and be completely detachable. They normally fasten, or are sewn, somewhere behind the elbow a little way up the rug, and clip on to another dee on the other side of the horse, a little below the hip; thus the right surcingle fastens on the left side and vice versa, so they exert a complimentary, opposing pull on the rug which helps it right itself.

The rug may have straps after the Australian style: these fasten on the front of the rug at the breast, pass between the forelegs and clip to dees in front of the stifle, with a fillet string behind the thighs under the tail to stabilise the back part of the rug. Or a rug may have New Zealand-type hindleg straps instead of or as well as the foreleg straps described. Some makes of rug employ yet another fastening method, an under-belly harness which is secured to both front and back of the rug.

All these new-style fastenings are far and away superior to the now outdated roller/surcingle method. As there is nothing passing round the girth there is no more pressure on the spine at all, and because of the lightness of the fabric and the improved shaping, pressure on the withers is very greatly lessened.

What happens if a blanket is required under one of these new rugs? Firstly, most of them are so much warmer than traditional rugs that this may well not be necessary. Secondly, if it is, many manufacturers make their own complimentary under-rugs, often fleecy but not always, which clip into the top rug, as already mentioned, so the problem of a separate blanket does not arise.

There is another intermediate type of fastening which is perfectly satisfactory but not as good as the cross-surcingle method and those like it. This is a wide surcingle, usually of the same fabric as the rug – for example quilted nylon – with elastic inserts into its nylon web, which fastens under the belly. This brings the rug snugly round the ribcage but without creating significant pressure on the spine. Another make has a very wide wrap, also of the same fabric as the rug, and which covers the whole belly area; this is intended for extra warmth, and is a design which also works well in practice.

So, to summarise: with the new designs and fastenings, all of which are very readily available, there is now no need, nor is there any excuse for heavy clothing, or for rubbed withers and spine, slipped rugs (which are dangerous as well as ineffective), or stifling pressure from a round-the-ribcage roller or surcingle. Horses, if they experience gratitude and could understand, must be eternally grateful for these latter-day improvements in their wardrobe! However, it is a sad fact – to my mind, at least – that not only are the bad, old-style rugs still being made, but people are still buying them! I hope the move to the more humane type – because that is what they are – will take place more quickly than so many of the other changes in the horse world.

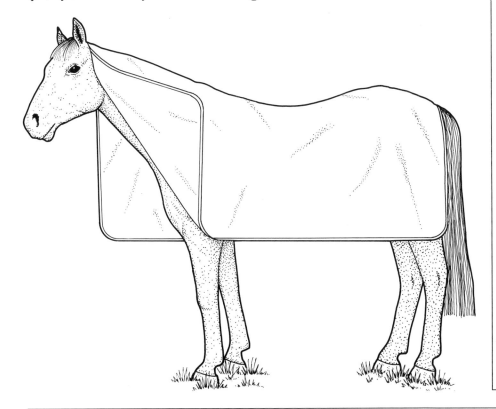

Blanket riding

Bareback riding is not really the aid to developing a secure, 'natural' seat it is often imagined to be.

The skin of a healthy horse's back and sides is quite flexible. If the rider holds on in the belief that this will help her stability she will find that the skin wobbles and moves around under her legs most unhelpfully.

In addition, most horses in healthy condition (that is, not fat) have spines which protrude somewhat — *extremely* uncomfortable to sit on! And there is also the problem of the withers, which the rider will frequently bump against.

Far more comfortable, conducive to relaxed riding and, therefore, to the development of a deep, secure seat, is blanket riding. A blanket is usually folded into a square and placed over the horse's back, and secured by a wide roller. There are no stirrups, and no relatively rigid saddle between the rider and the horses back, but the blanket does not slide around and offers some comfort and security.

Using a blanket: when using a traditional rug with a blanket underneath, place the blanket lengthwise on the horse, like this, and turn up the front corners to the neck. The rug is then put on and the blanket 'point' folded back over the withers part of the rug. It should be long enough for the roller to be put on over the blanket which helps secure it; blankets are notorious for slipping back and off from under rugs. It is particularly important with this arrangement to make sure the blanket is as smooth as possible under the rug, with few bulky golds or creases. Once the roller is in place you should be able to slide the flat of your fingers easily between it and the rug. Grasp the bottom edge in front of the roller and give it a little pull forward to release pressure on the shoulders; do this on both sides

Opposite: These **turn-out rugs** are shaped around the back seam but have nothing else to recommend them. There is no shaping around the neckline or at the elbow or stifle. Worst of all they have an uncomfortable and ineffective surcingle which attempts to secure them onto the horse. This will cause considerable spinal pressure, will not keep the rugs in place and will in fact keep them *out* of place when they slip or are pulled round when the horse lies down or rolls

Turn-out rug with tough rip-stop synthetic outer cover and under-belly crossing surcingles. The rug is well shaped along the back seam and would also have a fillet string or strap at the back to prevent its blowing up in the wind and frightening the horse

Turn-out rugs

New Zealand or turn-out rugs of good design have, in fact, had hindleg straps and shaping for a few generations. The true New Zealand rug is so called because it was invented in that country, where the climate is similar but slightly milder than ours, and horses live out much more. It has an undulating back seam, is shaped at the stifle and sometimes at the elbow, and has either darts or, more effectively, a drawstring inside the back edge which can be adjusted for a truly personalised fit. Made of heavyweight, waterproof canvas with leather breast straps and leg straps, it has stood the test of time and is still marketed and sold in several countries. However, there is no denying that these rugs are appallingly heavy when wet. They have a half-lining of wool (a full lining down to the bottom edge would easily allow damp to creep up inside) and certainly keep a horse warm, dry and cosy; but in my experience the weight is a disadvantage.

The new-style shaping and improved fastening methods, however, are available on many good new synthetic turn-out rugs, together with the same sort of variations as described for stable rugs. Furthermore, special expanding yarns have been devised for the stitching: these swell when wet to fit the needle holes, and so preclude leakage; and reproofers are available for post-laundering treatment. (Both synthetic and traditional turn-out rugs need reproofing from time to time.)

The Australian rug intended for outdoor wear has the foreleg type of fastening described earlier and in my opinion is not quite so effective as the New Zealand type. It has a fillet strap rather than hindleg straps.

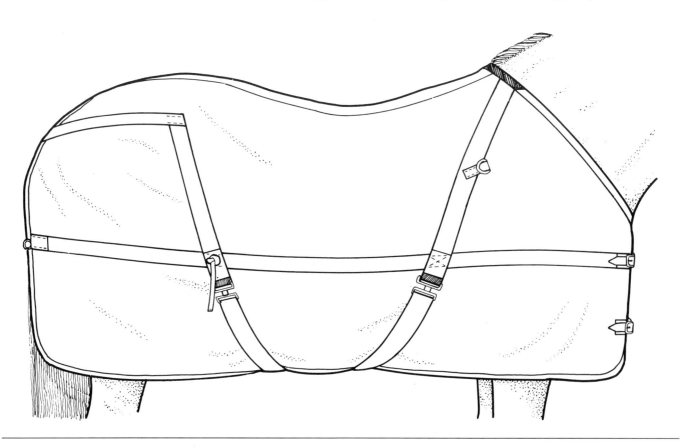

Synthetic rugs have nylon or polyethylene webbing straps and surcingles, with various patented clips and buckle-type fastenings. Sometimes the plastic 'buckles' break too easily, but again, in the best rugs these problems are being overcome.

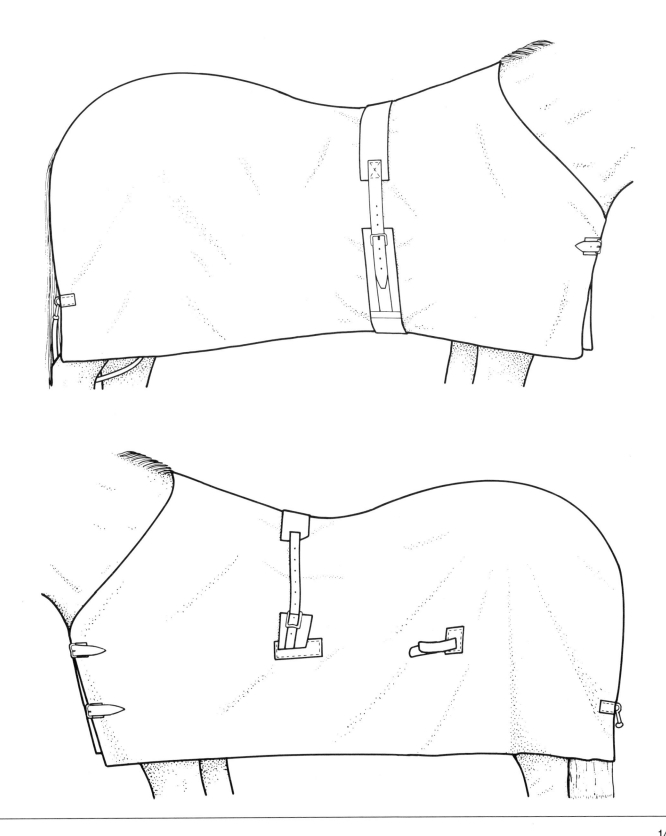

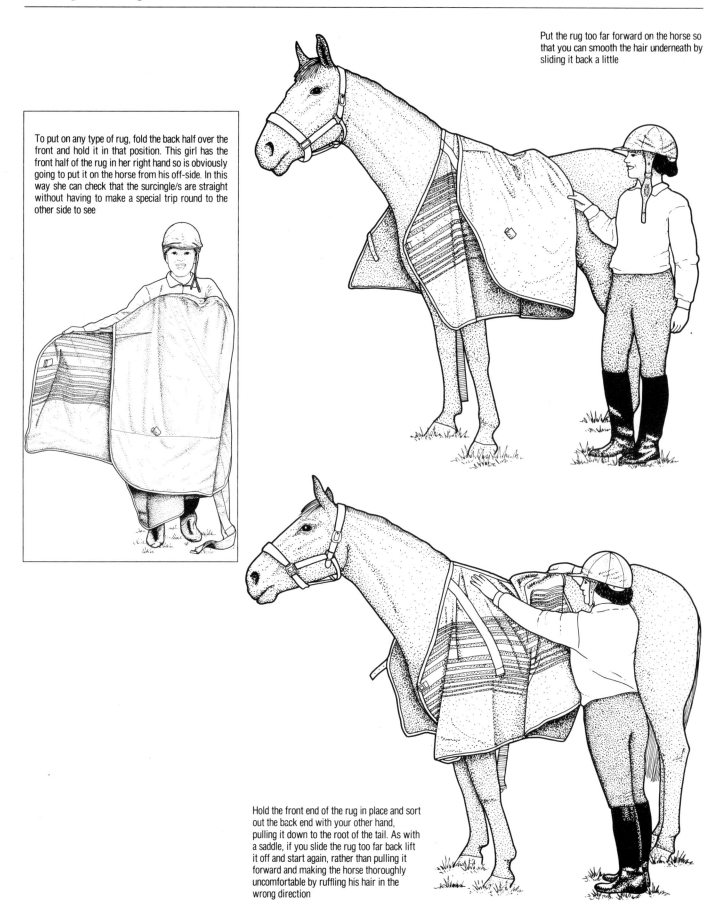

Put the rug too far forward on the horse so that you can smooth the hair underneath by sliding it back a little

To put on any type of rug, fold the back half over the front and hold it in that position. This girl has the front half of the rug in her right hand so is obviously going to put it on the horse from his off-side. In this way she can check that the surcingle/s are straight without having to make a special trip round to the other side to see

Hold the front end of the rug in place and sort out the back end with your other hand, pulling it down to the root of the tail. As with a saddle, if you slide the rug too far back lift it off and start again, rather than pulling it forward and making the horse thoroughly uncomfortable by ruffling his hair in the wrong direction

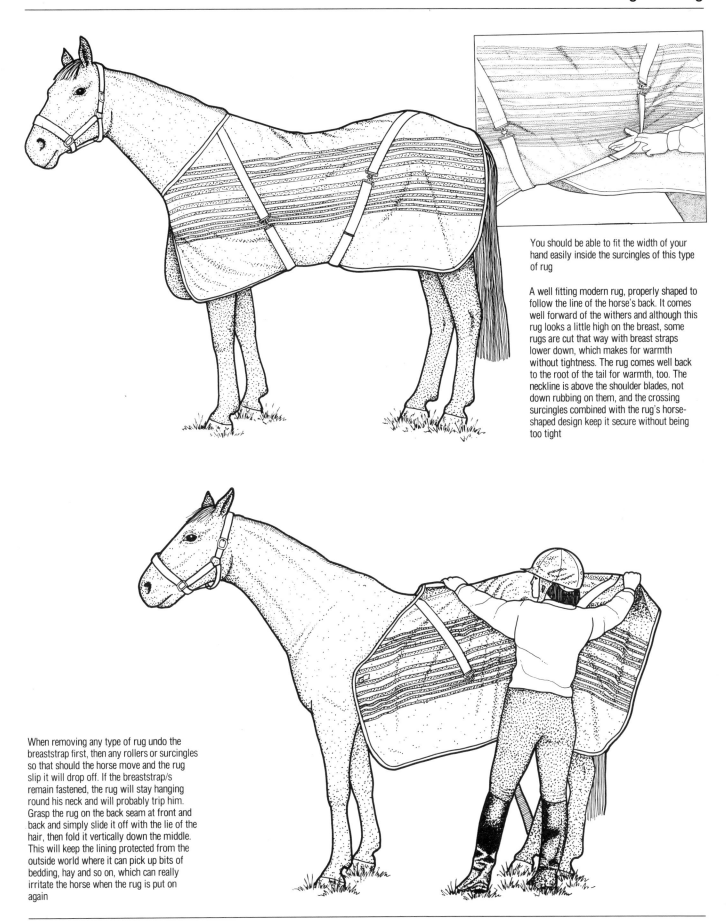

You should be able to fit the width of your hand easily inside the surcingles of this type of rug

A well fitting modern rug, properly shaped to follow the line of the horse's back. It comes well forward of the withers and although this rug looks a little high on the breast, some rugs are cut that way with breast straps lower down, which makes for warmth without tightness. The rug comes well back to the root of the tail for warmth, too. The neckline is above the shoulder blades, not down rubbing on them, and the crossing surcingles combined with the rug's horse-shaped design keep it secure without being too tight

When removing any type of rug undo the breaststrap first, then any rollers or surcingles so that should the horse move and the rug slip it will drop off. If the breaststrap/s remain fastened, the rug will stay hanging round his neck and will probably trip him. Grasp the rug on the back seam at front and back and simply slide it off with the lie of the hair, then fold it vertically down the middle. This will keep the lining protected from the outside world where it can pick up bits of bedding, hay and so on, which can really irritate the horse when the rug is put on again

Comfy rugs

Rugs rubbing the coat are a major reason for tatty looking horses in winter. There is much more to finding a suitable rug than simply getting the size right: style and shape are just as important as correct fit. If a rug rubs it does not fit properly. Any irritation from rubbing, tightness or general discomfort will annoy and distress the horse, as will being too hot. No wonder so many horses are positive Houdinis when it comes to getting out of rugs and so many rip them to shreds in their annoyance. Rugs lying around on the floor or hanging down where they should not are obvious sources of tripping and falling in the box, as are leg straps or harnesses which are too loose. Consideration of these factors is as important as size alone.

It is a good practice to alternate styles of rug on the horse. Rugs of the same make and shape invariably

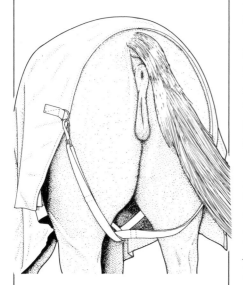

Hindleg straps are normally found mainly on turn-out and New Zealand rugs. Most people find the most effective way of fastening them so that they keep the rug in place without chafing the sensitive skin inside the hind legs is to link them through each other, like this, so that the right strap fastens on the right and vice versa. Each strap holds the other away from the legs.

Fitting a rug

Correct fit is just as important as good design and it is amazing how many horses are standing in rugs which patently do not fit them. Rugs go up in 3in sizes, although some are now sold in metric sizes. To assess the right size for your horse, measure him from the centre of his breast in front, down his side to the back edge of his thigh. The elements of good fit are as follows: first, a rug should come *in front* of the withers at the front and extend right back to the root of the tail. So often rugs are seen resting on top of, or even behind the withers, and finishing halfway up the quarters. This is quite wrong, it must be uncomfortable, and is fairly useless. In depth, the rug should come just below the horse's elbow and stifle; extra-deep rugs, particularly in turn-out styles, are now available as well, designed to minimise the circulation of air (draughts!) under the belly. Then the neckline of the rug should come up to the base of the neck – not be down round the shoulders as is so often seen – and its front must be roomy enough so that there are no creases radiating out from the point of the shoulder; these would indicate pulling and pressure here. With good shaping this is less likely, but it is still important to have the size and roominess. The breaststrap/s must fasten so that the horse can get his head down comfortably to root in his bedding, turn his head and neck right round, or graze (if a turn-out rug) without discomfort and without creating an unreasonable pull on the withers; yet these must also effectively prevent the rug from slipping back, which it will do readily if too big. You should be able to slide your hand easily all round the neckline and over the withers.

If a stable rug has no hindleg straps, there must be a fillet string (usually a braided, coloured cotton cord) which can be fixed one end to each side of the back edge level with the thighs and under the horse's tail, to prevent the back of the rug blowing up and frightening him if he is led about outside.

As a general rule, turn-out and New Zealand rugs should be a slightly roomier fit than stable rugs, and at the back should extend a few inches past the root of the tail for extra protection. Some of the better makes have tail flaps attached at the horse's rear to give protection from the weather: this is a very vulnerable area capable of considerable heat loss, particularly if the horse has a pulled tail. On a normal-depth rug you should only just be able to see the hindleg straps below the bottom edge.

Neck covers and hoods

The horse's neck is also an area of significant heat loss, and neck covers and hoods (for the head) are now available; some neck covers have a head hood combined. Most need to be a complementary part of a particular rug, as they have matching fastenings round the front of the rug a little way back from the neckline to keep the hood in place and prevent rain seeping under the rug's neckline. The hood will also have tapes or straps on the underside to further secure it and keep it in place, albeit fairly loosely; these fasten under the horse's neck. Sometimes, if no head hood is present, they have fastenings to attach to the horse's headcollar: and if a headcollar *is* used for this purpose a browband is essential to keep the whole arrangement in place and fairly comfortable.

At least one brand of neck cover/head hood can be obtained which is made of light stretchy material and fits the horse very closely. The purpose of this particular style is to keep the head, neck and mane free of mud rather than for warmth; not all horses like the close feel of this hood – the usual sort drapes over the neck rather than fitting round it. In the old days, steeplechasers and hunters were travelled in woollen head and neck hoods which matched their travelling/day rugs; however, this practice seems to have gone largely out of fashion.

Exercise clothing

Opinions vary as to the merits of working horses in clothing. Some say, why clip so much if you know it will be necessary; others believe that the horse gets used to clothing when exercising, so that when he actually comes to 'proper' work (hunting, racing and so on) when he won't have his clothing on, he will feel the lack of it and it may affect his health and/or performance. Nevertheless, clothing can be useful in very cold weather for horses who simply hate winter – and many do – and since exercise is normally less strenuous, and therefore heat-making, than actual work, it may not be such a bad idea to exercise these horses in a purpose-made rug.

rub and pull in the same places. Their is less chance of the coat being rubbed if different styles are used, thereby altering the pressure points.

This is particularly valuable if using traditional canvas turn-out rugs which can become very heavy when wet. Horses should really have two rugs so that one can be dried and cleaned up a bit while the other is in use. With heavy rugs, change of style alternately gives the horse a break and a different feel.

Synthetic linings are much gentler on the coat hair than in the past and linings of natural fabrics such as wool, cotton or sheepskin are probably the least likely to cause rubbing. Sheepskin, sheared or not, may be used for lining turnout rugs (particularly round the shoulders) to help lessen friction and rubbing, and old silk scarves do as good a job, better than polyester. Even woollen linings, however, become harsh if dirty, caked with horsehair and grease and not laundered properly.

Clothing is intended to keep the horse warm, not to make him sweat up. Too much clothing can result in over-heated, itchy skin and actual hair loss, and not the desired sleek, flat look. If the horse is pleasantly warm in his body there is no need to put a neck hood on him, unless you wish to keep the area clean. The head and neck take their cue from the body and the hair will remain quite sleek here.

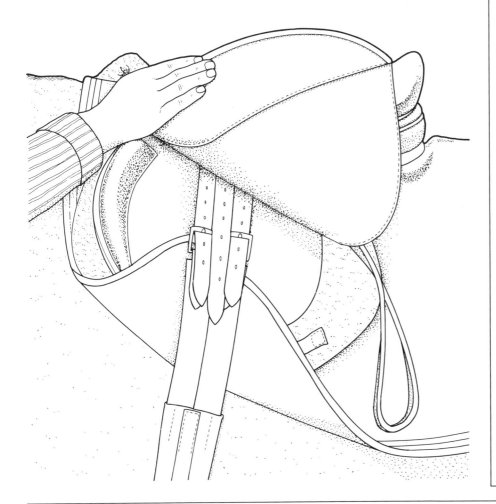

Exercise sheets sometimes have a loop on the bottom edge for the girth to pass through, to keep them in place. If this is absent, just fold up the front corners and secure them under the girth, like this. You can improvise an exercise sheet from an ordinary stable rug by folding up the front parts in this way. Pull the rug well up into the saddle gullet

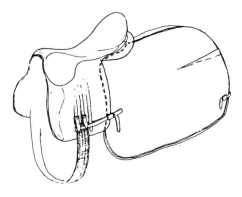

Lansdown quarter rug (see p137). The diagram shows the fitting of the rug.

Thus, the exercise sheet or rug is a rug without the breast part, worn under the saddle with a loop on the bottom edge each side for the saddle girth to pass through to secure it in place, and a fillet string, which is an absolute necessity. They come in traditional wool fabric or in some of the new synthetics, and they are also available in waterproof textiles which is most useful if you don't want your horse to get a soaking during his necessary exercise in wet weather. The Lavenham sheets have a cut-out shape for the saddle and velcro fastenings over the withers so the horse's shoulders are covered as well; other traditional styles do not provide for this.

It is possible to improvise an exercise sheet from an ordinary stable rug by simply folding the breast parts back beneath the saddle flaps and securing them under the girth and girth straps. As with a numnah, a rug or sheet used for exercise should be pulled well up off the withers and spine into the saddle gullet to prevent otherwise considerable pressure once the rider is mounted.

Anti-sweat rugs

A mesh anti-sweat rug. This is normally used alone or under a top rug; if it is used over straw for thatching a surcingle would be needed to ensure it did not slip round, as shown here

Mesh anti-sweat sheets were originally produced in the UK by the Aerborn Rug Company, and are still justifiably popular despite the appearance of permeable rugs. The theory behind them is that, when covered by an ordinary

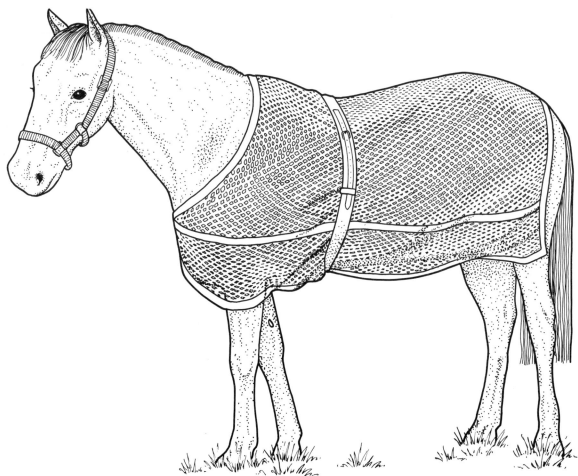

rug or light sheet, their mesh structure maintains an insulating layer of air next to the horse's skin, so helping him to dry off quicker than he would with conventional clothing, and obviating the need for thatching him when he is wet or damp. In fact there is no way an anti-sweat rug can actually *stop* a horse sweating so the name is slightly misleading. However, they do the job of drying a horse very well, and are particularly helpful in yards where straw is no longer used. The makers also suggest they can be used instead of an additional blanket, since they hold an 'extra' layer of body-warmed air next to the horse.

The original intention of the anti-sweat rug was that it should be used under a top covering; those who watch racing may therefore be confused by the sight of these sheets being used on steaming horses without any other rug at all. In practice, it has been found that the mesh creates little currents of air over the surface of the horse which has the effect of drying him off more quickly than if he wore nothing at all. However, anyone who has worn a string vest alone will know that this also makes you feel colder, and in winter, it may not be a good idea to cool a hot 'chaser, hunter or pointer down too quickly in this way, as it will make him feel cold. In summer, or at least in milder weather this may be in order, but not in cold weather.

These rugs should fit like any ordinary rug. Very often they are seen to be much too small for the horse, and do not even cover his quarters.

They can still be useful even when old, stretched and holey, because cut into squares they can be used under leg bandages, where they are most effective in helping to dry wet legs.

Rain sheets

These are lightweight sheets, normally made of proofed or waxed nylon or cotton, and are used to dress a horse in warm weather when you want to turn him out but don't want him to get wet or muddy. If nothing else, they save the horse from the discomfort of wearing a full winter-weight turn-out rug in summer.

American coolers

These are rugs-and-a-bit! Long, deep and lightweight, made of cotton, light wool and synthetic, they tie to the horse's headcollar and cover him from ears to tail and down to knees and hocks. Originally an American idea for cooling off a hot horse in cold weather without chilling, they seem fortunately to be catching on here, to the advantage of British horses. They tie with tapes under the neck and at the breast and are used solely for leading the horse round till he has cooled down; the fact that the neck is also covered is an excellent feature of this rug. Americans often have them made up in their barn (stable) colours, together with their individual logo; perhaps more of this sort of thing will be seen in the UK in due course. Again, a headcollar with a browband is imperative for a cooler.

A quick wash and brush-up!

Putting tack or clothing on top of dried-on sweat and particularly mud is never a good idea. Mud consists of tiny grains of silica or rock and the pressure of tack or clothing on top of such an irritant can soon rub the horse sore.

The new permeable rugs can be put on top of a wet coat and the horse will dry off without the need for thatching. An anti-sweat mesh rug will have the same effect, but although mud will dry it can still cause soreness, as can dried stiff sweat. In addition, both will soon work their way into your blankets or rug linings and either start to rot them (in the case of natural fabrics in contact with dried sweat — a decomposing organic substance) or wear and cut the fabrics in the case of mud grains.

If you belong to the old school of thought which believes you should let mud and sweat dry on before brushing off, at least thatch the horse or put on an anti-sweat rug and brush him clean as soon as possible. If, like me, you believe it is quicker, easier and more comfortable and better for the horse to rinse off the sweat and mud, you can then either thatch him or put on an anti-sweat rug, or put a permeable rug straight on, and let him dry off in comfort and with no danger to his skin or clothing.

Summer coats

Excessive clothing is a common and sad sight in showing stables where the aim is to get a summer coat as soon as possible, preferably in time for the early spring shows. However, it is *lighting* which will mainly achieve this, plus just enough clothing to keep the horse comfortably warm and, of course, correct, not excessive, feeding to simulate the growth of spring grass, increased daylight and warmer temperatures.

The light rays pass through the pupil of the eye and are registered in the brain, which causes hormones to start circulating to prepare the body of the horse (of either sex) for the forthcoming breeding season in nature. Fortunately for us, this works in domesticity as well, and also with geldings! You can take advantage of it as follows.

From Christmas, start leaving the light on in the horse's box in the evenings (a 150 or 200 watt bulb will do) to extend the amount of light falling through the eye to sixteen hours a day. The light must be fairly bright, and it is best to use a full spectrum bulb.

Daylight (known as white light) is made up of all the colours of the rainbow — red, orange, yellow, green, blue, indigo and violet — from the infra-red end to the ultra-violet end of the spectrum. If you spin a disc with portions of these colours marked on it it will appear white, hence the term white light. Most candescent (non-fluorescent) bulbs consist of the red-to-yellow parts of the spectrum while most fluorescent lights consist of the blue-to-violet end. Natural daylight, of course, consists of all of them, but you can mimic this by using full-spectrum bulbs or strips in your boxes. Plant lights such as used in commercial greenhouses and aquaria are ideal.

To rug or not to rug?

An apparently simple decision, yet the question of how much to rug a horse up is one aspect of management where mistakes are often made. The most obvious situation when rugs *should* be used is on a clipped animal in winter, but even then the *amount* of clothing may be hard to decide upon. Normally it is possible to tell whether or not a horse is warm enough, or chilly, or downright cold by simply feeling the base of his ears, his belly, flanks and loins. If they are cold then so is he. Temperature guides are not particularly helpful as horses, like humans, vary widely in their sensitivity to cold; so the individual horse must be the guide. It isn't difficult to recognise the two extremes of temperature: too hot, and a horse will sweat under his rugs; too cold and he will shiver, with or without rugs – but the various degrees in between are a little harder to determine and you simply have to use your common sense.

It is certainly not a case of rugging up a horse, or ceasing to do so, just because a certain date has arrived on the calendar. Once the horse is clipped in the autumn he will need clothing, and the less he is clipped the less clothing and food he will require – and vice versa. Also, the wise horsemaster will use his or her imagination and sensitivity about how much to vary the amount and type of clothing throughout the winter; this will depend not only upon the ambient temperature (that of the surrounding air), but also the 'feel' of the weather. In conditions of a given temperature, horses and humans alike feel much colder on a damp or windy day than on a dry or still one. It is mainly the wind and wet when combined with cold which affects horses adversely, not just cold itself; an unclipped horse can tolerate cold, still, dry weather very well.

An animal's coat may seem to stare (when the hair stands stiffly away from the body) for two reasons: he could be cold, but it is also a sign of illness, and it is important to learn to distinguish the symptoms. If a horse is ill he could look depressed and dopey as well; he might have an abnormal temperature, and betray other physical signs such as patchy sweating or a nasal discharge; if he is out he might well be keeping away from other horses (if he is in a group), or not moving around much at all; or he may be lying down a lot. If he is perfectly healthy but cold, his coat may stare but he will probably seem tensed up (as we are when cold); he might shiver; and although he might look unhappy he will nonetheless be alert and probably eager at the sight of humans who may be coming to bring him in or put more rugs on. If he is out and feeling cold, he might well hang around by the gate hoping to be brought in; or be frequenting his normal shelter areas.

The natural insulating effect of the coat is lost not only when the horse is clipped, but also when the full coat is flattened by rain or sweat. The wet coat clings to the skin, so the heat radiating out from the blood through the skin has little resistance – indeed its outward passage is helped by the moisture, as water is a good conductor of heat, and it escapes all the quicker. The horse loses body heat faster than he can make it up from his inner resources, and can become seriously chilled; furthermore wind, even a slight breeze, will compound the problem and you could soon have a serious case of hyopthermia on your hands – and the weather need not be particularly cold.

Whatever the situation, it pays to watch your horses really carefully. For example, just because you happen to be using a rug and two blankets or under-rugs at Christmas it does not mean that this combination will be appropriate for the rest of the winter, and that you 'must' keep using it until the warm spring weather arrives. On mild winter days your horse could become uncomfortably hot and sweaty dressed like this, and his clothing would well become damp with sweat if it is of the traditional heavy woollen type; moreover as he cools down it will remain damp, and the result later on could be a distinctly chilly horse. So, never be afraid to alter the rugs a horse wears: it is perfectly logical to use more clothing at night than during the day, and to alter it according to the temperature, other climatic conditions and the response of the horse himself.

The question of whether or not to rug up an unclipped horse is one which often causes novices confusion, and not unreasonably so. Some people argue that if an unclipped horse is turned out in a turn-out rug during the day, a stable rug should be put on when he comes in at night as he cannot walk around to keep warm. This is a rather nebulous argument. In an ordinary, well-designed stable there should be no actual draughts to bother him, and if he has a good clean, *dry* bed and a night-long supply of hay, he won't need to walk around very much anyway to keep warm – he will be thoroughly snug even without a rug. Eating creates heat, and one of the best ways of keeping a horse warm is to give him an *ad lib* supply of hay. The energy provided by hay and similar roughages is of the 'slow-release' type which is converted partially to body heat – as opposed to the 'quick boost but soon gone' variety provided by starchy concentrates. By all means feed the horse his largest concentrate feed at night, but not because it will help to keep him warm: for that the horse will need enough hay, hayage or his usual roughage to keep him occupied during the regular eating bouts he likes to enjoy throughout the night and following morning. Ideally there should always be a little hay left when he is seen first thing; this should indicate that not only has he been correctly fed, but also that he has been able to keep his 'central heating' efficiently stoked to withstand even the bitterest of nights.

It is worth remembering that if you put a rug, however light, on an unclipped coat you will flatten it and partly remove the insulating warm-air layer next to the skin; and the heavier the rug the more air-layer you destroy. Thus on a still day it is probably better not to put a turn-out rug on an unclipped horse, except to keep him clean, and then use the lightest rug available. If it is windy and/or wet, however, it is probably best to put a rug on, as the wind and rain, singly or together, will largely nullify the horse's natural protection. In persistently wet weather a waterproof turn-out rug, or simply a lightweight sheet, will keep him dryer and therefore warmer; it can also help to protect against rain-rash.

Horses and ponies with Thoroughbred and/or Arab blood (and also Barbs and Caspians, and horses of any other oriental origin) will need clothing very much more than animals of more northern origins. Thus many of the native and native-type ponies and cobs, and also the British and continental European native horse breeds, are undoubtedly tough enough, if unclipped, not to need rugging up in winter except perhaps in really nasty weather.

A *particularly* unattractive practice in my opinion is to turn out native ponies in the heat of summer all dressed up in heavy New Zealand or other turn-out rugs: this is a very common sight, and people do it, even in dry weather, to

Whatever you use, the brain will record the lengthening daylight, as it sees it, believes it is spring and time for breeding condition to be ordered, which includes the casting of the winter coat and the growth of the short summer one. If you can arrange it with a timer switch, only one extra hour of light between 2am and 3am will do the same trick. However, it is kinder for the horses if the light comes on gradually in the middle of the night — as can be appreciated!

As your horse's coat starts to cast, you will find that his clothing becomes clogged with hairs quickly. The coat grows a little and then casts a little, and it is very tempting to over-groom the horse to get rid of all the loose hair.

You can protect the linings of your rugs or your blankets by putting an old bed sheet underneath his ordinary clothing during this period or a summer sheet.

However, resist the temptation to over-groom as this could result in the coat being lost too quickly and the horse growing a longer and thicker-than-usual summer coat.

keep the animals clean! This is actually just as much bad management as turning them out clipped with no clothing in winter. The poor creatures must be desperately uncomfortable and may become dangerously hot on certain days, possibly even succumbing to hyperthermia or plain heatstroke. This is not an exaggeration. If it is considered absolutely essential to put something on an animal when turned out in summer, the lightest sheet possible should be used and *certainly* not a conventional winter-weight turn-out rug of any kind. Driven frantic from the discomfort, the animal may make desperate attempts to get out of his rug, or start rubbing himself, with all the potential problems that such behaviour brings.

Summer sheets were intended to keep dust and flies off a stabled horse's groomed coat in summer, but in dry weather they can easily be adapted, as long as they are well shaped, for use on animals that are turned out. The summer sheet's cotton or linen fabric, or the modern permeable textiles, will not cause sweating, and any moisture will be able to escape easily. Cross-over under-belly surcingles can be put on, and to some extent such a rug will help to keep biting flies off the horse's body. So, if you really want to rug up your turned-out horse in summer for whatever reason, try this method; and if the idea is to save yourself the work of cleaning him up in warm, wet weather, just use a lightweight, preferably permeable rain-sheet. These are readily available now and ideal for this sort of situation.

Breeding stock is not normally rugged at all, particularly when other youngsters are around, as it is considered far too risky – one more item for young legs to get caught up in. However, some top breeders of 'blood' horses do take the precaution of training their youngsters, from yearlings upwards, to wear New Zealand and other turn-out rugs so they can be left outside longer for essential exercise in winter. There is nothing particularly special about this, nor anything controversial provided the youngsters *are* trained to accept the rugs properly; sometimes mature horses also need this training.

Any rug with surcingles or a harness in unfamiliar places (under the belly, or between forelegs or hindlegs) must be introduced carefully. In the first instance put the rug on in the stable, having made sure it is scrupulously well designed and the right fit, and lead the animal around the box, perhaps with an assistant on the other side. You can then progress to leading him round the yard, and then leave him loose in his box with the rug on, although initially someone should stay around to supervise for a few minutes. Schooled horses can be lunged in their New Zealands, before finally being let loose in a small paddock (so they cannot get up much speed) and ideally with a very quiet companion who won't charge about. From this point, it is no big step to turning them out properly in their normal field with the rug on.

Little foals can be rugged in various types of foal rug; these are really intended for sick foals, or for those which seem thin-skinned and sensitive and are born at an inclement time of the year – for example most Thoroughbreds because of their official 1 January birthday. Invariably it is considered too risky to turn a foal out into a paddock wearing any kind of rug with cross-over surcingles or leg straps. Foal rugs of lightweight quilted synthetic fabrics, with a soft, carefully fitted, round-the-girth surcingle of self-fabric (such as the Lavenham foal rug) are used in certain cases, but experienced breeders' opinions vary on this.

6
PROTECTIVE EQUIPMENT

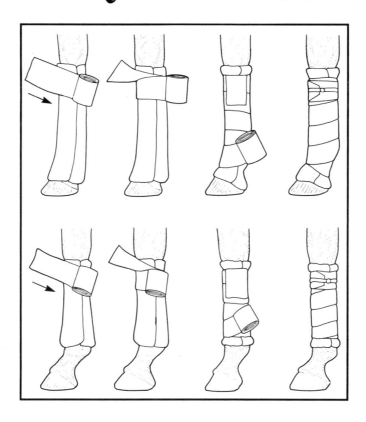

Conformation

Boots and bandages are often needed to protect a horse from his own actions. Faulty conformation or action can cause brushing or whatever. In athletic pursuits it is reasonable to expect some self-inflicted injuries, but generally the way to avoid many of them is to buy horses with good conformation and action. Young or unfit horses must be given time to develop strength which will enable them to avoid hitting themselves and a good farrier can help correct faults in action and conformation and shoe a horse appropriately for his make, shape and work. Up to six months of age, a farrier can do a great deal to put right faulty conformation and action. After that age the bones begin to harden and this becomes much more difficult. Even mature animals, however, can be helped to some extent, particularly if their faults have been acquired due to poor foot dressing and shoeing.

Horses do get into the habit of going in a particular way, even if it is not natural to them, to protect themselves from real or anticipated pain. If they have been used to going in such a way as to protect themselves from the pain of a specific injury, they may continue this faulty way of going out of habit after the injury is healed. There are various professional yards usually involving remedial schooling and physiotherapy which can correct such behaviour, maybe advertised in the equestrian press or recommended by a vet or physiotherapist.

The elements of good conformation are fascinating to concerned and interested horsemen but too detailed and complex to go into here. Basically, you should look for a horse who stands naturally with 'a leg at each corner': the legs should appear straight (bearing in mind that horses

Boots

Probably protective boots are the most obvious in this category of equipment and there is a wide range of boots aimed at protecting the horse's legs. Boots of all kinds are now available in traditional fabrics such as woollen box cloth, felt or leather, and combinations of these, or in various synthetic materials; the padding may be polyethylene, plastic, nylon or polyester; straps and fastenings may be of synthetic webbing and velcro instead of leather straps and metal buckles; and where there is a shield which covers the inside of the fetlock and inside of the leg as, for example, on brushing or speedicut boots, fibreglass or other such hardened material will be used.

Brushing boots

These must be the most widely used sort of boot in circulation and are intended to protect a horse that hits the inside of one leg with the opposite hoof. Usually the damage is low down on the leg; if it is higher up it is called speedicutting, in which case *speedicut boots* are available – these are just like brushing boots, but are longer. Boots for the hind legs are longer than those for the front legs anyway, since the hind cannon bones are longer.

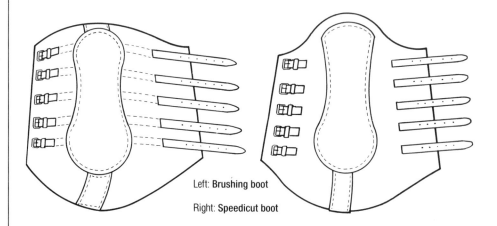

Left: **Brushing boot**

Right: **Speedicut boot**

For brushing and speedicut boots, the protective hardened shield may or may not be padded on the inside. The boot itself fastens on the outside of the leg (as does any boot) so there is no risk of the horse's action breaking or tearing the fastening and causing the boot to be forced off, or to slip down the leg and over the hoof, where it could obviously trip the horse and perhaps bring him down, with potentially disastrous results. The straps may be buckles, or clips on elasticated straps, or velcro, and they always fasten facing backwards; they are then less likely to become caught in undergrowth, or heather, or hedge growth when jumping, and come undone.

A nicely fitting speedicut boot should come just below the fetlock on the inside, and just above it on the outside of the leg, to just under knee or hock; brushing boots should be a little lower. Both these boot types should be wide enough for you to be able to fasten the straps easily without over-stretching or over-tightening them; if they are too long they will not be snug enough to be secure, nor should there be lots of strap left flapping around. The horse has to move very actively in these boots and if they are too tight or too loose they will either cause injurious pressure or they will rub. It is a point of fine discretion to satisfy the demands of fit, safety and comfort – but basically the boot should seem firm, but should not be pulled tight on the leg.

Learn how to hold the boot in place on the leg whilst you fasten the bottom strap first, thus stopping the boot from slipping down the leg as you fasten the other straps – if it were to descend right over the hoof it could trip the horse should he move about. For the same reason, when undoing the boot undo the top strap first and work down. Make sure the edges of the boot are smooth and not wrinkled or turned under on themselves as this might create a potentially injurious pressure point, as with any item of tack or clothing.

Fetlock or **ankle boots**: a shorter version of the brushing boot, and are employed for the same purpose. They may have three straps or sometimes only one, and have the usual hardened shield covering the inside of the joint and a few inches above it.

Some brushing boots fit not only round and over the inside of the fetlock, but also behind and just under it to protect the ergot which is on the point of the fetlock. *Heel boots* will also protect these parts. They are used on horses doing fast work when the fetlock is often pressed right down to the ground with the force of the speed, and/or when landing from a jump (some show jumpers also wear them) when the ergot and underside of the fetlock may be injured.

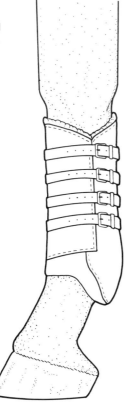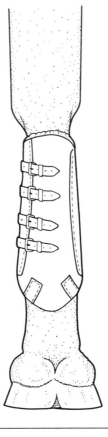

Heel boots. These come down under the fetlock to protect the ergot (not actually the heel) and under-fetlock area in fast work. Combined brushing/heel boots are available

do not have ramrod-straight legs like a table) with the fore hooves under the points of the shoulders. Drop an imaginary straight line from the point of the shoulder, through the centre of the knee, down the cannon bone and straight down the front of the toe. At the back, you should be able to run such a line down from the point of the buttock, through the hock, down the back of the cannon bone and fetlock and, it is said, bisecting the heels of the hind feet. In practice, most members of the horse family are very slightly cow-hocked — that means their hocks point *slightly* inwards. This may only be noticeable to the sharp-eyed.

Viewed from the side, the front legs should appear straight to the extent of having a line dropped from the point of the elbow, down the back of the forearm, touching the back of the fetlock and thence to the ground. At the back, a line should be able to be dropped from the point of the buttock, touching the back of the hock, hind cannon and fetlock, and on to the ground.

In action, the legs should seem to 'follow each other': in other words, the hind legs should follow in the flight path of the forelegs without deviation which could cause brushing or speedicuting.

Boots may also be used as a matter of course during certain types of work. Work involving circling (such as lungeing youngsters), work across country, particularly on slippery going or over fences, or rough or uneven going of any sort can always cause a mis-step which will result in injury and it is normal practice to boot or bandage a horse or pony under such circumstances. Many people like to exercise in knee pads of other boots because hard roads can often be slippery and broken knees, not to mention treads and cuts, can be avoided.

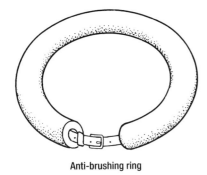

Anti-brushing ring

A **fetlock ring boot**: generally fitted only to the leg which needs protecting. It is a rubber ring fitted just above the fetlock and acts simply by keeping the opposite, offending leg away from the leg it is on. On some horses it works well, but others may be upset by the way the ring 'interferes' with their action; horses have also been known to trip because of this.

A **sausage boot**: this is not the same thing: it is much thicker, and is fitted round the pasterns to prevent the horse bruising his own elbows on the heels of his shoes when he lies down.

Yorkshire boots: are very simple, and are effective on horses whose brushing and interference are not too bad. A Yorkshire boot consists of a piece of thick, rectangular cloth, usually felt, with a tape sewn along the middle of its length. The material is straightened out and placed round the leg so that the tape (on the outside) is tied just above the fetlock (only tightly enough to keep it up, not to press on the tendons); then the upper part of the felt is folded down over the tape and the lower part, giving double-thickness protection.

The Yorkshire boot: simple but effective. Place it round the lower leg with the tape above the fetlock. Fasten it in a bow on the outside of the leg, just tightly enough to secure it. Fold down the fabric, as shown, which not only covers the fastening but provides a double thickness of protection

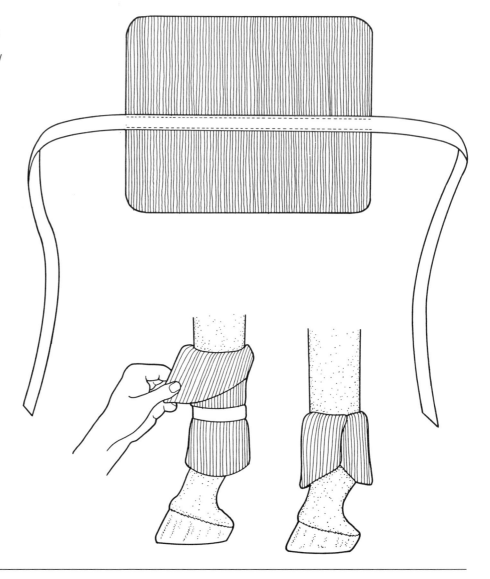

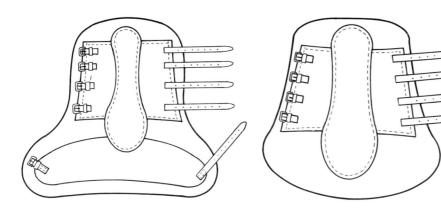

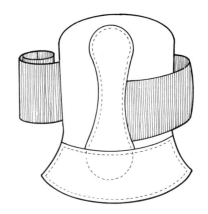

Left and middle: **Polo boots**

Right: **Polo or schooling boot** secured by bandage

Polo boots: like heavy-duty brushing boots, but often come right down over the pastern and coronet with a fastening around the pastern to stop them flapping around. They can be fastened with conventional straps, or with bandages which can be sewn on, or secured by means of strong adhesive tape, or both.

Over-reach boots: each like a rubber bell in shape, these fit round the pastern and protect the heels and coronets. However, fitting them is not as easy as the experienced make it look! Hold the horse's front hoof between your knees as a farrier does, turn the boot inside out and, with the bottom edge towards you, and gripping hard to this all the while, haul it on over the hoof. Once its top is around the pastern, turn the boot down the right way, making sure the turning is smooth and even to reduce the chances of rubbing. Even so, these boots can rub sensitive horses round the pastern.

There is another type which is easier to put on, where each boot is split down one side and then secured round the pastern with a leather strap.

A continuing problem with over-reach boots is that they frequently turn upwards and inside out during work – in this instance they become not only useless but irritating, and sometimes a positive danger as occasionally they can cause a horse to change his action so much in his efforts to avoid the boot, that he comes down. To obviate this, there is a type of boot which consists of a number of overlapping leaves, or 'petals' of tough synthetic material, threaded on to a plastic strap which then fastens round the pastern. Extra petals can be

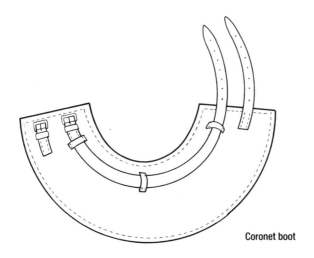

Coronet boot

Conventional over-reach boots which protect the coronet and heel

bought in a pack separately, to make up size or to replace any petals that are damaged. These boots are more expensive but are much superior to the 'ordinary' sort.

Over-reach boots are a wise precaution when travelling, since the horse may adopt all sorts of unnatural and weird actions and postures in an effort to keep his balance; some people put them on the hind feet, too, to help avoid treads. Strictly speaking, horses should be travelled with proper partitions between them – but some are not, and are then in danger of treads from their companion as well as from themselves. *Coronet boots* can be worn instead of over-reach boots for travelling. These are usually of semi-circular leather and strap round the pastern, but they are not really as effective as over-reach boots.

Tendon boots: these sometimes cause misunderstanding. They do not, and cannot in any way support the tendons: what they are for, is to stop the horse hitting into the back of his lower front legs with his hind hooves. For this reason they have a thick pad which fits down the back of the tendons, often with a leather-covered bar-shaped pad on the inside running down both sides of the tendons which helps keep the boot in place. They strap on like brushing boots, and some designs combine brushing and tendon boots in one article.

Shin boots: padded down the front rather than the back, to protect the front of the cannon bones against knocks when jumping.

Travelling boots: these are a boon on busy travelling days. Instead of having to fit knee pads, hock boots and over-reach boots on maybe all four feet, and stable bandages over thick padding – which is all quite a palaver! – travelling boots do the whole job in one easy-to-apply operation. They provide full lower-leg protection, and are made of padded material, usually synthetic these days, because this has a degree of flexibility thus allowing the leg to move, particularly as each boot extends from above the knee or hock right down over the coronets and heels; generally they fasten with Velcro. These boots enable you to do in five minutes what could take half an hour – for a novice at least! However, choose carefully, as some of the cheaper ones are not too effective, being rather light on padding and of not very tough material.

Knee pads: these come in two types, one intended for travelling, the other for exercise and called *skeleton knee pads*. Obviously they come in pairs, each pad consisting of a padded upper band to which leather straps are attached, usually with a strong elastic insert. From this pad a hard leather shield extends downwards; the travelling sort is surrounded by woollen cloth and is bound with braid, usually in colours to match the day/travelling rug. The top strap fastens securely, but not tightly, above the knee and there is a bottom strap which you should fasten as *loosely* as possible, so it does not interfere with the horse's leg action. The skeleton exercise pads have no woollen cloth and are lighter.

When travelling, knee pads provide some security against the horse banging his knee joints, usually when loading or unloading, or injuring them should he come down. The skeleton pads protect the knees should the horse slip and fall

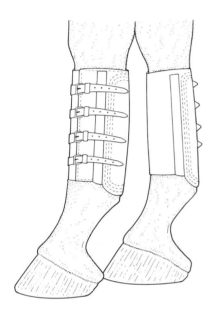

Tendon boots. The reinforcing, protective 'bars' can be seen down the sides, plus the padding down the back. It is a common mistake to use these boots back to front as shin boots as pictured below!

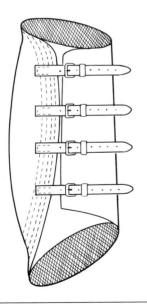

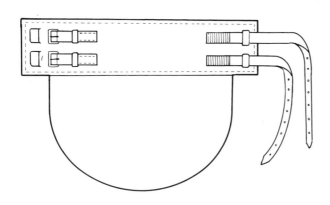

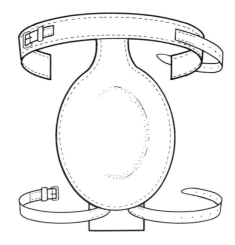

Left: **Knee boot or pad**

Right: **Skeleton knee pad** for exercising

when exercising. Some people like to use knee pads as a protection when jumping, but for this their use is controversial: those against maintain that they are dangerous as they are likely to slip down the leg during such athletic activity, unless the top strap is fastened really tightly – in which case the horse will not be working in comfort, and if this strap is too tight it can actually injure the leg.

Hock boots: protect the point of the hock against knocks when travelling or, in some cases, in the stable. Generally, however, it is not a good idea to leave them on for any length of time: for example, for horses which scrape their bedding to one side and lie on the hard floor as a few perverse individuals insist on doing, the boots would have to be fastened tight enough to stay on all night and the pressure could injure the leg; and if they were to slip down the leg they could certainly annoy, frighten and trip the horse.

Hock boots are made of wool or synthetic cloth, bound and with a blocked leather cap for the point of the hock; they fasten by means of two straps across the front of the hock, top and bottom.

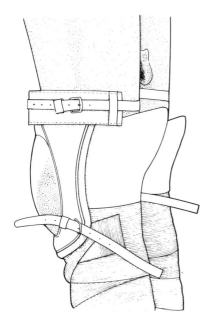

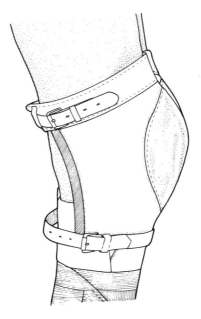

Left: **Knee pads** used here for travelling in conjunction with stable or travelling bandages and padding. Skeleton pads are used for exercising by some people

Right: **Hock boots,** used mainly for travelling

Boots or bandages?

Whether to use boots or bandages often causes disagreement. As badly applied bandages can do so much damage to a horse's legs, it is certainly safer for novices to use boots provided they get the tension right — neither so tight as to cause discomfort or pressure injuries, nor so loose that the boots slip round or down.

The problem with boots is that it is much easier for dirt and grit to work down inside them and rub the horse very sore, resulting in either a raw patch or a swollen, 'blown up' leg. This is less likely with bandages which are put on over padding, but not impossible.

Both boots and bandages can rub much more easily when wet. Some paddding (notably Gamgee Tissue) goes to nothing when wet, and crepe work bandages can shrink slightly. The best plan of action is to use top quality products and apply them properly to minimise problems.

Bandages

Bandages are a useful part of a horse's wardrobe, depending on his job and lifestyle: almost more important, however, is to master the art of applying them so that they are effective without doing harm – this is essential to the horse's well-being and may even influence how sound he remains. Basically bandages are used for work, when they are called exercise or work bandages; and in the stable or for travelling, when they are called stable bandages. (There are also certain specialist bandages, and of course surgical bandages for first aid and veterinary use, but these do not really come under the heading of tack.)

When bandages are put on incorrectly they can do a great deal of damage, and very unpleasant injuries can be caused by uneven and/or tight pressure: the legs can become badly swollen, and the skin may even rupture to reveal the tendons, the result of traumatic bruising and pinching of the skin and underlying tissues, also interference with the blood circulation and functioning of the tendons. An old trick was to apply elasticated work bandages when the horse's leg was flexed, as these would then become cripplingly tight when the leg was straightened – the aim was to 'stop' the horse in a race, which of course this did do very effectively. Tapes fastened tighter than the bandage, and bandages put on without protective padding underneath also cause injuries.

Rings of crooked hair down a horse's legs indicate incompetent bandaging – this is a not uncommon sight in the disciplines of dressage and show jumping, and moreover can be seen at the highest levels of competition! White hair in rings around the legs signifies actual injury, where the pressure has been so bad as to damage the roots of the hair which subsequently grows back white. Tightly applied tail bandages have the same effect – wavy and/or white hair on the dock, and scabs or sores under it. It is not unknown for the nerves and even the bone of the tail to be damaged due to impaired blood circulation.

Loose bandages have perils of a different sort, usually of coming unravelled and tripping the horse; and of course too loose, they are not doing their job.

Exercise bandages

These are best made of some slightly stretchy fabric such as crêpe, elasticated fabric or (less stretchy) stockinette (a fine knitted cotton in double thickness). However, the problem then may be that they will be pulled much too tight during application and cause injury. They have a self-tightening effect anyway, and it is very easy to put them on too tightly – apply one to yourself as tightly as you would put it on a horse, and you will soon feel the tightening effect! However, when correctly applied, the stretch quality does allow for movement of the horse's leg, which must not be interfered with during work.

Exercise bandages (as most other bandages) must be put on over some kind of padding, firstly to cushion their effect, but primarily as extra protection to the leg against knocks and self-inflicted kicks and interference during work, particularly fast work. If they become wet they must be removed as soon as possible after work as they can easily shrink and tighten slightly on the leg. For this reason it is advisable not to use them for long rides, like a day's hunting.

It is widely but quite wrongly believed that bandaging is a significant help in supporting a horse's tendons and ligaments during work. It probably helps reduce the damaging vibration in the leg caused by jarring when the horse is worked fast or jumped on hard going (which should not be done anyway), but bandages can only be of any *support* to the leg if they are applied so firmly as to interfere significantly with the movement of the joint – and it is a moot point as to how effective they are in this respect. Exercise/work bandages are normally applied from just below the knee or hock to just above the fetlock in order *not* to interfere with the fetlock's function, so cannot possibly be actually supportive to this part. Vetrap bandages are sometimes applied to below the joint, particularly at the back to protect the ergot, but the support provided by this method of using Vetrap bandages must be minimal, if anything. We should remember that the average riding horse weighs half a ton, so whatever we apply to his legs in the form of ordinary work bandages cannot possibly do much at all to lessen the effects of that weight, particularly when it is compounded by the speed at which he is going and the weight of the rider on his back.

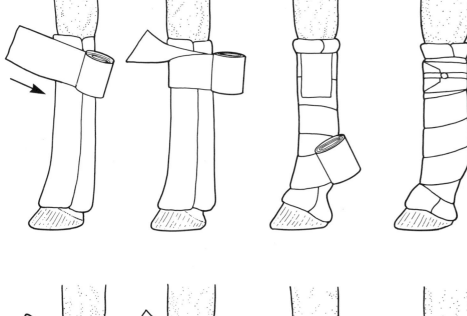

PUTTING ON BANDAGES

a) **Stable/travelling bandages**. Wrap your padding smoothly around the leg (damping the hair slightly helps keep it in place), and learn the trick of holding it on whilst applying the bandage. There are various methods, and this one is as effective as any. Leave a little end of bandage free and place it across the leg as shown. Take a turn around the leg and let the end drop down. You can now either bandage over the end, or leave it free as you bandage down the leg. You should aim to cover half the previous turn each time. Take the bandage well down under the fetlock to the heel, where it will take a natural turn upwards, and bandage back up again. Cover the free end (if not done before) and tie the (smooth) tapes only as tightly as the bandage. Finish in a firm bow and tuck the ends in. If possible, cover the bow by turning down a fold of bandage over it

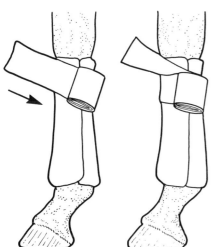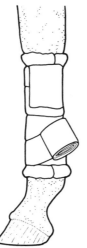

b) **Exercise bandages** are put on in essentially the same way, but they do not normally go below the fetlock joint as this would interfere with the horse's action. However, some competition horses have their bandages applied well down round the fetlock, ostensibly for extra protection

Roll-A-Bandage

One of the most irritating jobs to be done in many yards is rolling bandages but the Roll-A-Bandage hand-operated machine, shown here, takes the tedium out of it. Its inventor, John Parry of CCLA International Products (address, p195) said: 'A bandage that takes two minutes or more to hand roll is, with very little practise, rolled by this machine in as little as ten seconds, and it is done so neatly it will even fit back into its original package. You can't do that by hand'. The machine comes with easy self-assembly instructions. The end of the bandage is placed between the primary and secondary winding shafts leaving about 30mm of the bandage as a lead protruding through them. The handle is turned anti-clockwise and as you roll you feed the bandage over the inside of your hand on to the primary winder shaft. The bandage is easily removed from the shaft provided you have not over-tightened it during rolling.

When real support and immobilisation are needed, veterinary surgeons can apply air casts, plaster casts and synthetic casts, or a Robert Adams bandage which envelops the whole leg in thick padding and several bandages down its entire length. Otherwise, ordinary crêpe exercise or tail bandages can be used to cover a dressing, as long as they are clean and put on without stretching so that their self-tightening property does not cause further damage to an injured part.

Exercise bandages are normally sold in sets of four; each one is about 8cm (3in) wide and roughly 2m (6 to 7ft) long. They can fasten with cotton tapes (which must be kept ironed flat so as to help spread their pressure) in a bow (tucking in the ends for neatness), or with Velcro strips; they can be sewn on (particularly secure for fast work), or wide adhesive tape (Elastoplast tape or masking tape) can be passed right round the leg over the end or fastening. All fastenings must be only as tight as the bandage itself.

The accompanying illustrations and captions show how to put on exercise bandages and also stable/travelling bandages. To remove any bandage, undo the fastening and pass the bandage quickly from hand to hand as you unwind it, bundling it up and making no attempt to roll it – this is done later. It is normal to rub the leg upwards, with a final smooth downwards, to stimulate circulation in the skin.

To roll a bandage of any type start with the outside pointed end – when you have finished bandaging a leg this will be on the outside – and fold the tapes (if present) neatly and flat across the end; they will form a 'core' inside the rolled-up bandage. Then hold the bandage up between fingers and thumbs and roll it downwards towards you till the straight, inside end is on the outside of the roll; or, once the roll is started, roll it down with the flat of the hand on your thigh, or a wall or a table top.

Stable bandages

The most effective stable bandages are knitted wool jersey or, for summer, knitted cotton stockinette; thermal, synthetic fabrics have the propensity to keep a leg either warm or cool as required; and expensive, stiff velour is also available, but this is very difficult to use and does not mould itself to the leg at all well. Stable bandages are a little wider than exercise bandages and should be a good 8ft long (very roughly 1.5m), though many of the ones you buy these days are too short. With these, you can compensate for the insufficient length either by starting to bandage just above the fetlock; or you can buy two sets and sew them together: take two bandages and sew them at their straight ends, then cut off one of the pointed ends, oversewing the raw edge firmly to prevent fraying, and you have one super-long stable bandage. These extra-long bandages enable you to make a much better job, for whatever purpose they are required: securing padding for warmth, or protection in the stable or when travelling; or to provide slight pressure to help keep down filled legs – when the leg swells somewhat, usually in animals left standing too long in the stable and not exercised sufficiently.

Tail bandage

Most people use a single exercise bandage for doing the tail, the crêpe type being the easiest to use. Putting on a tail bandage without injuring the tail can be tricky, as padding is not usually put underneath; the bandage must be kept smooth with no wrinkles or turned-under edges, and as with all bandages, not applied too tightly – just snug enough to stay on and to keep the dock hair smooth which is its day-to-day purpose. It also protects the tail during travelling, preventing it from getting rubbed against the lorry side or trailer ramp.

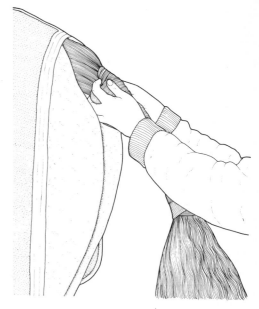

To remove a tail bandage, just grasp it without undoing it at all and pull it straight down and off the tail

The Sandown bandage

Not very widely seen, the Sandown bandage has its own built-in, fleecy padding so that when used consistently on the same leg of the same horse, it moulds itself to a perfect fit. Again available in sets of four, these bandages are normally made of wool and can be used as stable or travelling bandages with no need for separate padding.

The bandage is put on from the fleecy end, and as you roll it on, you will eventually come to a non-padded part which continues over the fleecy part to hold it and keep it firm. Sandown bandages are also available in stockinette and these are used by some people as work bandages.

Padding materials

Gamgee Tissue (a brand name of Robinsons of Chesterfield) consists of cotton wool inside a fine gauze covering which gives it much more strength than ordinary cotton wool. It is ubiquitous in the horse world, and is used under bandages and as part of first aid and surgical dressings. It is very good when fresh, but soon loses its resilience – sometimes after only one use – and particularly if you wash it when it quickly becomes quite useless. It works out rather expensive because of this, even though it is more hardwearing than cotton wool; however, one advantage is that it comes in rolls of various sizes so you can cut it to size as you wish.

Fybagee is a synthetic fabric like felt, but it has the advantage in that it can be used time and again, and is hardwearing and washable. It is resilient, yet not too stiff to mould fairly well to the leg.

Foam rubber is a poor padding material, since it becomes easily compressed, and also tends to rub the skin. It is not recommended.

Felt pads are not as good as Gamgee Tissue or Fybagee, either: they are hardwearing but stiff and somewhat inflexible.

Legs can be dried off by using anti-sweat rug pieces or coarse mesh dish-cloths under stable bandages, or hay and straw which can be wrapped round the legs for the same purpose; obviously 'formal' padding is not needed as well.

Preventive devices

Poultice boots

These are not used as widely as they were in the past, because advances in drugs and veterinary medication mean that the injuries and diseases a boot might have been needed for, are treated more effectively by drugs than by poulticing. However, there is a good deal of misunderstanding about poulticing, and a boot still finds a place in well-equipped yards. It is a rather clumsy-looking contraption of canvas, rubber or some synthetic fabric, with straps or drawstrings to fasten it on; though it is more effective, nonetheless, than creating a makeshift dressing out of old sacks and bandages which can be bitten off easily by the horse. Remember that some horses are frightened by the feel of a poultice boot – it is not sufficient just to put the boot over the dressed injury and then disappear if the horse is not used to wearing a boot. Stay around, talk to him and reassure him, let him get the feel of the boot, as with any new item of tack or clothing, and don't leave until you are sure he won't react adversely.

Poll guard

This is a hardened 'cap' with holes for the ears, and is used primarily when the horse is in transit, when loading into the transport, when travelling, and when unloading. Its purpose is to protect the top of the horse's head should he either rear or throw up his head during the process, at risk of causing himself serious injury. A poll guard straps to the headcollar and is padded on the inside. Synthetic ones, sometimes with ventilation, are now available; these are very much stronger and lighter than the heavier leather ones, and are therefore more comfortable for the horse whilst still being effective.

People sometimes improvise poll protection by wrapping the headpiece of the headcollar around with Gamgee Tissue or other padding; however, this protects only one small area, and as the strap lies behind the ears, not the poll itself. It is better than nothing, perhaps, but quite inadequate compared with a proper poll guard.

Tail guard

This is put on over a tail bandage when travelling or in the stable to prevent the horse dislodging it if he rubs his tail or leans on it during travelling. Normally a guard is made of jute rugging on the outside, usually bound to match the travelling rug, and lined with wool blanketing; it has a strap or tape passing from the top to the roller which keeps it up in place, and is fastened round the tail by means of several tapes tied with bows, or velcro-tipped tapes, or straps and buckles. A tail guard can also be used to protect a dressing on the tail should the horse have an injury or disease in that part.

A good type of poll guard, made of leather-covered fibreglass. It slots on to the headcollar's headpiece and is worn for travelling. Unfortunately, these can be rather hot in summer; you can occasionally find guards made of strong synthetic open mesh to obviate this problem

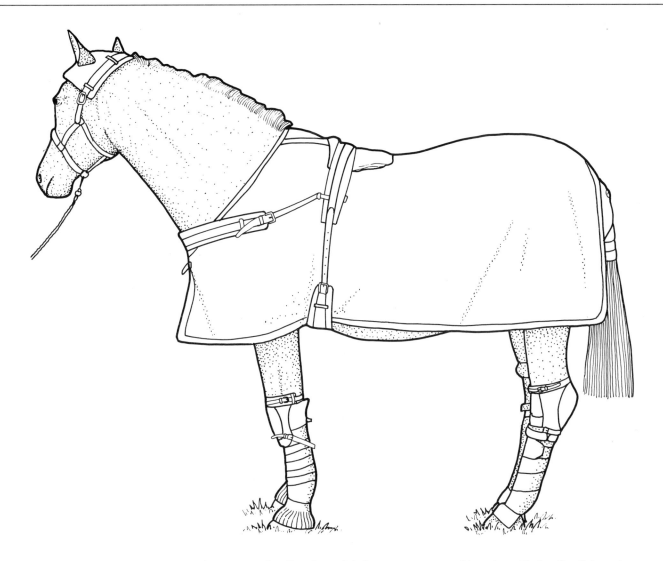

As with a tail bandage, the guard must not be fitted so tightly as to cause irritation, injury or interference with the circulation, and it must be kept clean simply for reasons of hygiene.

Leather guards must be dressed regularly with leather dressing to keep the leather soft.

A horse dressed for travelling. He is wearing a headcollar and lead-rope, poll guard, rug with roller, padding and breastgirth (to keep the roller forward) and a tail bandage. His legs are protected not by full travelling boots but by knee and hock protectors, bandages over padding and over-reach boots on his forelegs

Neck cradle

Usually made of wooden or synthetic rods, this is like a cage tapered to fit the shape of the horse's neck, the narrower end near the head and the wider end down near the withers. The purpose of this uncomfortable contraption is to prevent the horse biting at dressings or any injured part, as it completely prevents him turning his neck. However, he is also unable to scratch or bite himself to relieve an ordinary itch, and a neck cradle should really only be considered as a last-ditch effort when trying to protect dressings and so on.

As with any equipment which is restricting, some horses panic when prevented from moving normally, and so when a neck cradle is first put on it must be expertly supervised.

Rug chewing

Rug tearing and chewing is one of the most annoying and expensive vices a horse can develop.

The habit can be stopped if you soak the parts of the rug within his reach with one of the proprietary liquids (the pastes are just too messy) which taste foul. One bite and the horse is usually cured. An old recommendation was to use the horse's own urine, or to smear the rug with his droppings. Both of these practices may work but are not very hygienic, and won't improve the fragrance in the stable!

Some thought should be given to why the horse is tearing his clothing. If it is irritating him then he is trying to do something about it. People who habitually put clothing down on the bedding and do not bother to remove every scrap from the inside of the rug or blanket before putting it back on the horse can only expect the poor creature to be uncomfortable. If the horse has some kind of irritating skin condition he may take to tearing his clothing while trying to relieve the itch. A few horses just do not like wearing clothing at all so if they really have to (for instance if they have to be clipped for work in winter) try to make the clothing well-fitting and comfortable.

Skin irritations can be caused by the clothing itself if it is washed in harsh detergent, particularly biological washing powders and liquids. The safest and most effective thing to wash horse clothing with is washing soda. It should be rinsed out very well; resist the temptation to use fabric softener as this could be the culprit.

The horse can be fitted with a bib hanging from the headcollar so that when he turns round his teeth make contact with the bib and he cannot get

Muzzles

A considerably less restrictive piece of equipment is the muzzle since it allows the horse to turn round with complete freedom; although he may knock or touch the area he wants to reach with his muzzle, he cannot get his lips or teeth on it. Equally he cannot, however, eat and drink with some designs of muzzle which he can do, of course, with a neck cradle. A muzzle is put on when handling an animal which is vicious or has a propensity for biting – a stallion, for example; it also prevents a horse eating his bedding, chewing wood, tearing clothing or crib-biting.

Muzzles normally consist of a metal or synthetic (hard plastic) cage which fits over the entire muzzle area; they are usually padded around the inside top edge to prevent rubbing, and are kept up by a simple strap which passes up the side of the horse's head, over the poll, and buckles to a shorter strap the other side. Some muzzles are made of hardened leather, and these will have air holes which are essential.

Dealing with vices

In my book *Behaviour Problems in Horses* (David & Charles), Dominic Prince gives an excellent discussion on the whole subject of vices which insufficient space prohibits reprinting here. So let it just be said that a 'vice' in the horse is often merely a self-comforting reaction to stress, and preventing it will simply make him even more miserable; furthermore, it could well result in yet some other 'undesirable' behaviour which the poor animal adopts to relieve his own wretchedness. Thus while there may well be a case for restricting a horse with some device or other for his own protection in the very short term, there is none for its permanent application. The answer lies in either putting up with the 'vice' (if it is totally impossible to get rid of it), or – better by far – changing the horse's management and, very often, the owner's or manager's attitude towards him, so that he greatly lessens or even stops his undesirable behaviour. The root cause of all vices lies in inappropriate management for the individual concerned, and all are thus caused by Man. It is wrong and quite insensitive physically to force a horse to stop performing his neurosis or comfort behaviour: the aim should always be to make him stop *wanting* to perform it – otherwise, as Dominic Prince points out, it is like stopping a child biting his or her fingernails by pulling out the nails.

Bibs

A bib is a flap or a shaped half-cup of leather or synthetic material which straps to the headcollar behind the horse's head and chin to prevent him turning round and tearing his clothing or possibly getting at dressings on wounds. However, it does allow him to eat and drink. Obviously in the first case the answer is really to make sure the horse's clothing fits and is comfortable, and is not made of a textile to which he is allergic – watch also for laundering products which can remain in the fabric and cause allergic reactions; also, make sure that his skin is comfortable and not diseased or generally dirty and itchy. Many horses are over-rugged and over-clipped, both of which contingencies can cause problems themselves.

Anti-cribbing strap

Although this sounds like a good idea, it does not really work in the long term, and like so many such devices, simply increases the horse's discomfort. It is a strap with a padded part in a U-shape which fits round the horse's throat and reaches high up behind the ears, the windpipe fitting into the U-shaped part: there is a blunt metal blade which digs into the horse's throat behind the rounded jawbone when he tries to assume the arched-neck position needed to crib-bite (or wind-suck). Again, the animal may be prevented physically from performing this behaviour, but it will not stop him doing so when not wearing the strap, and will certainly not stop him needing to perform his vice – the strap will obviously do nothing to make the horse mentally or physically any more content.

Flute bit

The flute bit is also designed to stop the horse crib-biting or wind-sucking – though physically only. It consists of a straight, hollow metal mouthpiece with loose rings, with holes in the mouthpiece and at its ends which effectively preclude the formation of the vacuum necessary for the horse to gulp down air, the whole point of crib-biting and wind-sucking. The bit is suspended from the headcollar with little straps and has to be left in permanently to be effective. In theory it is possible for the horse to eat with the bit in, although drinking is extremely difficult, but it does become clogged with food and makes the eating process much less of a pleasure for the horse. And when you consider that domesticated horses, when correctly fed with adequate roughage, will eat for about two-thirds of the day, you will appreciate that flute bits are not really much use.

hold of the rug, yet he can still eat and drink normally. It is still best to eradicate the cause if at all possible, as it is extremely stressful to the horse to have to put up with this kind of discomfort, and the stress may produce other vices.

Youngsters teething (up to four years old) sometimes chew things, including clothing, so consult your vet for some remedy to rub on the gums to alleviate the soreness. Baby products work well.

Protective Equipment

Page 171:
Medipost Ltd (address, p195) produces an interesting range of items all based on a material called Vulkan Thermoskin which the company claims acts as an insulator of the horse's own body heat. The heat is accumulated in the material and reflected back to the body, so increasing the temperature of the area beneath whatever item is being worn.

Most performance-horse owners are familiar with the need to adequately and gradually warm up equine athletes in order to avoid soft-tissue damage, such as, for example, to muscles and tendons, due to working harder than the blood supply can cope with at any particular stage – the harder a horse works the harder his blood has to 'work' to cater for the supply of oxygen and nutrients and the removal of toxic products formed during work. Hard work before circulation and body temperature have increased overstresses tissues and injuries can result. Medipost state : 'Proper warm-up prior to exercise heats the muscle, increasing its elasticity. The collagen fibres making up the ligaments and tendons also have an increased stretchability when heat is applied. In short, warming an area increases flexibility thus reducing the likelihood of damage when the muscles, tendons and ligaments are asked to work to their full potential.

'For rehabilitation purposes the heat increases the blood circulation to the site of the injury. Increased circulation speeds up the removal of accumulated fluids that cause stiffness and swelling, this in turn speeds up the natural healing process ensuring a quicker return to fitness.'

The Thermoskin material is described as offering 'a microscopic massage of the covered area, promoting blood circulation and arousing the skin. The special structure of the material allows the skin to "breathe" so maintaining a healthy, therapeutic environment by dissipating excess heat and sweat which accumulates during physical activity. Thermoskin is able to provide up to 12 hours wearability without skin irritation or discomfort.

(30) Tendon boots: The company produces two types of tendon boot, standard and extra-padded types. They are said to offer 'compression and support' and to help relieve acute and chronic pain in the lower leg, plus assisting in rehabilitation of tendon injuries. They stretch and contract with the horse's movements, helping ensure even tension. Medipost states that putting on the boots an hour or an hour and half before exercise 'ensures maximum elasticity of the collagen fibres in the tendons, helping to reduce the likelihood of strains occurring.' Because of the heat-reflecting properties of the material, the boots are said to assist healing of tendon injuries by maintaining an optimum heat level.

(31) Leg wraps: The leg wraps are claimed to assist in the treatment of bruises, sprains, kicks and other injuries and consist of Vulkan Thermoskin material secured with an elastic bandage. They are recommended to be used before or after work and during travelling.

(32) Hock boots and (33) knee boots: The hock and knee boots are claimed to offer 'effective compression and support' to these joints, the accumulated heat helping in the treatment of acute and chronic pain conditions, knocks and blows.

PAGE 172:
In addition to their range of boots and leg wraps (p171), Medipost (address, p195) also use their insulatory material, Vulkan Thermoskin, in a range of rugs, sheets and numnahs.

(34) The Vulkan Rug, Exercise Sheet and Racing Sheet are waterproof and 'breathable'. Medipost claims that the rug ensures that the horse is fully warmed up and ready for work. The exercise or quarter sheets, put on during tacking up, maintain body heat in the loins and quarters during exercise. Medipost also produces a half sheet designed to fit over the quarters aimed at maintaining warmth whilst the horse is saddled and waiting to start competition. It can be quickly slipped off without unsaddling.

(35) In addition to heat-reflecting properties which help prepare the back muscles for work, the numnah is described as having been 'specially constructed to dissipate forces over a greater area. The forces are distributed by different shock-absorbing layers. The design is specially suited for long working days and strenuous exercise.'

(36) The 'Professional's Choice' Sports Medicine Boots marketed in the UK by Peter Nutt Agencies (address, p195) seem to be a real breakthrough in supportive wear for the equine athlete. For generations it has been mistakenly believed that exercise bandages conventionally applied from just below the knee or hock to just above the fetlock actually support the tendons and ligaments. Normally, the only way actual support can be given would be to hamper the action of the associated joint (in the case of equine athletes it is normally the fetlock joint which comes in for most injury). Now, however, it seems that sports boots have been developed which really do seem to lessen stress and offer a significant degree of support to the lower legs without interfering with fetlock action.

Developed in the USA and tested over two years in the field and during clinical research at major universities, the boots are described as 'the most thoroughly researched boots ever offered in the horse industry.' A summary of the results from the University of Wisconsin reads: 'The purpose of support devices (boots and bandages) placed on the lower limb of athletic horses is to absorb a portion of the energy that is generated as the hoof impacts upon the ground. The more energy absorbed by the bandage, the less energy available to deform and injure the soft tissues of the limb. The Professional's Choice Sports Medicine Boot provides very high levels of energy absorption (24.54%) which will help to prevent injuries associated with hyperextension of the fetlock. In addition, horses that are rehabilitating from bowed tendons and suspensory ligament injuries will benefit from the ability of these boots to absorb high levels of energy if they are worn during their exercise and training activities.' A quote from William H. Crawford, DVM, MVSc, BSA, BApS, reads: 'I was very pleased to see the boots perform so well in the laboratory tests. Congratulations on a quality product that will provide injury protection for our equine athletes'. A report on the high speed gait analysis conducted at the University of Minnesota, by Calvin N. Kobluyk, BSc, BSA, DVM, DVSc, reads: '[the boot] was tested on five Thoroughbred racehorses exercised at a gallop on a high speed treadmill. The boots were found

to have little effect (or restriction) on the horses' gaits when compared to the same horse not wearing the boot. It also appeared that the horses exhibited increased comfort wearing the boot as they shifted their weight forward. Combining the high level of protection and energy absorption (24.54%) with minimal effects on the gait, the Sports Medicine boot is a valuable tool in prevention of lower limb injuries during training and performance, as well as a valuable addition to the treatment régime for rehabilitating horses with limb injuries.'

The boots are made of neoprene with an 'ultra-shock' lining. The material has a four-way stretch and it is 'recommended that the boot is put on 'as snugly as possible' so as to provide the optimum support to tendons, fetlock and lower suspensory ligaments and to protect the sesamoid area. The boots are claimed to 'increase circulation to actually tighten and condition the legs, bringing the horse to a higher level of performance'. As well as providing support, they also appear to absorb energy from concussion (a well-known cause of injury) and so reduce the potential of trauma and stress-related injuries to the legs of the horse.

Also available via the same source are the Quik-Wrap Bell (over-reach) Boots, apparently renowned for staying on in 'deep dirt, sand or mud' if applied correctly. Made of tough synthetic material, they are of wrap-round design providing two thicknesses over the heel area and secured with velcro straps and hooks.

(37) Following in the wake of all-in-one travel boots, JAI Equine Products (address, p195) have brought out combined knee pads and exercise boots which have been thoroughly tested on performance horses. They are made from a tough PVC outer skin with a high-density, impact-absorbing foam interior and have a fleecy lining to prevent chafing. They are fitted with elasticated velcro straps for quick, firm application. They were designed to overcome the problem of knee pads slipping down during canter exercise. The boots protect the lower leg and also the knee. JAI Equine Products claim that the impact-absorbing foam helps to reduce concussion and eliminates the likelihood of a 'big knee' as well as broken knees (where the skin on the knees is broken).

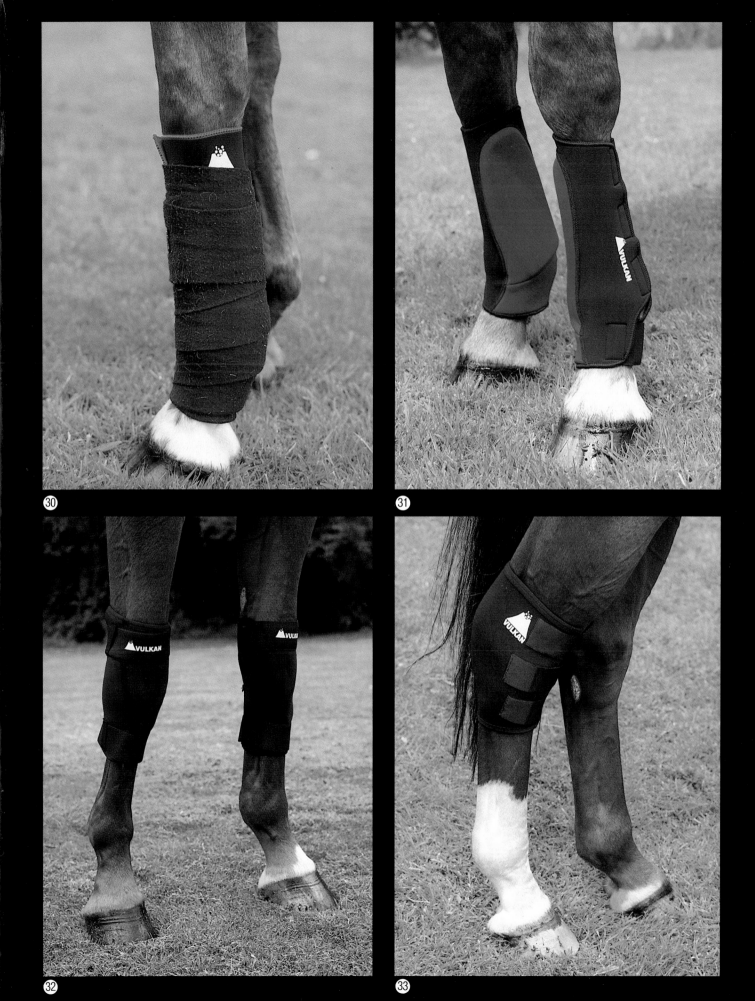

㉚

㉛

㉜

㉝

34

35

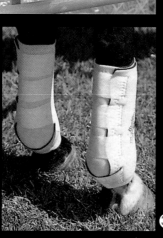

36

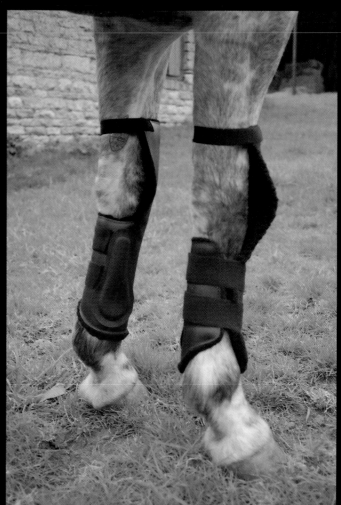

37

7

DRIVING EQUIPMENT

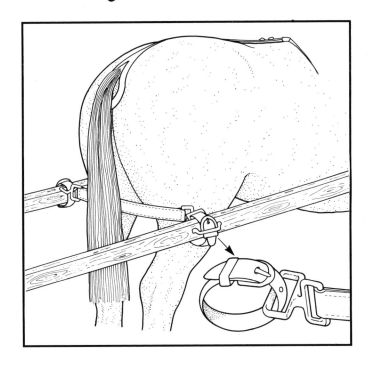

The development of driving harness has a longer history than riding tack, as driving is a technique of using horses which began earlier than riding them. Modern harness has not actually improved much over the last few hundred years, and the basic principles are the same now as they were in Tudor and even mediaeval times. There are modern developments such as synthetic 'leather', but nothing revolutionary such as adjustable collars or new designs or materials to improve driving bits.

There are various ways of driving horses, but all the different techniques and developments stem from single harness, and this is what will be described here. Pairs, tandems, unicorns, troikas and so on are all developments of the basic single harness, and anyone taking up driving usually starts with a single horse or pony. It is, incidentally, an ideal discipline for an outgrown child's pony or the family horse, which can thereby remain involved in family activities and perhaps even provide a useful alternative to the car or a second conveyance for local shopping and errands – not to mention the fun and satisfaction the competitive sport of driving can bring.

The Harness

Collars

Probably the most critical piece of harness is the collar, as this is the horse's sole means of moving the vehicle forwards – the breeching behind the thighs, either as part of the harness or fitted to the traces (described later), assists in stopping or backing the vehicle. In fact the horse does not actually pull the vehicle, but pushes the collar forwards with his shoulders. The traces are the long leathers attached to the collar and the vehicle and are the vital link between the two, the means by which traction and movement can take place.

The fit of the collar is as critical as that of a riding saddle because the shoulders take all the pressure and friction created by pushing. The collar itself is roughly oval in shape, but wider at the bottom than the top to accord with the shape of the horse's lower neck and shoulder region. It is made of leather, and where it touches the horse may be lined with a softer leather or with linen, serge or checked wool. It is stuffed with horsehair, straw or flock, or sometimes these days with a synthetic stuffing.

As with a saddle, it should be flat where it touches the horse so as to spread the pressure and create an even contact; it should not be stuffed so full that the inner part of the collar rounds out, as this results in a smaller, hard bearing surface which will concentrate the pressure on too small an area and result in bruising and maybe galling. Just as a badly fitting saddle can cause riding problems, so a badly fitting collar may cause the horse to become reluctant or difficult – quite apart from the aspect of the horse's own welfare.

Collar fitting, particularly for the uninitiated, is best done in person by an expert, as it can certainly be as tricky as saddle fitting. A collar may be a wide, medium or narrow fitting, and it may be piped (a 'windpipe' collar) which means the bottom is shaped to prevent pressure on the horse's windpipe. Whatever its design, the collar should fit evenly, smoothly and flat against the shoulders,

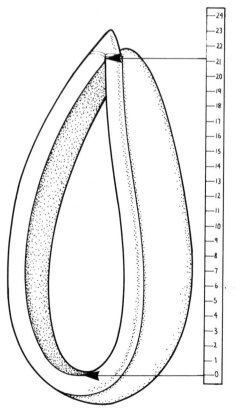

The **collar** is measured between the two points shown.

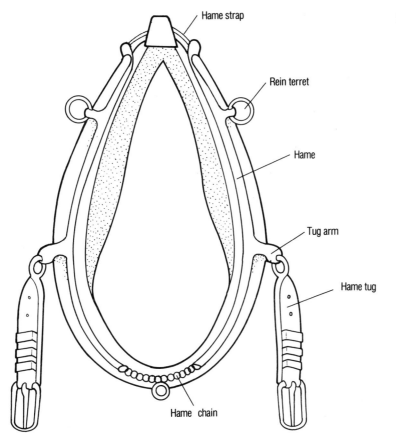

Parts of a collar

Labels on diagram: Hame strap, Rein terret, Hame, Tug arm, Hame tug, Hame chain

and you should be able to pass your hand between the bottom of the collar and the windpipe. It should not shift and rock about against the shoulders, nor should it squeeze, rub or ride up; moreover as with a saddle, the horse's condition and muscular development – or loss of it, according to his work load – will affect its fit, so a close eye should be kept on it.

A collar is always put on upside-down so that the widest part passes over the widest part of the horse's head. Also, it is common practice to stretch the collar a little first of all, by putting your knee against the inside and pulling on it. Once on, the collar is turned the right way up at the throat, the narrowest point of the neck, in the direction of the lie of the mane; it is then lowered carefully down on to the shoulders, making sure the hair lies comfortably flat under it and that the mane hair is not being pulled.

The Hames

The hames are steel branches which fit closely into grooves in the collar, one on each side. They can be plated with yellow- or white-coloured metal which, of course, requires a certain amount of 'bull' to keep brightly polished. The collar leather on the outside is frequently polished with boot polish, in the same way that military and police riding tack sometimes still is today. On the bottom third of each hame is a projection called an *anchor pull* to which the traces fasten; sometimes there is a ring instead. Further up are two other rings for

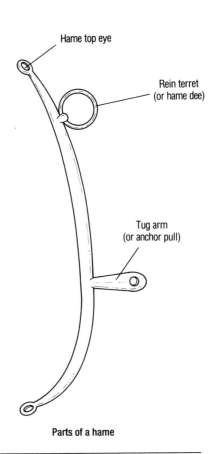

Parts of a hame

Labels on diagram: Hame top eye, Rein terret (or hame dee), Tug arm (or anchor pull)

the reins to pass through, and at the top two metal eyes for the hame strap, a critical piece of equipment which secures the hames together – if this strap breaks the collar can fall off and the horse be off without his vehicle! At the bottom of the hames are eyes or hooks to which another hame strap or chain can be attached, for further security.

Breast collars

Most single horses are driven in neck collars, but sometimes a breast-type collar is seen: this is like a sturdier version of the breast-strap used on a riding horse to keep the saddle forward. They are simpler to fit, consisting of a fairly wide, padded strap (sometimes with sheepskin on the inside) which passes round the breast above the points of the shoulders but not pressing on the windpipe, with a further strap passing vertically upwards and over the neck just in front of the withers. Breast collars are suitable for light loads only, as the pressure is obviously concentrated on a much smaller area. Also, they are not considered 'smart' turnout, particularly for display or showing or (in the old days) for town or city work; even country turnouts usually used neck collars. Having said that, competition carriage teams wear breast collars for the endurance phase as they are lighter, and the loads involved are not heavy. Hackney ponies are always shown in breast collars.

Parts of a breast collar

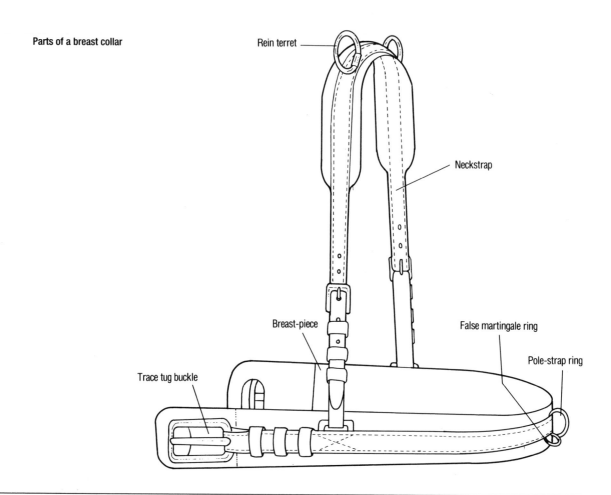

Rein terret

Neckstrap

Breast-piece

False martingale ring

Pole-strap ring

Trace tug buckle

Furthermore, despite the fact that breast collars are said to be unsuitable for heavy loads, it is interesting to note that many of the horses of the King's Troop Royal Horse Artillery are fitted with a wide, strong type of breast collar to pull the limbers and guns – several tons in weight – which are used in displays and for firing salutes at royal events. Presumably it would be impractical to have individually fitted collars for so many horses of a changing equine population, and breast collars can be made to fit almost any horse with only minor adjustments; most items of the King's Troop's harness have been used on many generations of horses, and the type, size and fit of the harness is the same as that which was used in warfare last century.

As discussed, the anchor pulls or rings on the collar hames take the traces, and so there are strong buckles on each end of the breast collar for the traces. There are also rein terrets (rings) on the strap passing over the neck, for the reins to run through.

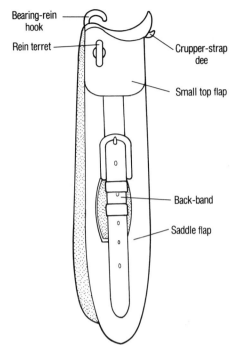

Parts of a driving saddle

Saddles and pads

Single horses wear a *driving saddle*: each shaft of a single-horse vehicle 'rides' in a strong reinforced loop called a 'tug', one on each end of a leather called the backband which passes through a channel under the top of the saddle; thus some weight is transmitted to the saddle (although in a properly balanced vehicle this should be small) and thence to the horse's back. Fitting the saddle has basically the same requirements as a riding saddle: there are well-stuffed panels on each side leaving a central gullet, with no pressure at all on the spine. At the front of the saddle there may be a ring or hook to take a bearing rein (see illustration), although this is almost never used these days except on hackneys; and on each side near the top there are terrets through which the reins pass. At the back of the saddle there is a dee for the crupper strap. A girth strap is also used to secure the saddle, passing through the same channel as the backband and underneath it. The backband itself is secured, though less tightly than the girth, by a separate belly-band (under the belly, obviously) which passes through a loop on the girth to stabilise it. It is there purely to keep the shafts in position.

A *driving pad* is lighter than a saddle and less sturdy, and is used in pair harness where there are no shafts but a centre pole and breast pole, and where no weight is taken on the back.

Tugs

As already mentioned, tugs are strong leather loops through which the shafts of the vehicle are slotted to keep them stable, though with a little leeway. However, if a four-wheeled vehicle is used with a single horse, a special type of tug is needed, which holds the shafts firmly: these are called Tilbury tugs. The shafts are usually individually hinged on such vehicles, and are secured by the end of the leather which forms the tug passing back through the end of the buckle.

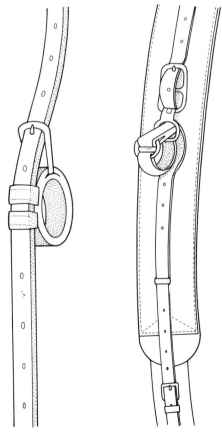

Left: **Back-band with open tug attached**

Right: **Tilbury tug**

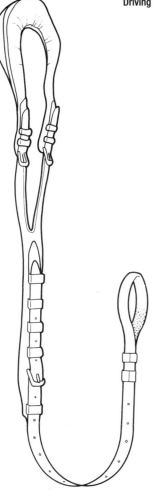

Driving crupper

The Crupper

The crupper dockpiece is comprised of a thickly padded loop of leather through which the whole tail is passed; the dockpiece itself buckles on to the crupper backstrap which then buckles on to the back saddle dee. Made of leather, the dockpiece must be kept very well cleaned and oiled so as not to cause chafing of this very sensitive and thin-skinned area. The job of the crupper is to keep the saddle (or pad) in position on the back, and to prevent it riding forwards towards the withers where the girth could cause galling, or might bring pressure to bear on the shoulder muscles and behind the elbows so that the horse becomes sore and is hampered in his action and attitude. The crupper should, therefore, be adjusted so that the dockpiece fits comfortably and snugly under the tail but *without* pulling on it.

The crupper may be designed with a buckle on each side of the dockpiece for easy adjustment so you can position the widest part centrally under the tail. This also means you can pass the dockpiece under the tail when fitting it, instead of having to double up the tail and pass it through the loop, a process to which some horses object. Whichever method is used, care must be taken that there are no hairs trapped between the skin of the dock and the dockpiece as this will cause chafing and soreness.

In the so-called martingale crupper, the dockpiece and backstrap are made as one unit, with a single buckle for fastening to the saddle dee. This looks neater and there is no chance of the reins or whip catching on the buckles of the dockpiece or crupper backstrap, but the method of putting it on (as described earlier) may be a disadvantage with some horses.

Breeching

The breeching is simply a wide, strong strap which passes round and behind the quarters, about mid-way between the root of the tail and the point of the hock; its purpose is to enable the horse to take the weight of the vehicle when going downhill or backing – though the whip should, of course, apply the brakes appropriately when descending a hill or slowing down. The breeching is supported by loin straps which pass up through the crupper backstrap. There are also dees on the vehicle shafts: the ends of the breeching fasten to these by means of short lengths of breeching strap with buckles.

Another fairly common type of breeching is *false breeching*: this is not part of the horse's harness, but is a wide strap fixed between the vehicle shafts just behind the horse's thighs, attached to dees on the shafts. With false breeching it is usual to fit a kicking strap to the horse, a strap passing through the crupper backstrap and attached to dees on the shafts, its purpose being to stop the horse raising his quarters to kick, a practice which can be very dangerous in harness.

Again with reference to the King's Troop Royal Horse Artillery, it is interesting to note that the massively heavy gun carriages, drawn at the gallop during the troop's spectacular displays and formerly in war, have *no brakes!* The two wheeler horses (those nearest the gun carriage) are solely responsible for stopping the carriage with the breeching (which is *not* false

Full breeching

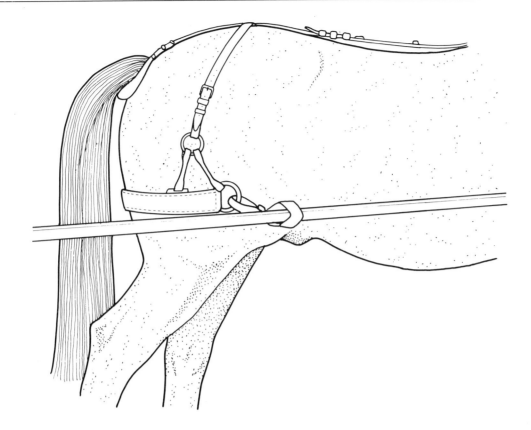

False breeching

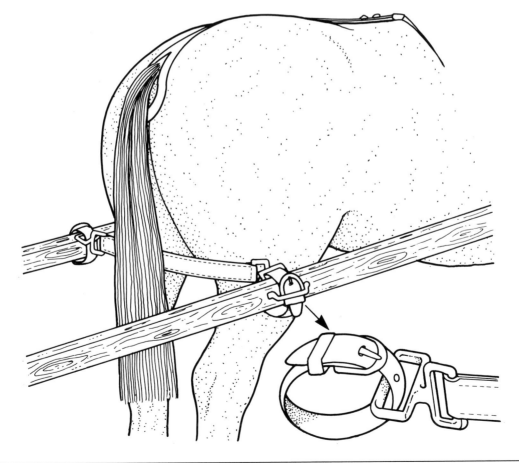

The development of harness

Driving harness is extremely complicated. Its evolution has taken place over 5,000 years or so, ever since early civilised peoples realised that the horse could pull much more weight than he could carry. Initially used for pack work (not to mention meat, hide, hair and milk), when it came to pulling loads rather than carry them the horse proved far superior to any other animal.

Probably the first harness and 'vehicle' was a simple tree bough with its branches which had perhaps been used to transport animals killed for food and initially pulled along that way by man himself. He must have realised that it would be easier to get the horse to do the pulling and devised a means of attaching the horse to the bough, probably by means of ropes of either rawhide or braided grasses. This may not sound very effective but plaited and braided grasses and straw were used for this purpose until very recently. There is a neck collar and padding for underneath a driving pad made of plaited and woven straw in the Highland Folk Museum in Scotland and it is still often the practice to stuff neck collars with straw.

The travois was used by the American Indians and by earlier peoples. It consisted of two poles with a carrying platform between them, the poles dragging on the ground behind a horse. Probably preceding the wheel in most cultures, it is, in practice, more effective than the wheel in certain ground conditions such as deep mud and over ice.

Simple sledges were initially made of large tough animal skins, such as bearskins, and developed from there.

When wheeled chariots came into being they were used for battles and

breeching) – they often actually sit into the breeching with their hind hooves off the ground and propping with their forelegs, a supreme feat of equine muscle-power and physical strength.

Having said that, many competition carriage teams do not use breeching on the endurance/cross-country phase, their whips considering it provides just one more thing to cause tangles and snags; the horses must therefore take the weight – albeit comparatively light – of the competition carriage on their saddles (and cruppers) and girth. Some competitors will use a false breeching.

Traces

Obviously the traces are the vital link between the horse and the vehicle. They are made of layers of leather sewn together with up to four rows of stitching, and are normally adjusted from the hames' buckle end, although it is sometimes possible to do this at the trace-hook end by means of a buckle on a separate short length of trace.

The horse should be positioned by means of careful adjustment of the traces so that he is close to the vehicle but with his quarters well clear of the footboard. Whatever kind of breeching is used, it too should be fitted so as not to interfere with his movement in any way.

Martingale

In driving harness, a strap called a martingale is often used, to stop the collar riding up: it is fixed to the bottom of the collar, then passes down between the horse's forelegs to the girth; it is normally passed round both the collar and the hames to keep them together. Unlike riding martingales, it does not attach at all to the bridle or reins.

Bridle

The driving bridle differs from the riding bridle in that, besides being of sturdier construction altogether, the cheekpieces carry the noseband as well as the bit, and also the winkers (blinkers) where these are worn. A bridle with winkers is termed 'closed' and one without, logically enough, 'open'; however, opinions vary as to whether it is a good plan to drive horses in winkers. The vast majority are worked wearing them, of course, and have been for centuries, but many categories of horse – including military horses, commercial delivery horses and some private turnouts – work perfectly well without them.

So, are they necessary? The horse has virtually all-round vision, an asset which has obviously enabled the species to survive to the present day. Because of this ability, however, some people feel that the horse is bound to be terrified by the sight of the vehicle following (chasing) him at such close quarters, and particularly by the wheels (which travel at twice the speed of the vehicle) which may seem to be actually overtaking him. The logical assumption is that he will associate all this with an imminent attack by a predator. But the fact that so many horses work just as well, and some even better, without winkers, rather puts paid to this argument. Racehorses sometimes wear blinker hoods which are said to concentrate their attention ahead, and their performance improves as a result; and there is no reason why this could not apply to some driving horses, too. On the whole, however, I feel that winkers should not be used on driving horses just as a matter of course, but only when a horse has shown he needs them. Though I doubt that the situation will change in the foreseeable future!

Basically, the fit of a driving bridle must follow the same requirements as that of a riding bridle. Browbands are frequently decorated with white or yellow metal, and there will probably be a metal disc, rosette or boss at each end, frequently inscribed with perhaps the family crest or maybe the company insignia.

Winkers are partly supported at the top by winker stays, small straps which pass under the browband and buckle to the centre top of the headpiece. These stays must not be too tight or they will cause the winker to press painfully against the head. The winker must be positioned so that its widest part coincides with the point of the eye.

Bits

The two bits most commonly used for driving single horses are the Liverpool bit or curb, and the Wilson snaffle.

The **Liverpool Curb** is basically a pelham, but only one rein is used. Some are still made with a smooth and 'rough' (ridged) side, but nowadays these are quite rightly out of favour as being far too harsh. The mouthpiece may be straight or have a gentle port. As you will see from the illustration, the bit has circular cheeks with eyes for the curb chain hooks, and a sliding mouthpiece.

The reins may be fastened to the circular part of the cheek, when the position is called 'plain cheek' and the effect is purely that of an ordinary snaffle; or to the cheek inside the ring, when it is called 'rough cheek' and gives a little leverage; or to the upper or lower of the two slots on the cheek extending below the circular part. On the top slot, the position is called 'middle bar', and

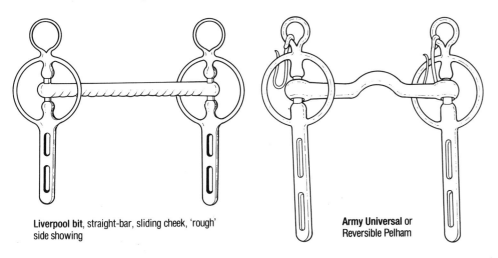

Liverpool bit, straight-bar, sliding cheek, 'rough' side showing

Army Universal or **Reversible Pelham**

racing, not for general transport. Early forms of harness show a neck strap with two ropes (early traces) running back to the vehicle, which probably had to be stopped manually as there were no brakes, and the vehicle would regularly run into the animals' back legs. Vehicle poles and shafts were devised (many say by the Chinese) to prevent this.

The neckstrap type of harness was also not particularly good as it interfered significantly with the horse's breathing. Gradually, as padding was used on the horse's back to prevent the injuries caused by weight (of the vehicle and load) and friction there, a girth/surcingle was devised. A strap was then fitted, running from the bottom of the neckstrap to the girth to prevent the former riding up and to help with the breathing problem.

Another type of harness, incorporating a breast collar and breeching, both kept up by straps over the withers and croup, was more successful. The poles and/or traces were attached to the horizontal strap forming the breast collar-cum-breeching on the horse's side and over the withers.

The modern collar evolved as man realised that the horse could pull far more weight with his shoulders than simply by means of a strap across his breast.

Another type of harness used on horses for thousands of years and stemming from that used for oxen was the yoke, initially used about 2,000BC. The shaped wooden bar fitted over the ox's neck and the vehicle pole or poles attached to it. When horses took over from oxen this arrangement continued, later combined with breast collar and traces. The yoke was also used on the horse's back in some forms of harness, with a pad underneath, a common method used on chariot pairs in some cultures.

on the bottom one 'bottom bar'; the middle bar position is often used, but the bottom bar should only ever be used for a hard-pulling, difficult horse as it is very strong and obviously produces a formidable curb effect.

There is also an ornate version of the Liverpool curb called the *Buxton bit*, but this is usually used only on pairs and teams on special occasions.

Wilson snaffle

The **Wilson snaffle** is a plain, loose-ring, jointed snaffle with four rings, one pair hanging loose around the mouthpiece and one passing through the ends of the mouthpiece as normal. The reins are normally fastened to both rings, although the design of the bit is really so that they can be buckled to the 'true' rings only, and not those hanging loose – this produces a much stronger effect, with not only the conventional nutcracker action where tongue and bar pressure occur, and maybe roof-of-the-mouth pressure as well, but the free rings will also squeeze the lips together. This combined action is very severe, and should only be used in exceptionally difficult cases.

The Army Reversible (Universal or Elbow Bit) can also be used on a driving bridle (see p181), but this is not common.

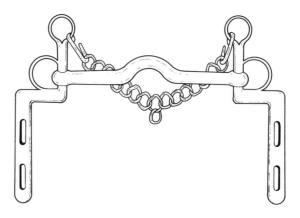

Liverpool bit with ported mouthpiece

Reins

Driving reins are plain, though sometimes they may be stitched, they are obviously much longer than riding reins, and are always brown even if the rest of the harness is black. It is quite normal for them to *buckle* to the bit – in a riding bridle this is considered very 'down market' – and they normally buckle at the 'hand' end in the usual way, although some whips prefer them to have no buckle but a strong, fairly tight keeper only, so that in the event of an accident they can be quickly and easily separated.

Harnessing

Harnessing up

The collar is the first item to go on, in the way already described. The hames are put on, and the top hame strap fastened securely before the collar is turned and lowered on to the shoulders. The hames strap is tightened up, and the bottom hame strap or chain is also now done up. The false martingale, if used, is buckled round the collar and hames.

Next step: the saddle, backband, tugs and belly-band, girth, crupper, breeching and breeching straps are put on in one piece. First, position the saddle in the middle of the back, and then the breeching; next, fit the crupper

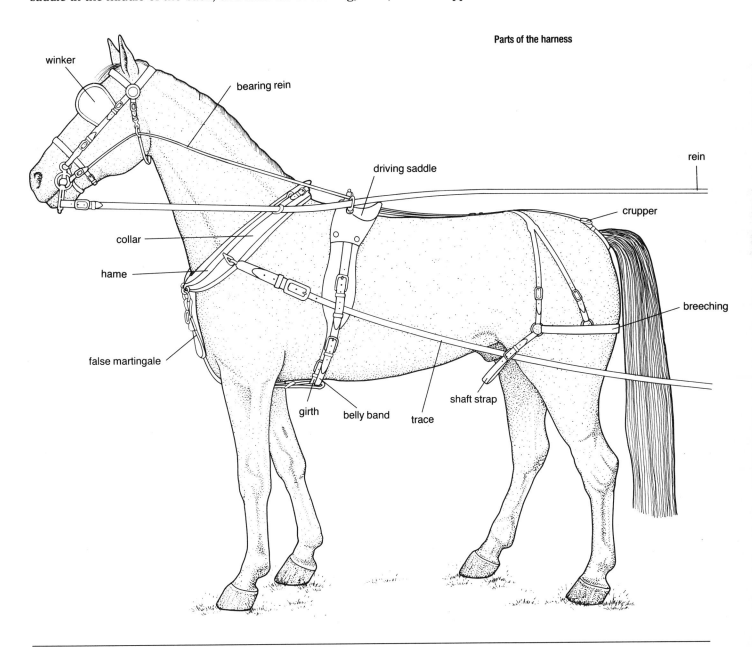

Parts of the harness

winker

bearing rein

driving saddle

rein

crupper

collar

hame

breeching

false martingale

girth   belly band   trace   shaft strap

dockpiece. Lift the saddle forward (don't drag it against the lie of the hair) and position it again well back from the withers. Fasten the crupper backstrap, and then girth up, looping through the false martingale if appropriate, and not too tightly at first (as with a riding girth).

Prepare the reins for fastening to the bit, having first passed them through the saddle and hames terrets; fold up the hand-end, and tuck it under the backstrap of the crupper.

Next, put on the bridle and buckle the reins to the bit.

Putting to

This is the term used for actually harnessing the horse to the vehicle: note that the vehicle is brought to the horse – the horse should never be backed into the vehicle. The vehicle is brought towards the horse with the shafts raised well above his quarters, and the shafts are then put through the tugs until the latter come up against the tug stops on the shafts. Until this stage is reached the traces are left coiled around themselves, hanging from the hames: now, they are undone, and hooked on to the trace hooks on the vehicle, taking care that the trace straps are not twisted. The traces pass between the girth and the belly-band.

The breeching straps are now passed round the shafts and buckled to the shaft dees; they should be adjusted so that the breeching hangs about four inches away from the horse's thighs – this is enough to prevent irritating him and interfering with his action, but sufficient to take the weight of the vehicle as soon as required.

If a false breeching is used, this is fastened on to the rear breeching dees on the shafts before the horse is put to.

Finally the belly-band is passed over the traces and done up. As regards tightness, you should be able to pass the flat of your hand fairly easily between the girth and the horse, though it should not be *loose*, as such; the belly-band is fitted a little looser than the girth.

Taking out

Unharnessing and removing the horse from the vehicle is called 'taking out'. The vehicle should be empty before you begin. The reins are tucked through the offside saddle terret well forward of the tug stops on the shafts so that when the vehicle is pushed back from the freed horse they do not catch and give the horse a nasty jab in the mouth. The belly-band and breeching are undone, and the traces unhooked from the vehicle. If Tilbury tugs are used, these are also undone.

It is not advisable to lead the horse out of the shafts, although many people do so – just as many back the horse into them – as it can encourage the horse to move out of his own accord before everything is freed, which could possibly cause an accident. The vehicle is pushed back from the horse, and only when it is quite clear is the horse led away. This also instils discipline into the horse, which learns that it does not move until accompanied by a human.

8
CARE OF
EQUIPMENT

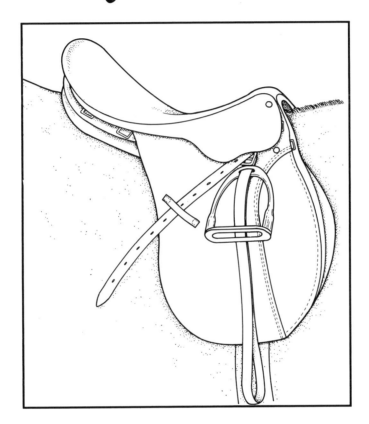

Tack, clothing and harness is expensive so it obviously pays to look after it; and this is important not only from the economical point of view, but also because neglected equipment deteriorates – leather dries out and weakens and is then prone to snapping without warning; stitching rots and wears; metal parts wear and become cracked or weakened, or they become sharp and can injure the horse. The fabric used for numnahs, clothing, bandages and so on can wear and rot, or become damaged. Hard, stiff leather will also readily chafe the horse; this will hurt him and can understandably make him difficult to ride, drive and handle – and this is the only way he can tell us of his discomfort or pain.

Leather

Nearly all leather items, from expensive saddles and driving collars to the straps on a pair of boots, can have basically the same sort of treatment; the exception is modern tack which has been given specialised treatments during manufacture, particularly in relation to colouring dyes. These items must be cleaned and maintained strictly in accordance with their manufacturers' instructions if their appearance, at least, is not to be ruined.

The traditional way of cleaning and maintaining tack is still appropriate for all other leather items used for riding horses. Driving harness (and, indeed, much military and police riding tack) is treated differently in that boot polish is used (conventionally, just like cleaning shoes) on the outside of the leather to give a hard shine; saddle soap and leather dressings are used on the underside of the leather which can absorb them, to clean it and keep it supple. This is the old traditional way of achieving the shine on, for example, show harness and certain military tack (though not items made from patent leather). However, there is no doubt that boot polish hardens and dries out leather, as can be seen from the many tiny cracks in, for example, a pair of old, consistently polished pair of shoes or boots. The object with tack and harness used on horses is to keep it supply enough to use easily and not to chafe; and if boot polish *is* used on it, special attention must be paid to regular dressing and oiling of the underside to counteract the drying, stiffening effect of the boot polish.

As well as the traditional saddle soaps which may or may not contain glycerine to condition the leather, there are various proprietary cleaning agents which aim to both clean and protect in one operation; some of these work quite well, whereas others just seem to work the dirt into the leather along with the conditioner! New dressings based on lanolin and glycerine have also largely replaced the various greases and, to a lesser extent, neatsfoot oil which have always acted as conditioners and softening agents rather than as cleaning agents.

Those leather items which can be cleaned in the traditional way – that is, which have had no specialist treatment – can be kept in excellent condition (if used and cleaned regularly) by means of washing and soaping with glycerine saddle soap. There is virtually no need to apply any oils or dressings to such tack as the glycerine conditions the leather every time it is soaped. The basic procedure is as follows:

To be most effective you should completely undo every strap and piece of equipment: saddles should be stripped (girths and stirrup leathers removed), and bridles have all their straps undone and laid separately on a flat surface. However, it is quite possible to do a reasonable cleaning job on a bridle by undoing the buckles and either refastening them on a different hole so that the normally buckled section can receive full attention, or by running the straps through the keepers (those fixed loops of leather below each buckle – the loose ones are called runners) so that the straps can be moved around easily. Personally, I find it as quick in the long run to take a bridle apart and clean it straight off, without wasting time fiddling with straps, fastenings and keepers here and there; but many will not agree.

Straight lengths of leather such as girths, stirrup leathers and some items of harness can best be cleaned by hooking the buckles on to a firm hook in the wall or ceiling and running the sponge or cleaning cloth up and down them with one hand whilst holding the item taut with the other. A bridle to be cleaned but not taken apart can be hung on a special bridle hook – designed to take three or more bridles – suspended from the ceiling, or can be dealt with on its own peg or bracket; this is easier than cleaning it on a flat surface. A saddle is most easily cleaned on a proper saddle horse with a top section which will turn over to hold the saddle so that you can get at the underside. But you can clean it just as well by resting it on your lap, or on the back of a kitchen chair, though this is rather more awkward.

Regular **saddle maintenance** is essential

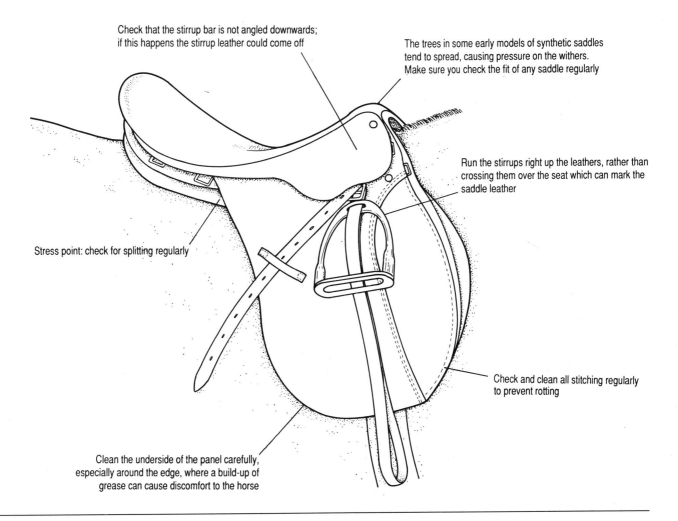

Check that the stirrup bar is not angled downwards; if this happens the stirrup leather could come off

The trees in some early models of synthetic saddles tend to spread, causing pressure on the withers. Make sure you check the fit of any saddle regularly

Run the stirrups right up the leathers, rather than crossing them over the seat which can mark the saddle leather

Stress point: check for splitting regularly

Check and clean all stitching regularly to prevent rotting

Clean the underside of the panel carefully, especially around the edge, where a build-up of grease can cause discomfort to the horse

Leather must first be washed to remove mud and grease, and also dried sweat from the horse himself. Note that mud is composed of soil grains which are really miniscule rocks, and it can very easily scratch leather if it is rubbed off at all hard; and scratching not only spoils its appearance but gradually degrades and weakens the leather itself. Mud should therefore be washed off very carefully with the washing sponge (which must never be mixed up with the soaping sponge); very muddy tack *which is not padded* (ie not saddles and collars) can be swished in a tub or trough of water (not the horses' drinking water, of course), or held briefly under a running yard tap – this will remove most of the mud with no risk at all of scratching. However, leather must not be left to soak for more than a minute or two, as excessive exposure to water can strip it of the oils and greases which were put into it during manufacture to protect and preserve it. If leather gets a real soaking, perhaps during a rainstorm or because the horse falls in water, or if it is accidentally left soaking, it must be given a thorough dressing with oil or a proprietary dressing, preferably while it is still slightly damp as it will absorb the dressing better in this condition. Salt water must be soaked out as well as possible; my horse and I once fell in the sea whilst using my favourite saddle: it oozed salt out of the panel for weeks, but after about a month of repeatedly soaking and pummelling it in clear water, then thoroughly dressing it with leather conditioner (Hydrophane Leather Dressing was the one used) we managed to save its skin, if you'll forgive the pun. The saddle gave many years of further service with no permanent ill-effects even to the stuffing inside the panel.

In spite of what some people say, cold water is absolutely useless for washing grease off leather; hot water will strip too much oil and grease out of it: lukewarm water is both safe and effective. For very greasy tack, use lukewarm water with just a dash of a mild washing-up liquid added, or pure soap liquid or flakes, as this will break down the grease without overdoing things.

The side of the tack which touches the horse will obviously need most attention, but the leather should be washed thoroughly on both sides and round all the edges; those stubborn little black blobs of grease (called jockeys) should be removed gently with a coin or blunt knife. Once clean, let the leather dry a little at a natural temperature – never near a radiator or fire, or in a hot, dry room – before soaping it.

With 'ordinary' saddle soap, glycerine or not, damp the soap, never the sponge: either spit on it, or splash water on it if in a tin; if a bar, dip the end in water and then rub it on the soaping sponge – the soaping sponge itself must *never* be wetted. If the soap and sponge are too wet, the soap will lather and this reduces its effectiveness.

For saddles and any flat expanses of leather, rub the soaping sponge firmly all over the surface in small circular movements until a deep sheen is achieved. Strips such as reins, bridles, traces, stirrup leathers and so on are best hung on a hook, held taut with one hand, and the sponge wrapped round the leather with the other then run firmly up and down the strip. Rug and boot straps, and other small pieces of leather, can be cleaned by resting them on a table or even your knee if necessary, and working the soap in.

Pay extra attention to the underneath, or 'flesh' side of the leather – the slightly duller and, in some tack, rougher side – as this is the most absorbent and can take in the soap and glycerine more readily. Pay special attention to any

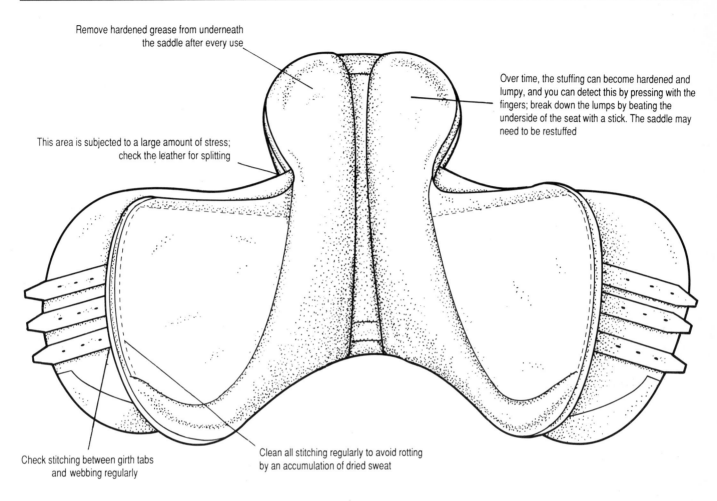

Remove hardened grease from underneath the saddle after every use

Over time, the stuffing can become hardened and lumpy, and you can detect this by pressing with the fingers; break down the lumps by beating the underside of the seat with a stick. The saddle may need to be restuffed

This area is subjected to a large amount of stress; check the leather for splitting

Check stitching between girth tabs and webbing regularly

Clean all stitching regularly to avoid rotting by an accumulation of dried sweat

curves or stress points in the leather, for example where the stirrup iron eyes rest, inside hook studs and billets where the bit-rings go, the girth straps and suchlike, giving these parts plenty of soap.

Those parts of the horse's tack which remain relatively clean, such as the seat of the saddle, need not be washed and soaped every time – though when you do tackle this part, be careful what type of soap or dressing you use on it, as light-coloured breeches can be easily stained!

Metal parts such as hooks, buckles, stirrups and bit-rings or cheeks should be cleaned with metal polish, but never mouthpieces. Nickel (if you absolutely have to use it) should really be done every time as it soon goes dull, but stainless steel will stand a longer wait, although in time a dull coating appears; however, this can be removed easily with Duraglit or something similar. Try never to get metal polish on leather – this can be rather difficult, but if you do, clean it off at once or it will rot the leather. Bit mouthpieces should be washed thoroughly in warm water after each ride so the horse is not presented with a dirty, unhygienic bit next time round.

Make a point of checking all stitching as you clean your tack, as your life really could depend on the state of its repair; the most important areas are the stirrup leathers and girth straps.

After soaping, go round all the holes in the straps and poke out the soap with a matchstick, twig or nail. Put the right stirrup leather back on the left side of the saddle and vice versa, and do this each time you clean the tack as the

Out of sight does not mean out of mind: the **underside of the saddle** requires just as much attention

leathers may stretch somewhat with use, particularly if you always mount from the ground on one side. Otherwise you will end up with one leather significantly longer than the other, and the numbered holes (which should be present on all good leathers) not matching up, so you will either be riding lopsided or won't be able to level up your stirrups properly.

Suede leather is fine when new, and excellent for helping to keep a rider in the plate, but it does wear smooth fairly quickly. It can be revitalised by brushing hard with a wire suede brush, but this will eventually wear out the leather. Needless to say, it should never be soaped or oiled on the suede side, and being rained on doesn't help it, either.

If your girth is leather, clean it as described and when finished, lay it over the seat of the saddle, which should be put on its rack, stripped or otherwise.

All tack should be put away, or hung up carefully so that it keeps a good shape. The bridle can be hung on a semi-circular bracket (often integral with the saddle rack in branded products, though a finished saddle soap tin nailed to

It is important to check all parts of the bridle for wear and tear

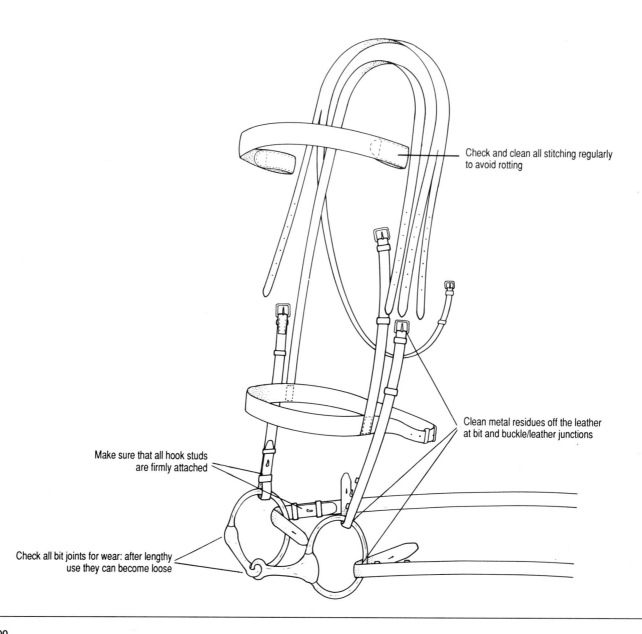

Check and clean all stitching regularly to avoid rotting

Clean metal residues off the leather at bit and buckle/leather junctions

Make sure that all hook studs are firmly attached

Check all bit joints for wear: after lengthy use they can become loose

the wall will suffice) usually just under the saddle, and the stirrup leathers may be either laid over the saddle or hung from their buckles on hooks next to the bridle. The stirrups themselves can be hung on nails on the wall, or may be put back on the saddle with the leathers to save time before your next ride.

Harness has special racks to hold it in good shape but, again, you can either put it away made up, or separately.

If boot polish is used on driving harness, keep a special eye on the stitching as this will rot relatively quickly. Patent harness should be cleaned with proper patent cleaner, and according to the instructions. Modern saddles and other tack made of specially treated leathers are sold with special cleaners, and you must follow the instructions for these implicitly if you want to keep the tack looking good and in good condition.

Synthetic tack and fabrics

Synthetic tack such as saddles, or harness can often be cleaned by just hosing down or rinsing in water, with a good brushing with a dandy brush in between times. Rubber-covered reins should have the handparts washed with no more than a damp sponge; obviously soaping will not do any good, and will just make the reins slippery. Fabric girths may be laundered in a washing machine using non-biological washing products, or scrubbed gently with mild soap and a nail brush on a flat surface; they should be rinsed very thoroughly (using fabric softener if you wish) and hung up to dry by both sets of buckles so they are hanging in a U-shape – this prevents water running down on to the buckles which will encourage rusting if the buckles are not rustproof. Special synthetic fabric girths must be washed according to the manufacturer's instructions: some sorts can be ruined by inappropriate laundering.

All natural fabric items such as cotton reins, natural-fibre girths, summer sheets and numnahs, can be washed: use a washing machine at 40°C on a short or medium programme; if using a bath or a tub outdoors use a good non-biological washing product – biologicals often cause skin irritation. Woollen day rugs are usually sent to the cleaners (yet if you wash them subsequently you'll be shocked at the dirt which still comes out!); woollen blankets can be cleaned or washed at home. The trick with wool is to wash and rinse it in water of the *same temperature* otherwise it will surely shrink; cold to just warm water (up to 30°C) is fine for wool. Spin or warm-tumble it, and ease it into shape while still slightly damp, drying it off over a fence, hedge or clothes' rack. Fabric conditioner is a good idea for wool, and indeed for many of the synthetics as it removes the rustle and static, which some horses find unpleasant and alarming.

Boots and all other extraneous items can be washed according to the general instructions given, depending on what they are made of. Heat-retaining and permeable-textile rugs, under-rugs, girths, numnahs, saddle cloths and so on must be carefully washed according to the maker's instructions; failing any written instructions, treat them as for real wool. Hot temperatures can actually melt the fabrics or their linings, which then congeal into a solid block so the garment becomes absolutely useless.

Bandages can be put into a pillowcase with a zip, tape or velcro fastening across the top to prevent them tangling in the machine and taking hours to undo; this also prevents them becoming over-stretched in the wash. Tapes should be ironed to spread the pressure when they are fastened.

Fancy browbands made of metal, velvet, white leather and so on need special treatment. There is virtually nothing you can do with velvet browbands, although water marks from rain can often be removed with talcum powder. White browbands should have ordinary whitener put on, and brass or other metal done carefully with metal polish as for buckles. Work your metal polish into awkward corners of metal items like buckles or curb chains with a matchstick or toothpick, buffing them up in a duster afterwards.

Never leave any items lying around, wet and dirty, for long. Organic matter such as dried droppings and urine, or sweat and grease, will soon start to rot almost any material – clothing, leather, even synthetics are not rot-proof and can become badly discoloured, if nothing else.

Storing equipment

The ideal conditions for storing your equipment are at room temperature (about 20°C) in a dry-ish atmosphere. Damp, humid, over-dry and over-hot areas should be avoided, as all these will spoil fabrics, and leather in particular. Insects will make their homes even in synthetic items, so some kind of insect-proofer with as little smell as possible (available from saddlers) should be used on items to be stored for any length of time.

Leather which is going to be stored should be washed thoroughly, and dressed with perhaps neatsfoot oil or a good proprietary dressing. The best way to apply it (including a thin layer to buckles and so on) is with a paintbrush – but don't overdo it, as you can soften and weaken leather this way. This should also be done on leather only cleaned about once a month, even if this is with glycerine saddle soap; but never on leather which is polished with boot polish. Apply the dressing mainly to the underneath 'flesh' side of the leather.

Apart from saddles, leather is best stored unbuckled and laid flat. In the old days it would have been laid carefully in layers in drawers or on shelves with oiled cotton or some other thin fabric in between with the top layer obviously covered over, if on an open shelf, to keep the dust off. Saddles should be stored on their racks, each in a soft natural fabric bag which allows ventilation. Nylon is not good although it is commonly bought; and polythene should never be used for storing any leather as it encourages condensation and mildew. Fabrics should be stored sensibly as you would store home linen: in a dry atmosphere, flat, having been thoroughly laundered and repaired first. Smear all buckles with oil or petroleum jelly.

Blanket chests and trunks are good for rugs and other fabric equipment; so are deep drawers. It's a good plan to take them out and air them periodically if they are going to be out of use for any length of time.

Turnout rugs can present problems, particularly the traditional canvas and wool ones. Hang these up by the rings on their back edge, probably to strong hooks fixed on an outside wall, and hose off the mud from the canvas. Vacuum the wool lining and scrub it, laid out on the floor, with warm water and mild soap; then hang the rug up, lining facing you, and thoroughly hose all the soap out. Lay the rug out again and spread towels over the lining; then walk on it, to soak up as much water from the wool as you can. Lay it over a hedge to dry out – the hedge will spread the garment, yet still allow air to get at the underside, too. Failing a hedge, a clothes rack high up in the ceiling of a kitchen or warm tack room is good; or in fine weather you can lay it over a fence to dry out, turning it regularly. This will take quite some time, maybe days if the drying conditions aren't favourable. Do not try to hang a canvas New Zealand rug on a clothes line when wet as it will almost certainly break it.

Synthetics should be laundered as per the manufacturer's instructions.

Common sense is really all that is needed to back up even just a little knowledge when looking after tack and clothing. If in doubt, ask an expert; otherwise ask yourself how you would treat a garment of your own made of these materials. This way you won't go far wrong!

ADDRESSES

Ortho-Flex saddles and Biothane bridlewear,
Yvonne Tyson, 68 Milton Hill, Worlesbury,
Weston-Super-Mare BS22 9RF

A. J. Foster Saddlemakers,
22 Station Street, Walsall WS2 9JZ

G. Fieldhouse Saddlery (Walsall) Ltd,
18–19 Green Lane, Walsall, West Midlands
WS2 8 HE

Safehorse (UK) Ltd,
Glenfield Park, Glenfield Road, Nelson,
Lancashire BB9 8AR

Albion Saddlemakers Co. Ltd,
Albion House, Caldmore Road, Walsall WS1 3NR

Cottage Craft,
Cottage Industries (Equestrian) Ltd,
Crown Lane, Wychbold, Droitwich,
Worcestershire WR9 0BX

Hydrophane Laboratories Limited,
Ickleford Manor, Hitchin, Hertfordshire
SG5 3XE

Lansdown Rugs,
Beachwood Cottages, Lansdown, Bath,
Avon BA1 9DB

The Schoolmasta training aid
Masta Horse Clothing Co Ltd,
Crosland Moor Mills, Blackmoorfoot Road,
Huddersfield HD4 5AH

Equi-Weight schooling aid
Mrs Carin Newman,
Ryall's Farm, Ryall's Lane, Bishops Caundle,
Sherborne, Dorset DT9 5NG

CCLA International Products,
Lyminster Road, Lyminster, West Sussex BN17 7QQ

Medipost Ltd,
100 Shaw Road, Oldham, Lancashire
OL1 4AY

JAI Equine Products
Dairy Farmhouse, Courteenhall, Northampton
NN7 2QE

INDEX

Index